Teaching Secondary School **art**

Contents

Preface

However, it can be said that whatever a teacher does in stimulating creativeness greatly depends on three factors: (1) his own personality, of which his own creativeness, his degree of sensitivity, and flexible relationships to environment are an important part; (2) his ability to put himself into the place of others, and (3) his understanding and knowledge of the needs of those whom he is teaching.

VIKTOR LOWENFELD,
Creative and Mental Growth, 3rd Edition,
New York: Macmillan, 1963, p. 3

This text is planned for prospective teachers and experienced art teachers who wish to share in the artistic adventure of teaching art to junior and senior high school students. The information is aimed at revealing the wonder of art and suggesting some of the ways in which it can be taught. These ideas are based on the premise that art in education is a fundamental need for all students who would discover their personal artistic vision of the world. The book aims to spark future teachers with enthusiasm by helping them to catch the spirit of art teaching. It is intended to provide provocative insights into the methods of teaching art and provide an avenue for grasping the substance of art as history, skill, and idea awareness.

Teaching Secondary School Art is intended to be a pathway of discovery to help prospective teachers understand the teaching of art in its many aspects at the junior and senior high school level. It urges the future teacher to experience the world of art and the world itself in intense detail. Another aim is to indicate directions from which sequential and comprehensive curricula can be established in the junior and senior high school art programs. This author believes that definitive objectives and goals for a critical awareness in art can take place at the junior high level and proceed through the senior year of high school. Carefully reasoned art goals are discussed as the challenges in presenting and developing an in-ventively structured, comprehensive program at the secondary level.

Chapter One discusses the objectives and aims for teaching secondary art. Clearly stated goals are defined and amplified which help to clarify the meaning of art teaching at the junior-senior level. Central objectives include the teaching of art as historical content, studio skill, and the development of personal artistic and perceptual awareness. Contemporary emphasis is placed on an understanding of art in context to the world.

Chapter Two discusses the difficult but intriguing question of what makes an excellent teacher. Data has been drawn from experienced art teachers throughout the United States. Additional information has been interpreted from hundreds of art students who responded to selected questions aimed at revealing some aspects of good teaching in art. Most of all, many expert teachers provided illuminating insights into the day-by-day challenge of teaching.

Chapter Three discusses the characteristics and attributes of secondary students. Developmental and behavioral levels are considered in relation to what the art teacher needs to know in order to teach successfully. The necessity for understanding the drama of adolescence in its countless unfoldings is discussed in detail, with ways of communicating with students carefully explained.

Chapter Four focuses on the art curriculum, including motivational considerations, organizing lesson plans, ordering art supplies, establishing art environments, and examining possibilities for evaluation of students in art. Throughout the entire text, selected statements by experienced art educators, studio artists, and art historians provide a continuing dialogue regarding various aspects of the nature of art and art teaching. Extensive references are cited at the close of most of the chapters to enable the art teacher to pursue further ideas which are suggested in the body of the text.

Chapter Five discusses the means and methods for planning the art history phase of the curriculum. Various suggestions for learning how to bring the art of the past to light is amplified and meaningfully related to art of the contemporary world. Other considerations in teaching art history include slide preparation, planning art lectures, and selecting key material for teaching. Chapters Six, Seven and Eight present a composite picture of much information pertinent to the development of a foundational program in art history at the secondary level. These chapters include many key references to the great achievements of past cultures as well as contemporary accomplishment in art. The great masters from Antiquity, the Middle Ages, the Renaissance, and Contemporary Art are presented through discussion, chronological charts, and check lists aimed at stimulating further search. This section on art history is intended to be open-ended in order to suggest avenues of inquiry, although factual information is included as a basis for investigation.

Chapters Nine, Ten, Eleven and Twelve discuss various aspects of the studio art program. This includes what should be taught and how, idea sources, a revealing conversation with a contemporary pop artist, and also a conversation with an art educator who is seriously involved with current problems relating to the "inner city" student. The remaining sections of the book are intended to encourage artistic action through the presentation of specific art ideas for the secondary studio program.

Throughout the book, carefully selected photographs are intended to serve as a visual motivation to prompt student and teacher to inquire further into the aesthetic world of art. As such, the photographs are planned as a visual text in themselves; therefore, extraneous commentaries are avoided wherever possible. The underlying premise of both verbal statements and photographs is to provoke directions for pursuit, in contrast to providing ready-made answers. *Teaching Secondary Art* is intended to be a beginning foundation for art teachers, and not a final document in the field.

This revised edition of *Teaching Secondary School Art* expands, clarifies and continues the original edition. All chapters have been carefully reviewed, with additional material added to take into account current philosophy and methods in art education programs.

Included in this revision is new information relative to developing artistic vision in the student, and several practical suggestions for its implementation. Also discussed is a section that deals with the special steps to follow to become a fine artist. Many new career possibilities in the arts is also added.

Also pertinent to prospective teachers is valuable information by a junior high teacher and a senior high teacher who discuss curriculum and provide insights dealing with grading, discipline, membership in professional organizations, art history, art skills, lesson plans, and the need to communicate with students.

Many additional photographs have been added throughout the text to provide greater visual direction. Selected bibliographical information has been expanded to include material published recently.

It is my sincerest wish that this book will serve as a helpful and challenging tool in your art teaching for years to come. May your creative spirit spread to your students.

Earl Linderman
Arizona State University

"I Just Asked the Band to Play
Honeysuckle Rose"
by Earl Linderman
48" x 56"
Oil on Canvas

Acknowledgments

The following art museums supplied many helpful photographs from their collections:

Albright-Knox Gallery, Buffalo, New York
The Cleveland Museum of Art, Cleveland, Ohio
Museum of Modern Art, New York, New York

The following galleries supplied many excellent photographs:

Arizona State University Art Collections, Tempe, Arizona
Cordier & Ekstrom, Inc., New York
James Graham and Sons, Inc., New York
The Hansen Gallery, San Francisco
The Pace Gallery, New York
Leo Castelli Gallery, New York
Andre Emmerich Gallery, Inc., New York
M. Knoedler & Co., Inc., New York
Martha Jackson Gallery, Inc., New York
Marlborough-Gerson Gallery, Inc., New York
Allan Stone Galleries, Inc., New York
Richard Feigen Gallery, New York
Wise Gallery, New York
William Zierler Inc., New York
Tally Richards, Gallery of Contemporary Art, Taos, N.M.

The following publishers granted permission to use quotations:

Association for Supervision and Curriculum Development for the quotes by Earl C. Kelley and Carl R. Rogers, from the book PERCEIVING, BEHAVING, AND BECOMING.

Charles A. Bennett Co., Inc., for the quote by Howard Conant and Arne Randall, from their book ART IN EDUCATION, and Carl Reed from his book EARLY ADOLESCENT ART EDUCATION.

The Center for Applied Research in Education, Inc., for the quote by Howard Conant from his book, ART EDUCATION.

Davis Publications, Inc., Worcester, Massachusetts, for the quote by Viktor Lowenfeld in the October, 1959 issue of School Arts Magazine.

Harper & Row, Inc., for the quotes as follows: Frederick Logan from his book, GROWTH OF ART IN AMERICAN SCHOOLS: Italo DeFrancesco from his book, ART EDUCATION: ITS MEANS AND ENDS; Abraham Maslow from the book, CREATIVITY AND ITS CULTIVATION.

Harvard Educational Review for the quote by William Meredith from his article "The Artist as Teacher, the Poet as Troublemaker."

Harvard University Press for the quote by Jerome S. Bruner from his book, ON KNOWING: ESSAYS FOR THE LEFT HAND.

International Textbook Company, Scranton, Pennsylvania, for the quote by James Schinneller from his book, ART: SEARCH AND SELF-DISCOVERY; and Robert Burkhart for the quote from his book, DELIBERATE AND SPONTANEOUS WAYS OF LEARNING.

Jossey-Bass, Inc., San Francisco, California, for the quotes by Edward L. Mattil from his article, "Teaching the Arts," from the book, THE ARTS IN HIGHER EDUCATION.

National Art Education Association for several quotations.

University of Nebraska Press for the quote by Manfred Keiler from his book, THE ART OF TEACHING ART.

Nation's Business Magazine for the quote by William M. Allen from his article "Lessons of Leadership: Accelerating the Jet Age," August, 1967.

Ronald Press Company for the quote by Manuel Barkan from his book, A FOUNDATION FOR ART EDUCATION.

Saturday Review Magazine, for the quote by Donald W. MacKinnon from his article "What Makes a Person Creative?".

Wadsworth Publishing Company, Belmont, California, for the quote by June McFee from her book, PREPARATION FOR ART.

W. Gordon Whaley for supplying the photos from his article in the *Texas Quarterly*.

The following artists, historians, and teachers supplied statements relating to the teaching and development of students in art:

Paul Beckman	Larry Foster
Jack Bookbinder	Eugene Grigsby
Robert Burkhardt	Jerome Hausman
Howard Conant	Rip Hoffa
Victor D'Amico	Henry Hope
Jim Doerter	George Horn
Ivan Johnson	Jack Taylor
Phil Kennedy	Rudy Turk
Mel Ramos	Tom Wesselman
Randall Schmidt	Joe Wilczewski
Jack Stuler	Harry Wood

The following individuals supplied photographs or statements:

Anthony Calarco	Edward L. Mattil
Tom Eckert	Verle Mickish
Chuck Friedenmaker	Don Schaumburg
Bob Henry	Randall Schmidt
Dorothy Kimm	Ron Wagner
Muriel Magenta	Rip Woods

Special acknowledgment to Rudy Turk, Curator, Arizona State University Art Collections for supplying several excellent photos.

Special thanks to Harriet Dolphin for the typing of many parts of the manuscript.

A very special thank you to my wife, Marlene Linderman.

Teaching Secondary School **art**

eeching Secondary School

"Study: Falling Man" (Carman)
by Ernst Trova, 1966
Polished Bronze

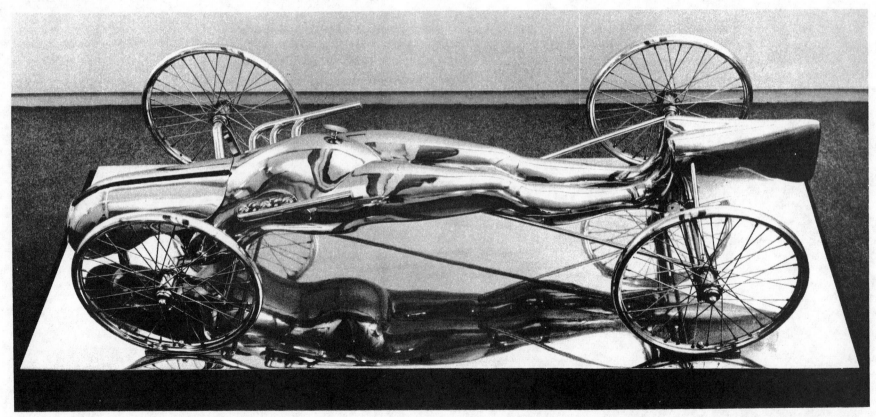

Chapter 1

Objectives and Meanings for Teaching Secondary Art

Secondary art teachers are the cornerstone for teaching artistic vision to youth. This is the time when lifelong experiences in making or thinking about art crystalize. Teachers-to-be need to bring exciting and imaginative systems into operation so that students will be challenged to the aesthetic life. Art is basic and natural to all individuals. It should not be thought of as abstract, impractical, or for the elite. Yes, talented art teachers can make artistic experiences a way of life.

We live in an age in which journeys to distant galaxies are already here. Secondary teachers who seek to invent the future are in a unique position to help change the artistic vision of tomorrow. The artistic life is a mainstream of joy and adventure that can be shared by all! Dynamic art teachers can make art experiencing practical for everyone. Art media today can be electronic, hand pulled, or traditional, for all of the usual stops are out as we enter a new era of exploration and creative endeavor!

The art teacher is the driving spearhead at this front edge of discovery. He is most aptly described by Conant and Randall.[1]

Courtesy of *The Hand and the Spirit Crafts Gallery,*
Scottsdale, Arizona

"White Hanging Feather Neckpiece
of heishe, brass bells and bird bones"
by Judy Corlett, Nez Perce Indian

No other person, no group, no amount of art materials, no physical facility, no community exceeds in importance the art teacher as the single element of greatest potential value in art education. No other person, thing, or place can make such penetrating contributions to art education A really superb art teacher can do more for the art education of individual pupils than any number of new and well-equipped art rooms, sympathetic administrators, cooperative classroom teachers, expensive art materials, top-notch communities, or educated parents.

The Art Teacher Is the Leader

An important method of getting students started on a path that will be positive for them, and for the teacher is to lay down the framework of the art course at the first meeting. This means letting the students know that you respect them and that they must respect the teacher also; that you will reward ambition, perseverance, hard work, achievement in any form in which it presents itself, and that you will be looking for experiences and evidences that indicate students are in there working as a team doing the very best they can. Students need to know that you want them to develop their art knowledge, their critical appreciative awareness, their art skills, and that you will be looking for accomplishment of this sort. It is important to lay down clear cut, well defined objectives of what is expected in a particular class. Explain also that you intend to prepare and encourage them for further extensive work; that you will try to make classroom lectures and demonstrations worth-while, that you are deeply interested in the class and enjoy teaching. This means approaching the students without appearing superior and overbearing, maintaining discipline, yet a friendly atmosphere in the class, exercising personal integrity, sound objectives and offering an open mind.

A teacher who is sincerely dedicated to his own work needs to like people and to feel a desire, a need to bring out the best in students in order to enable them to develop. When a teacher acts as though he enjoys teaching and wants to put an idea across enthusiastically, students can sense this and rapport comes. The teacher must command the attention of the class, but also must communicate and be able to hold the respect of the class. He must by his action demonstrate fairness, personal interest in pupils, enthusiasm for subject and profession, love of students, ability to keep the entire class moving forward even if different rates of progress are necessary. He must also understand students, show an interest in them outside of the classroom, have patience and understanding most of the time, be a good listener, sensitive to the student, have an extensive knowledge of subject, be original in thought and delivery, and work hard at encouraging students to see some genuine feeling of success in their work. Good teachers encourage students to reach out for greater knowledge. They try to be fair in evaluating students. They discard obsolete methods with fresh workable objectives. Good teachers don't put shackles on their students; instead they try to set students in motion. Good teachers encourage students to think on their own, to be individuals, and not just mimic the teacher. Good teachers like their students and treat each equally well. They have a high respect for their students, put a lot of time and effort into their preparations, and put their teaching first. Good teachers are proud of their abilities and of their class. They are careful not to ridicule, have strong personalities, energy to keep trying, demonstrate appropriate humor in difficult situations, and *always keep their word*. A teacher is not a programmed instructor, but a person who loves his work and shows it. They must be able to make students feel that they are an important part of the learning process. They must also have a great deal of patience and be willing to help students until they are certain the student knows and understands the material. Good teachers encourage students to learn. Teachers should inspire students to be anything they want to be. A good teacher is fair in his expectation and grading. He must consider their abilities, maturity, and interests when lecturing and teaching. Taking extra time outside class to help those who need help can be valuable.

Teachers need to be interested in life and reflect this concern of people in their own work. Teachers should listen to student suggestions and ideas. Good teachers will not tolerate students who are poorly mannered or who do not respect each other, for they do not respect themselves. Stress should be on a full and complete spirit of discovery and growth, that anything goes in the orderly search for aesthetic expression and that investigation, research, and learning are objectives to shoot for in the classroom. A truly magnificent art teacher can change the whole shape of the school's art program. His enthusiasm will permeate the resistance of any individual!

Teachers need to teach students to respect the works of others and to grow in their own development by sharing and becoming involved with the work that goes on around them in the classroom. Teachers can help to develop inter-people relationships by providing inter-people experiences. Art is not created out of indifference or in isolation or without feeling. Edward Mattil[2] states:

A truly creative student is not indifferent to what he does. Rather he dips deeply into his imagination, creates new and necessary symbols, develops personal techniques, and uses his tools with the maximum of skill.

The teacher creates the environment, whether it be rich or impoverished. It is the teacher who surrounds the child with experiences that keep him feeding on the stuff of learning, growing, and living. People, like snails, will come out of their shells for something enhancing and will stay inside when threatened.

Teaching Students to Work for Success

We need to develop an environment that demands the imaginative solution so that students in some measure of their potential will be lead to make discoveries in the direction of innovations and creativeness. Developing one's fullest potential means not only the development of one's own personal artistic skills, it means many things that relate to the opening up of the individual. It means imagining, pretending, understanding, aspiring, learning, wondering, supposing. In students at the junior and senior high level, we need to make them realize that fear can impede their inventive thinking. We need to encourage them to take risks (and ultimately to make mistakes), and not to be upset over a mistake if it happens, but rather to regard it as a step in the process of discovery. No learning takes place without difficulty, and in order to keep on learning there has to be tolerance for a certain margin of error. We need also to teach students to like each other, to do things with each other, to share ideas rather than to always compete in such a way that it destroys some at the expense of others. We need to work at encouraging students to be highly self-motivating. This is probably one of the prime objectives of an art teacher, or any teacher for that matter. We want them to try things on their own; to pursue beyond the existing problem in the classroom. We want them to quest after knowledge that results from what they have learned in the classroom. If, as art teachers, we can get students to enjoy what they are doing we have a greater opportunity to instill in them resources of energy and self-motivation. We need to encourage students to feel strongly about what they are learning. They need to do their very best.

Identification With Students

More than any other consideration is the need for art teachers to like students, and to respond to them as distinct personalities. The teacher has to give a considerable amount of himself in order to see results in those he teaches. It's important to think of teaching as an opportunity to help others by shaping and challenging thinking. It requires patience, determination, and much trial and error. Above all, it takes love for fellow man. But teaching can be a life long adventure where creating, responding, and sharing artistic vision can help youth to become sensitive, caring, and artistic human beings.

The Art Teacher Is the Model

A teacher must remember that he is a model. He is the primary model. Students will imitate the teacher in everything, just as a child is the spittin' image of his parents. If a teacher draws well, then students will work at drawing well. If a teacher draws poorly, then students will draw poorly or in a mediocre fashion. A teacher, after all, is an advanced student himself. He musn't be afraid to take chances, to involve himself, or to be in error occasionally, as this is part of learning.

Teachers need to encourage students to develop a vision of greatness, and to seek goals that are optimum in nature, instead of accepting the commonplace or average. They need to shoot for the stars; far and high, and not settle for second best.

Students need to take their thinking 10 steps beyond where they thought they could go.

The Aims of Teaching Art in Secondary Schools

What are the aims of teaching art in secondary schools? *Beyond a shadow of a doubt, the single, most significant objective for secondary art teachers today is to teach art in the secondary classroom.* All other aims become peripheral to this singular, broad objective. In teaching art, all other objectives *can be considered*, for art is a humanizing process, an aesthetic catalyst capable of opening up vast cultural vistas on the human plane. Art as creative process and scholarly awareness can reveal people, environments, and idea universes of varying constructs.

Three broad objectives are presented and described for the teaching of art in junior and senior high schools. They include:

1. The development of artistic and perceptual awareness in art.
2. The critical and appreciative study of art history and its analysis.
3. The development of a consistent degree of art skills in selective art media.

1. Developing Artistic and Perceptual Awareness in Art

Awareness can be artistic, intellectual, perceptual or any combination. It is the first stage in any creative process.[3] Awareness can be defined as the ability to perceive or recall in vivid detail the thoughts, perceptions, and feelings which comprise our experiences. It means letting in a steady, and constantly varying flow of stimuli which can be stored and ultimately converted into idea action at a future date. Without awareness, vision of the sort that makes artists *or* appreciators is limited or not possible. Awareness relates to the attitudes we develop concerning what art is or ought

Note how the artist, Henri Matisse has kept the figures simple, while filling the areas around the figures with decorative details.

Courtesy, Albright-Knox Art Gallery, Buffalo, New York
Room of Contemporary Art Fund

"La Musique"
by Henri Matisse, 1939
Oil on Canvas

to be. Awareness is the process by which we gather the details or raw fibers of our experiences. Our awareness forms the basis by which we are able to regenerate experiences into cognitive, aesthetic expression. Awareness means keeping our *mind-bank* flooded with varied and multiple stimuli. In another sense, it means establishing a child-like freedom in our responsiveness to ideas so that we can explore by all possible avenues the deepest aspects of an experience. This suggests moving far beyond the *recognition stage* of perception,[4] which is both immediate and superficial. Awareness encourages us to search for the most minute details. Lowenfeld[5] has said:

Unless we penetrate into an experience, whatever its nature may be, it will remain superficial and as such cannot serve as the basis for creativity. This penetration may deal with visual, tactile, kinaesthetic, or any other sensibilities and any combination of them. It may be emotional, intellectual, or social in nature or any mixture of these. The more we penetrate into the nature of the experience with our feeling, perceiving, and thinking, the more we relate ourselves to it.

Awareness has many facets. It can be intellectual in nature. To study Flemish art of the sixteenth century can reveal that Jan van Eyck, the great Flemish master, was one of the original inventors of oil painting, a highly regarded art medium today. Awareness can be the discovery that Matisse sometimes structured a face by drawing eyes, eyelashes, eyeball, nose, mouth and teeth with one continuous, uninterrupted line; or that Matisse often simplified the figure in his painting, while contrasting the background with highly detailed decorative treatments.

Developing Our Senses: Key Factor to Enriching Awareness

The principal intermediaries between the individual and the development of his awareness are the *senses*. Sensory experience refers to the manner in which we perceive or "take in" outside information.[6] Through the senses we are able to enrich our awareness of the world about us by increasing our capacity for utilizing our senses. For our purposes, this refers mainly to visual sensitivity or observing beyond surface impressions; tactile sensitivity, or learning how things feel to our touch; auditive sensitivity, or learning to listen sharply. It should be carefully noted here, that any outstanding artist, art critic, or art appreciator has a highly refined awareness to his world. Each possesses, through critical practice, awareness to ideas, a keen imagination, and perceptive powers that are aesthetically penetrating.

The significance of developing individual awareness becomes more evident when we observe the extreme absence of such an attribute. Laboratory experiments[7] have demonstrated the detrimental effects of sensory deprivation on human behavior. When human volunteers were bandaged, padded, and isolated from all sensory contact or normal approaches to their perceptions, they reacted in an unusually bizarre fashion. All of the volunteers experienced hallucinations, uncontrollable thoughts, and were otherwise "out of commission." Being out of touch completely with their previous world, they could not react in an organized or normal fashion. John Platt[8] has described the implications of such experiments:

These experiments seem to prove . . . that our bodies are not made to operate in a vacuum. Our brains organize, and exist in order to organize a great variety of incoming sensory messages every waking second, and can become not only emotionally upset but seriously deranged if these messages cease or even if they cease to be new. The fifth need of man is the need for . . . "information," for a continuous, novel, unpredictable, nonredundant, and surprising flow of stimuli.

Such experiments are indicative of man's natural need to explore, experiment, and invent in order to satisfy curiosity and expand one's cathedral of awareness. Experiences in art appreciation, in expanding the imagination, and in media exploration can provide essential cultural vehicles to the enrichment of the individual.

This student is using a camera to develop greater awareness and visual sensitivity to his world.

Courtesy of Dr. Edward L. Mattil, Chairman, Department of Art, North Texas State University, and Dr. Leon Frankston from Childrens Art Classes, Pennsylvania State University.

Openness Is Essential to Developing a Rich Art Awareness

Artistic growth in art takes place when students are "ready and open" to opportunities for experiencing their world as vividly as possible. Rogers[9] describes the value of being open to one's experiences:

In the person who is open to experience, however, every stimulus, whether originating within the organism or the environment, would be freely relayed through the nervous system without being distorted by a defensive mechanism . . . Whether the stimulus was the impact of a configuration of form, color, or sound in the environment on the sensory nerves, or a memory trace from the past, or a visceral sensation of fear or pleasure or disgust, the person would be "living it," would have it completely available to awareness.

Being open means that we are able to consider many alternatives in any given situation. We are able to move beyond the recognition or surface stage of our thinking to a more viable aesthetic sense. In art, our attitudes and assumptions toward it are determined from previous experiences. Surprisingly enough, it is not unusual for a college educated person to have an extremely limited understanding of the visual arts. Many adults, unfortunately, go through their entire lives with little if any understanding or enjoyment of art. Lacking such experiences in creating, or in learning to critically appraise art, many individuals shy away from it for fear of being exposed. As students in secondary schools are provided a meaningful curriculum in critically understanding as well as engaging in art, infinitely wider attitudes toward it will be encouraged. Past experiences in studying art will provide a basis for present evaluation. Barkan states:[10]

We see things through our past experiences. Our past experiences determines our "readiness" and our "point of view" from which we create our interpretations. For the active developing individual, a point of view is always temporary; it is always contingent upon ongoing active experience. The things we "see" are those that have been meaningful in our past experiences.

Fixed Points of View Block Awareness to Art

Fixed points of view implies that one does not venture from his rigidly constructed life style. However, if idea growth is to occur, one must step outside the security of his mental blanket and take some creative risks.

We need to move out of the narrow channel that can circumvent our lives. Most of us do not consciously plan to shut out parts of the world, but when we close our minds to fresh options for discovery in art, we begin marching backwards into the future.[11] Listed following are some commonly repeated statements of opinion which tend to limit one's point of view to art through clinging to fixed cliches. How often we have heard some students remark:

a. I can't see any point in abstract painting.
b. I'm not very original.
c. I can't even draw a straight line.
d. My kid sister can paint better than some modern artists.
e. Art is a waste of time unless a person has talent.

Statements such as these are defensive vehicles aimed at protecting one from the risk of discovering something new. Any initial confrontation with new subject material to ones experience can be painful. Studying art can be extremely distressing in the beginning, for it requires taking risks in exploring unknowns. Once we move beyond *surface inertia*, we can permit ourselves a more open attitude toward what we can discover about art.

John Gardner[12] states: "As we mature we progressively narrow the scope and variety of our lives. Of all the interests we might pursue, we settle on a few. Of all the people with whom we might associate, we select a small number. We become caught in a web of fixed relationships. We develop set ways of doing things."

Each of us needs some form of continuity in our lives, for without an ordering of our experiences we would be in a constant state of bewilderment, never knowing quite what to expect. For brief spurts, this could be an exciting holiday but continual uncertainty can often lead to distress. A more reasonable approach would be to try and experience one's world with fresh awareness at each opportunity. For some students, the development of their own potentiality and the process of self-discovery never ends, while others have great difficulty in using their imaginations or seeking experiences with the full vitality that awareness brings. As teachers, we need to work at discovering the ways that will open students to the imaginative, inventive, and self-renewing life.

Understanding What Mind-Stretching Can Do

Awareness requires mind stretching. Train your mind to work for you! Instead of closing off thinking too soon, open it up and let your potential come pouring out! Remember, awareness to art or life requires practice. Start today!

Another method of comparing your awareness potential is to contrast new words learned in the English language each year. For example, between the ages of six and ten, an average child learns 5,000 words a year. By comparison, the average adult learns fewer than twenty-five words a year.[13] When we read comparisons such as this it seems rather alarming to think that, for many of us, our learning rate has almost stopped. Most of us have a propensity for getting by with a minimum amount of functional words, sounds, or perceptions. Once recognition sets in, we switch off. It is natural for the mind to shut down once a solution pattern has been established, for this is the mind's way of being efficient. But minds, like waistlines, get fat. We need to reduce cranial bulge by practicing attitudes of awareness that help lead us to unique and original modes of response, especially to art. Teachers need to encourage students *not* to be satisfied with *just O.K.* Personal intellectual, aesthetic, and human success is achieved when one gives his best to an experience. This holds true for all of life.

The following points summarize the importance of developing awareness as the first stage in the art learning process:

1. Awareness encourages the growth of unique ideas.
2. Awareness practice takes one beyond the surface of an idea.
3. To be aware is to be more original in concept and action.
4. Awareness helps one to play his hunches and continue searching.
5. Awareness helps one to be more open to all sorts of possibilities.
6. Awareness is the first step in building ideas.
7. The development of one's awareness reaffirms the uniqueness of the individual.
8. Awareness sets the stage for artistic or appreciative endeavor.
9. Awareness prompts one to explore unknowns in search of a better idea.
10. Awareness helps one to see the world with fresh eyes.

Descriptive Comparison of Awareness in Teaching Art

The Teacher Who Has a High Degree of Art Awareness:	*The Teacher Who Has Average or Below Average Art Awareness:*
Realizes the importance of teaching subject content, art appreciation, as well as media exploration.	Continually gives project oriented lessons that avoid subject content or critical appreciative experiences.
Encourages students to be more perceptually alert by observing the world of art closely through reading art books and journals, visiting art galleries, evaluating art products.	Doesn't encourage students to go beyond a given art assignment in class. Accepts mediocre work as satisfactory.
Encourages students to resist their first ideas in order to push them to more unique, innovative, and imaginative solutions in thinking and in media processes.	Through lack of stimulus, keeps students within a given boundary, and often frowns on students who move outside the prescribed boundary.
Tries to build an artistic and aesthetic environment in the art classroom by visually interesting art materials at hand, with immediate access to books, art journals, art products. Makes certain that students contribute to the art environment.	Keeps the room "antiseptic" at all times, with a minimum of clean up problems. Clean materials, such as pencil or crayons are the order of the day.
Realizes that he is a model, and reveals his enthusiasm toward art, works in a media himself, and generally tries to impart the feeling that art is the most exciting thing around. Thinks uniquely at all times.	Sticks to tried and true methods, doesn't take unnecessary risks, has a pat system for everything, not interested in the students, lacks humor and is grumpy, fearful of other teachers, is conventional and rigid in his thinking.
Is imaginative, inventive, innovative, observant, skillful, enthusiastic, perceptive, understanding, and a sparkling human being.	In short, a very crabby apple.

Thinking Like An Artist

· One of the best ways to start your artistic thinking is to practice noticing details. Every natural object or form in the world is slightly different from its look-alike counterpart. In the imaginative world of the artist, things are often deliberately different. In figures A and B following, notice the great variety of ways to create eyes and noses. How many more can you add to the group? In figure C, complete the faces in an original manner.

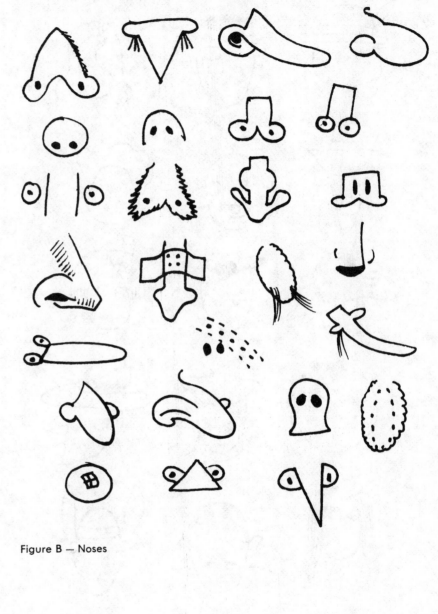

Figure B — Noses

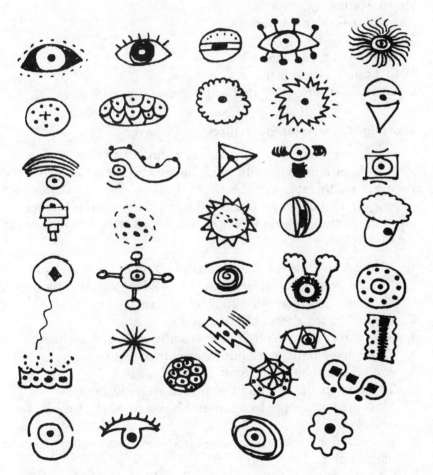

Figure A — Eyes

Figure C — Complete the faces
in an original manner

One of the earmarks of an artist is his originality in expressing ideas. The following artists created paintings, drawings, and sculpture with inventive solutions regarding eyes, noses, and other features. Se if you can find some examples of their work that illustrates this.

Pablo Picasso (Spanish)
George Grosz (German)
Rufino Tamayo (Mexican)
Alexi Jawlenski (Russian)
Henri Matisse (French)
Alexander Calder (American)
Paul Klee (Swiss)
Saul Steinberg (American)
Walt Disney (American)
Can you discover other artists and add to this list?

Sharpen Your Awareness through Discovery

You can sharpen your awareness for art by learning to be alert to hundreds of possibilities. Imagination is what gives you your original thrust in art. It is the experience of reassembling your memory in unique ways. Imagination can be nurtured by increasing your awareness for noticing details. Here are a few interesting details.

1. The vision of birds is approximately 8 times greater than man. (At the point of clearest focus, a hawk has 150,000 vision rods and cones, compared to 15,000 for man.)
2. Elephants are almost blind at 100 feet.
3. Ants can recognize other ants visually at 3/4 of an inch.
4. Clams have light mechanisms over their entire body.
5. A giraffe's tongue is a dark shade of purple.
6. The human brain weighs approximately 50 ounces.
7. Most dreams people have are in black and white, unless one is deaf.
8. You can remember information better before bedtime than in the morning.
9. Clarence Nash is the creator of Donald Duck's voice.

Courtesy, Chuck Friedenmaker

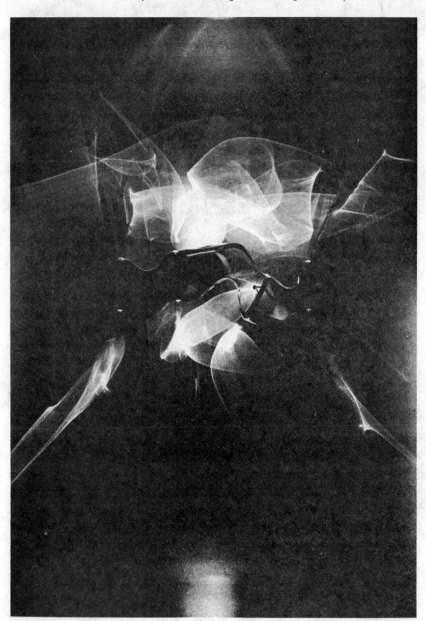

"Continuel Lumiere"
by LeParc, 1966
Light and Aluminum

Courtesy, Howard Wise Gallery, New York

The world of the student and that of the mature artist is one of degree. The trigger for artistic success may lie in the current art lesson. Note the relationship of the student work to the mature art work by the artist LeParc.

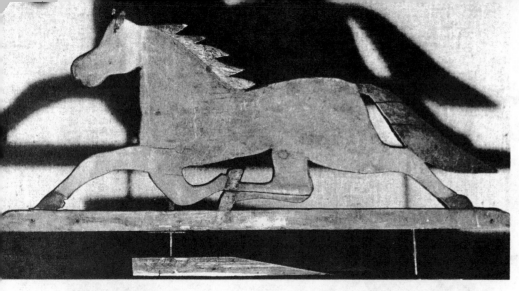

"Running Horse"
A carved weathervane
by an anonymous folk sculptor,
19th century

Courtesy, University Art Collection, Arizona State University
Purchase, The American Art Heritage Fund

"The Generals"
by Marisol (Escobar),
1961-62 Wood and
Mixed Media

Courtesy, Albright-Knox Art Gallery, Buffalo, New York
Gift of Seymour H. Knox

Each artist interprets the forms of
his art in his own way, although communication may indicate an identical
response. In this case, the image is
horse.

Positive Steps to Increase Artistic Awareness

1. *Track the uncommon — the unordinary.* Search for novel ways to see life, people, and your own individual manner of communicating and responding to experiences.

2. *Push your imagination to the furtherest limit.* Practice thinking up unique and interesting ways to express ideas or form solutions for problems.

3. *Develop an insatiable sense of curiosity.* Be interested in doing things and meeting people. Search out and discover what you like. Don't sit back and wait for it to come to you. Interest encourages new insights.

4. *Maintain a sense of openness.* Develop an open mind toward all things. Keep a tolerant attitude. Reject as little as possible in the beginning of any experience. Try new things. Risk more in terms of giving to others. Perceptual growth takes place when we let it come in.

5. *Seek information.* We need to bring in the data in order to increase perceptual power. We can express ideas if we have information to draw on. The more we learn about things, the greater our perception for future pursuing.

6. *Set reachable goals for yourself.* Set goals that you can achieve. Think 10 times greater than what you are currently doing in any experience. Let this be your reachable goal. Extend your goal each time you attain it.

2. The Study of Art History and Its Analysis

In the subject of art, teachers need to learn to articulate about artists and art works of both past and present. They should work at understanding what is going on in the contemporary art world, for this is most immediate. Some good sources for catching up and keeping up with contemporary art include:

Art News	Craft Horizons
Artforum	Graphis
Art in America	Art books (see references
Art Week	at close of each chapter)
College Art Journal	

Why The Study of Art History Is Important

Until recently, emphasis in secondary school art classrooms has been on the development of art skills through media exploration and practice. Without neglecting this aspect of creative expression, it should also be realized that a shift in thinking has occurred in secondary art education. First of all, many art students in junior high and secondary school programs choose art on an elective basis. Most of these students are potential consumers or appreciators, and will not major in art in college or life. However, through art classes at the secondary level they will have an excellent opportunity to develop a critical-appreciative awareness to art. The student who includes instruction in learning to understand the arts through critical assessment and study of masterworks will find himself increasingly in touch with an environment which places greater and greater emphasis on visually aesthetic commodities. Three points seem particularly significant for the study of art as history and for appreciative understanding:

1. The study of art history provides a scholarly springboard from which the great art of the past can be illuminated in the light of what is known about art today.

2. Understanding art in history enriches the artistic vision of the appreciator. Knowing the subject of art provides one with a basis for making evaluative judgments and comparisons to his own work and to the work of others.

3. Studying the subject of art increases one's capacity for engaging in aesthetic decisions immediate to life, including consumer product judgments and community decisions, especially architecture, parks, and city planning.

The person who is sensitive to the arts does not encourage ugly cities to be built, nor highways to be littered with billboards irregardless of aesthetic considerations. Without the farsighted thinking of a few sensitive individuals in responsible positions, many of our national parks, California redwoods, ocean beaches, and countless miles of beautiful America would have been ravaged long ago. Notwithstanding, these devastating forces are presently at work,

"Fur-Covered Cup, Saucer, and Spoon"
by Meret Oppenheim, 1936

Courtesy, Collection, The Museum of Modern Art, New York

but an outstanding art teacher at the secondary level can be a spirited light to sensitize the community leaders and average citizens of tomorrow who will play a major role in the determination of the aesthetic life.

Conant[14] speaks to the need for a more scholarly approach to the study of art:

These urgently needed changes in secondary school art education necessitate drastic modifications in the traditional roles of junior and senior high school art teachers. No longer can they function primarily as studio masters, spending most of their time guiding students' creative expression in drawing, painting, and occasional three-dimensional media. No longer can they stress their favorite art school subject, such as mask-making, watercolor painting, or copper enameling, neglecting the development of their students' overall art knowledge. No longer can art teachers regard youngsters in their classes as youthful prototypes of art school students. The role which art education now asks junior and senior high school art teachers to assume will be one which is more scholarly, initially less appealing, less dramatic, and more time-demanding; but, eventually, it will be seen to be rewarding both to themselves and to their students.

Art teachers need to teach the subject of art history in such a manner that it comes to life for students. Henry Hope[15] states:

In teaching the history of art, I would say that the first requirement is a thorough knowledge and understanding of the subject to be taught (not necessarily the whole history of art, but that part to which one's lecture or seminar is addressed). Second: one needs to develop a means of communication at the level of the students; clear and cogent statements, avoiding as much as possible both cliches and in art history one needs to be sure that the specialized terminology (even terms like line and color, but especially such concepts as forms, style, composition, volume, mass) as they apply to our critical understanding of works of art are clearly expressed and known to the audience. This would include showing in every way possible how art relates to life, through comparisons with other disciplines, through its role in history and through its presence in daily life in our time.

The artist can show us new interpretations of traditional forms, thus breaking barriers to more unusual possibilities and ideas for constructing aesthetic form.

Courtesy of The Hand and the Spirit Crafts Gallery, Scottsdale, Arizona, Photograph by Glenn Short

"Porkypine Basket" by Edith Bondie, Chippewa Indian Made from Black Ash

3. The Development of Art Skills in Selective Art Media

Even though most students may never choose some phase of art for continued career study, it is essential to the process of understanding art that students participate in the labors of creating it. Art works will never be adequately understood by someone who has never held a brush or practiced with a drawing instrument. Involvement in a series of experiences in making art is necessary to open up one's range of understanding to what art can be. The student who works with an art medium can better comprehend the difficult challenge of creating a masterpiece. Art is not a simple process of administering pigment to canvas according to a set formula and stepping back to admire the results. Indeed, as in all experiences of value, there will be frustration, heartache, despair, as well as the joy experienced in seeing improvement in one's own efforts. Students need to learn *not* to compromise too early in art. The art product a student creates must represent the complete and total effort of the student through his involvement, persistence, and dedication to the task in order to move his art work in process toward a hopefully successful conclusion. It would be erroneous to think that all art works attempted will turn out successfully. Even the best known artists of the world do not achieve perfection each time. In fact, many accomplished artists feel success if they achieve one good work out of ten. Success in art is relative to one's own goals. Being able to sense accomplishment from one work to the next can become the substance of artistic growth. Most of us will agree that every person varies in his native capacity to create art works. Some few are richly endowed, just as in any discipline. For most students, the joy of painting, or drawing, or working in some art media can be a most enlightening experience.

Students need to study art as both subject content, and as media exploration. Through both means, aesthetic awareness to artistic forms can be better grasped. Studying the work of various artists can reveal insights into the nature of how artists create. Students who have many opportunities to study great art works in both original or vicarious form can better relate their own feelings toward art. Studying masterworks of art can be extremely helpful in in-

Courtesy, University Art Collections, Arizona State University Gift of Mr. and Mrs. Orme Lewis

"Rembrandt Bareheaded"

by Rembrandt Van Rijn, Dutch, 1616-1669
Etching

"The Irish Girl"
by Robert Henri, American, 1900
Oil

Courtesy, University Art Collections, Arizona State University
Gift of Oliver B. James

Courtesy, University Art Collections, Arizona State University
Oliver B. James Collection of American Art

"The Young Clown"
by Walt Khun

creasing one's own art skill. It is usually not possible for students to have access to original works, except for those able to commute to museums in large cities. However, not matter, for as Malraux[16] has stated, the "museum without walls" of beautiful reproductions through books and slides can bring the world of art to the student. How to study art works can be approached in various manners. As an example, one might decide to investigate how various artists treated facial features, i.e., Matisse,[17] who drew features in continuous outline, or Picasso,[18] who merged profile and front view into one likeness. Another problem in seeing might be to study how certain artists structured light and dark patterns within their compositions, e.g., Caravaggio,[19] Rembrandt,[20] or Edward Hopper.[21] We may wish to examine how brush strokes and thickness of pigment can aid in building up the artistic form. Contrasting examples of pigment variations can be studied in the thick, pasty works of Van Gogh,[22] or the slick, varnished surfaces of William Harnett.[23] Each time subject exploration is undertaken, with subsequent evaluative appraisals, the student can reinforce his discoveries by working with art media in a similar manner. In this way, he becomes sensitive to what material can do, becomes more knowledgeable of the artistic masters, and gains fluency in his own individual expression.

The development of art skills can be different for each student. It can change, depending on age and maturity. Readiness is a factor to be considered throughout secondary education. For some students, exploring in one direction for an extensive period of time may yield positive results. For another student, handling many forms of media can suggest avenues of pursuit.

Two Types of Thinking in Art

There seems to be two distinct types of thinking in approaching art experiences. The two types[24] of thinking are (1) intuitive, and (2) analytic. Intuitive thinking in art occurs when the artist or student searches for expressive possibilities in specific art media. At the time of creating, he does not consciously note every stroke or movement of the brush or pencil. Rather, in an intuitive sense, he plays his hunches, and proceeds at a level just below conscious awareness. Intuitive thinking is not composed of set, concrete steps. Intuitiveness probably works best when there is a certain mastery of tools and materials. The student may arrive at answers or solutions in his art by an intuitive process, and not know why he worked in such a way except that he "felt" some inclination in a particular direction. Often, master artists will begin their work intuitively, and after working on a problem for some time, will step back to analyze what they have done. Students who are more willing to take risks, to explore new avenues, seem to be more able to proceed in their thinking about art by incorporating intuitive approaches.

"Typewriter"
by Robert Arneson, 1967
Ceramic

By contrast, analytic thinking in art evaluation-appreciation, or in creative processes involves concrete, plausible, and logical possibilities for arriving at workable solutions. Analytic thinking usually proceeds one step at a time, with each step building on the former until a product or solution is arrived at. Analytic methods can often be used after intuitive leaps have been initiated.

Experienced Art Teachers Offer Clues to What Should Be Taught at Secondary Levels

What we are basically trying to do in art is to cultivate excellence in every way possible. We might refer to excellence as the refinement of the aesthetic eye. Teachers should provide students with problems and exercises in art practice in order to help them gain a degree of mastery over the material. We want the student to be able to put the pieces together when he finishes and to eventually come up with his approach, his concept, his understanding. We want students to be richer aesthetically because of art—because they did engage in looking, evaluating, judging, and creating. Experienced teachers in art education can often provide valuable clues to teachers just entering the field. While research into what should be taught at junior and senior levels is not prolific by any means, experienced art teachers across the country offer insights into the type of art programs that should be initiated.

Frederic M. Logan[25]

The art teacher can start educating young people to know the arts, to begin understanding art in historical perspective, to expect that works of art will be a part of their lives wherever they may be. Only by persistently teaching "art" as history is taught, as literature and science are taught, is the teacher going to help students see art as humanistic, that is, as "thought or action centering upon distinctively human interests." Too many high school graduates think of art class as time spent in painting or in "doing" other projects which are important only in the classroom, to be put aside along with other memories of childhood and youth.

"Essex"
by John Chamberlain,
1960 Welded Auto Metal

Courtesy, Collection, Museum of Modern Art, New York
Gift of Mr. and Mrs. Robert Scull

The artist today uses unorthodox media in order to create unorthodox yet intriguing images that challenge us to respond and inquire further.

James A. Schinneller[26]

What one can expect from art is, of course, dependent upon what one is willing to give to the field. Effort and study increase knowledge, and active participation—from drawing and painting to carving or designing architectural forms—provides valuable insights and develops skills. Art activity should not be limited to only those who are preparing for a potential profession or career in art, for it can provide enrichment to all students no matter what their future vocations. It should aid those confronted with problems in building, selecting, enjoying, and evaluating. Knowledge of art should develop an awareness and appreciation of both nature and well-designed man-made objects ranging from paintings and houses to kitchen utensils. Art should aid in developing a belief in oneself and a desire for creating a more beautiful and meaningful world in which to live.

June King McFee[27]

1. Art is a visual history of the development of cultures. Objective: The history of mankind can become more real to children through empathic learning of other periods and societies.
2. Art is the basis of much of our communication system. Objective: Children should become aware of visual forms as communication. They should learn to judge what to accept and what to reject, rather than to be passive receptors.
3. Art is a live reflector of our present culture. Objective: Children can see art as a growing, changing part of life through their own participation.
4. Art is one of man's means for reflection of his personal and collective experience. Objective: Art activity helps a child objectify and organize his own feeling and interaction in living.

Irving Kaufman[28]

. . . art classes in high school should be closely and seriously allied to both the historical background of art and its current vitality of development outside the classroom. In all, the teaching of art should take on a more serious tone concentrating on intrinsic substance and critical evaluation at the same time that it enriches the symbolic development of aesthetic "play" and personal expression.

   The curricular base of art education requires an expansion, on all levels, to include more of the substance and particular processes which help in producing the mind that is prepared to know or engage in an art experience. A change in the direction of including contextual information about works of art, of aiming for intensified analysis of art works would complement the creative aims in a very sound and fruitful manner.

Elliott W. Eisner[29]

A second type of program, this one almost totally absent from the elementary school and only sparsely employed at the secondary level, has its major orientation towards the development of critical appreciative powers and toward furthering the students' historical understanding of art in human culture. In such a program students would be expected to develop their ability to critically appraise works of art by first being able to describe the qualities that constitute them and second by giving good reasons to support the judgments they make about them. Such a program might employ studio activities from time to time, but these activities would be understood by both students and teachers as instrumental to the development of critical and historical skills. The product of this program would be a person who understood the evolution of art in western and eastern culture; he would be able to evaluate the qualities that constitute works of art and would be familiar with major alternative conceptions of art.

Rein Hastie and David Templeton[30]

This shift in major emphasis for a high school art program has been a gradual one and is not new, having been underway and moving slowly for a quarter of a century. It suggests that the secondary school art program will be more an exploratory one, involving a wide variety of broad units of experience based on ideas and the role and function of art in all of man's activity. It will stress development of understanding and the art method. Less emphasis will be placed upon learning of a technical process for its own sake and on a specialized, sequential building up of skill as apprenticeship foundation for a more stringent college studio program. This also means that there will be evaluation in terms of the effects of the art experience on the student and his whole behavior, with the art product evaluated as only one part of the total continuum of the art process experience.

Edward L. Mattil[31]

To teach artists first implies that there are people who want, above all things, to become artists, and that these individuals can get into an institution where training is available. It also implies the availability of teachers, studios, art works, and libraries. The problem of teaching artists today is complicated by the fact that no one can say for sure what art is or what form it should take. In the past artists were trained "in the tradition," but what is today's tradition? Therefore, training artists amounts to directing the attention of prospective artists to the study and practice of their art through the study of mankind and of significant artists and their products, and through the creation of works of art.

"The Royal Tiger"
by Salvadore Dali, 1962
Oil

"Family Group"
by Henry Moore, 1944
Bronze

Courtesy, M. Knoedler & Co., Inc., New York

"Mother and Child" (Portrait of Mrs. Thurneyssen and her Daughter)
by Pierre Auguste Renoir, 1910
Oil on Canvas

Courtesy, Albright-Knox Art Gallery, Buffalo, New York

Mary Adeline McKibbin[32]

Art in the junior high school should be guided by the nature of the junior high school student, his interests, needs, and abilities. But it should always be concerned with the nature of art. Both in the student's creative experiences with tools and materials and in his approach to the traditions of art, he should be led to an awareness of form, color, line, and space, and a sensitivity to their interrelationships. He should be helped to a keener and more creative visual perceptivity through planned experiences. He should achieve greater skill in the use of the tools and materials of the artist and should realize through his own act of creating and through a study of the work of others that art is the organization of elements to communicate ideas, feelings, truths; that it is one of man's most effective means of communication and self-realization. He should understand that the artist is himself a part of every true work of art and should, therefore, come to value the uniqueness of the work of art and respect the integrity of the artist, whether fellow student or master, or indeed himself.

NAEA Position Statement[33]

Art has four aspects: seeing and feeling visual relationships, producing works of art, knowing and understanding about art objects, and evaluating art products. A meaningful school art program will include experiences in all of these areas.

Summary of Objectives for Teaching Art at Secondary Levels

In reviewing the chapter, the following objectives can be stated for teachers of junior and senior high school art programs:

Major Objectives

1. The development of artistic and perceptual awareness in art.
2. The critical and appreciative study of art history and its analysis.
3. The development of an operational degree of art skills in selective art media.

Specific Objectives for Teaching Art at Junior and Senior High Levels

1. Teach students to study and appreciate contemporary art.
2. Teach students to study the artists and art products that are influencing contemporary society.
3. Teach students the arts in historical perspective, and their relation to contemporary society.

4. Teach students specific art skills in art media, such as painting, drawing crafts, printmaking, photography.
5. Teach students to be aware of art and ideas through an increased sensitivity to aesthetic forms.
6. Teach students to have a discriminating eye in choosing beautiful forms in architecture, consumer products, paintings.
7. Teach students to see, feel, and discover.
8. Teach students that art enables man to express his feelings, thus reaffirming the uniqueness of the individual.
9. Teach students to examine critically why artists create art works.
10. Teach students how to judge and evaluate artistic forms.
11. Teach students to develop their awareness to the beauty of life.

References

1. HOWARD CONANT and ARNE RANDALL, *Art in Education*, Peoria, Illinois: Charles A. Bennett, 1959, p. 27.
2. EDWARD MATTIL, Meaning in Crafts. (II). and ed. 1965.
3. EARL W. LINDERMAN, "Curriculum for Awareness," *Art Education*, June 1964, Vol. 17, Number 6, p. 5.
4. JOHN DEWEY, *Art as Experience*, New York: Minton, Balch, 1934.
5. VICTOR LOWENFELD, "Creativity and Art Education," *School Arts*, October 1959.
6. WOLFGANG VON BUDDENBROCK, *The Senses*, Ann Arbor: University of Michigan Press, 1958.
7. SOLOMON, TRUMBULL, et al., *Sensory Deprivation*, Cambridge: Harvard University Press, 1961.
8. JOHN RADER PLATT, "The Fifth Need of Man," Horizon 1:106:July 1959.
9. CARL ROGERS, "Toward Becoming a Fully Functioning Person," *Perceiving, Behaving, Becoming*, Washington, D.C.: Association for Supervision and Curriculum Development, 1962, p. 23.
10. MANUAL BARKAN, *A Foundation for Art Education*, New York: The Ronald Press Company, 1955, p. 16.
11. MARSHALL McLUHAN, *The Medium is the Massage*, New York: Bantam Books, 1967.
12. JOHN W. GARDNER, *Self-Renewal*, New York: Harper & Row, 1965, p. 9.
13. NORMAN LEWIS, *Power With Words*, New York: Thomas Y. Crowell Co., 1964.
14. HOWARD CONNANT, *Art Education*, Center for Applied Research in Education, Inc., Washington, D.C. 1964, p. 80.
15. HENRY HOPE, from a letter to the author regarding the teaching of Art History, 1968.

16. ANDRE MALRAUX, *Voices of Silence*, Garden City, New York: Doubleday & Co., Inc., 1953.

17. JOHN CANADAY, *Mainstreams of Modern Art*, New York: Holt, Rinehart & Winston, Inc., 1966.

18. ALFRED H. BARR, JR., *Picasso: Fifty Years of His Art*, New York: Museum of Modern Art, 1946.

19. WALTER FRIEDLANDER, *Caravaggio Studies*, Princeton University Press, 1955.

20. ROSENBERG, J., *Rembrandt*, 2 vols., rev. ed., Cambridge: Harvard University Press, 1964.

21. CHARLES MCCURDY, Ed., *Modern Art*, New York: Macmillan, 1959.

22. SCHAPIRO, MEYER, *Vincent Van Gogh*, Agbrams, New York. 1950.

23. JOHN CANADAY, *Mainstreams of Modern Art*, New York: Holt, Rinehart & Winston, 1960.

24. JEROME S. BRUNER, *The Process of Education*, New York: Random House, 1960.

25. FREDERICK M. LOGAN, "*Artist in the Schoolroom: A Modern Dilemma*," *Studies in Art Education*, Vol. II, No. 2, Spring 1961, pp. 66-84.

26. JAMES A. SCHINNELLER, *Art: Search and Self-Discovery*, Second Edition, Scranton, Pa.: International Textbook Company, 1968.

27. JUNE KING MCFEE, *Preparation for Art*, San Francisco: Wadsworth Publishing Co., 1961, pp. 178–179.

28. IRVING KAUFMAN, *Art and Education in Contemporary Culture*, New York: Macmillan Company, 1966, p. 443.

29. ELLIOTT W. EISNER, "The Challenge to Art Education," *Art Education*, Vol. 20, No. 2, February, 1967, p. 29.

30. REID HASTIE and DAVID TEMPLETON, "Profile of Art in Secondary Schools," May, 1964, *Art Education*, Vol. 17, No. 5, p. 7.

31. EDWARD L. MATTIL, "Teaching the Arts," Chapter IV, *The Arts in Higher Education*, San Francisco: Jossey-Bass Inc., edited by Lawrence E. Dennis and Renate M. Jacob, p. 72.

32. MARY ADELINE MCKIBBIN, "Art in the Secondary Schools," from Report of The Commission on Art Education, edited by Jerome J. Hausman, Washington, D.C., National Art Education Association, 1965, pp. 92-93.

33. NAEA Position Statement on art objectives for Elementary and Secondary Schools, 1968.

Additional References for Reading Beyond

1. ARNHEIM, RUDOLF, *Art and Visual Perception*, Berkeley: University of California Press, 1954.

2. BROUDY, HARRY S., "Aesthetic Education in the Secondary School," *Art Education*, June 1965, Vol. 18, No. 6, p. 24.

3. COLLINS, HOWARD F., "Art History/High School," *Art Education*, May 1963, Vol. 16, No. 5, p. 6.

4. D'AMICO, VICTOR, *Creative Teaching in Art*, Scranton, Pa.: International Textbook Company, 1953.

5. DEFRANCESCO, ITALO L., *Art Education—Its Means and Ends*, New York: Harper & Row, 1958, 652 pp.

6. ECKER, DAVID, "Justifying Aesthetic Judgments," *Art Education*, May 1967, Vol. 20, No. 5, p. 5.

7. EISNER, ELLIOT, W., *Educating Artistic Vision*, New York: Macmillan, 1972.

8. FELDMAN, EDMUND B., *Becoming Human through Art*, Englewood Cliffs, N.J.: Prentice-Hall, 1970.

9. GAITSKELL, CHARLES and MARGARET, *Art Education During Adolescence*, New York: Harcourt Brace & Co., 1954, 116 pp.

10. GARSON, ANDREA and RUSSELL, MARTIN F., "Alternative Approaches to Teaching Art Appreciation," *Art Education*, June 1967, Vol. 20, No. 6, p. 8.

11. GRIGSBY, J. EUGENE, *Art and Ethnics: Backgrounds for Teaching Youth in a Pluralistic Society*, Dubuque, Ia.: William C. Brown Company Publishers, 1977.

12. HABER, RALPH NORMAN, editor, *Contemporary Theory and Research in Visual Perception*, New York: Holt, Rinehart & Winston, 1968.

13. HUBBARD, GUY, *Art in the High School*, Belmont, California: Wadsworth Publishing Company, 1967.

14. LANIER, VINCENT, *Teaching Secondary Art*, Scranton, Pa.: International Textbook Co., 1964.

15. LINDERMAN, EARL W., *Invitation to Vision*, Dubuque, Iowa: Wm. C. Brown Company Publishers, 1967.

16. LINDERMAN, EARL W. and LINDERMAN, MARLENE M., *Crafts for the Classroom*, New York: Macmillan, 1977.

17. LINDERMAN, MARLENE M., *Art in the Elementary School*, Dubuque, Ia.: William C. Brown Company Publishers, 2d ed. 1979.

18. LOGAN, FREDERICK M., *Growth of Art in American Schools*, New York: Harper & Row, 1955, 310 pp.

19. LOWENFELD, VICTOR, and BRITTAIN, WM. LAMBERT, *Creative and Mental Growth*, 6th ed., 1976.

20. MUNRO, THOMAS, *Art Education, Its Philosophy and Psychology*, New York: The Liberal Arts Press, 1956, 387 pp.

21. MURPHY, JEANETTE, "Art Education in the Secondary School, A Selected Bibliography," *Art Education*, November 1963, Vol. 16, No. 8, p. 22.

22. REED, CARL, *Early Adolescent Art Education*, Peoria, Ill.: Charles A. Bennett Co., 1957, 205 pp.

23. SCHINNELLER, JAMES A., "Art Programs for Secondary School Students," *Art Education*, March 1964, Vol. 17, No. 3, p. 11.

"Altar Portrait of a Deceased Oba"
Africa, Benin Tribe, probably 17th Century

Chapter 2

The mind is never passive; it is a perpetual activity, delicate, receptive, responsive to stimulus. You cannot postpone its life until you have sharpened it. Whatever interest attaches to your subject-matter must be evoked here and now; whatever powers you are strengthening in the pupil, must be exercised here and now; whatever possibilities of mental life your teaching should impart, must be exhibited here and now. That is the golden rule of education, and a very difficult rule to follow.

ALFRED N. WHITEHEAD,
Aims of Education,
New York: Macmillan Company, 1929, p. 18

What Makes a Good Teacher?

Measuring Excellence in Art Teaching Is Elusive

How often we hear students and faculty members remark on the superb teaching characteristics of certain instructors. What qualities do teachers of this caliber possess? It must be granted that the measurement of factors responsible for the difference between superb and routine teaching is often not evident from outward appearances. Some instructors may well believe that such measurement is impossible. Yet, excellent teachers exist at all levels of teaching. Most of us can remember at least one teacher in our background who served as a strong motivating force in helping us to mature and reach beyond what we thought we could do.

Harlan Hoffa[1] defines a good teacher in the following manner:

The definition of a good teacher is another matter. I think that I can recognize a good teacher when I see one in action but the qualities which such a person possesses are too elusive to easily define. Essentially, however, I suppose that a good teacher is one who provokes learning by whatever means may be appropriate to the situation and the individual students who may be involved. These qualities could include personal sensibility and political suavity, but may also involve performing like a trained seal, hustling like a circus barker, or preaching like a fire and brimstone parson. It is partly salesmanship, partly seduction, partly playing the pied

Courtesy, Edna Gilbert, Mesa Public Schools, Mesa, Arizona

Good teachers often do the unexpected. They are not afraid to try new possibilities, or seek new creative directions in their work.

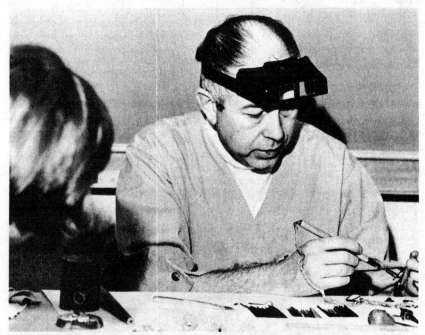

Courtesy, Mesa Public Schools, Mesa, Arizona
Photo by Michele Ditson

Alexander Kower, Scottsdale, Arizona jeweler visits a Mesa school

Courtesy, James Doerter, Southern Oregon College Art Professor

piper bit, and partly the IBM thing. A good teacher may be an iceberg of which the students see only a small proportion or a lighthouse which serves as a navigational beacon or a mountain to be conquered. The best teachers I have known, Margaret Stein, Jane Betsy Welling and Victor Lowenfeld, had one quality in common, however. They enabled me to transcend myself, to do more than I thought myself capable of doing, to seem disappointed rather than angry or blasé if I did not meet their expectations, and I worked like the very devil for them because of this. This may be too personal a definition but I only know good teachers from having learned with them. Perhaps this is the only way. The business of being nurtured by another is, after all, a fairly intimate relationship.

Ivan Johnson[2] states:

A secondary school art teacher is confronted with two phenomena not known to his predecessors: a quasi-existentialist view of art and an alienated, articulate youth sub-culture. Both phenomena are characterized by swift and continuous change. The substance of what is taught in art as well as how it is learned are prime considerations of the secondary art teacher.

Courtesy, Edna Gilbert, Mesa Public Schools, Mesa, Arizona

An effective high school art teacher must be:
—deeply committed to the educative process as a means for social and cultural change.
—sensitive to the needs and learning style of those he teaches.
—personally competent and active in studio production.
—capable of honest and reasonably objective self-appraisal.
—discerning and energetic in his attention to his own professional development as an art educator.

The ultimate or over-riding goal of the secondary art teacher is to evoke in his students optimum learning in and about art in order that it may be meaningful.

Good Teachers Are Not Machines

It should be remembered that good teachers are also human beings, capable of human error. Not being machines, they react with emotion, feeling, intelligence, and perception much in the manner of any person. That is, superb teachers, while possessing special talents and traits did not become excellent because such traits of excellence were not attainable. They started out as any highly motivated student would begin his teacher preparation. They reached their goals through desire, exemplary achievement, and optimum effort.

Good teachers are special kinds of people, not because they are poured from the same "success" mold, but because they are able to more fully utilize their own potential. It matters little if the good teacher's voice is somewhat squeaky or nasal, for his dynamic nature and spirit are what counts. Good teachers can be tall and thin, short and stocky, fair of complexion, black, brown, yellow, green, or polka-dot. They can have high piercing, or deep booming voices. At certain times, they can be, like anyone else, comfortably disorderly, sloppy, chaotic, vague, doubtful, uncertain, indefinite, approximate, inexact or inaccurate.[3]

Building Self-Confidence

One characteristic of good teaching seems to be an intrinsic positive attitude toward seeing oneself as a teacher. The teacher (or teacher-to-be) must believe in his own ability to do good teaching. In this respect, he is his own image-builder. He needs to become teacher-success oriented. If a person does not hold a strong sense of self-worth toward his abilities to teach, then self-doubts may develop, thus a loss of confidence and the onset of fear. Kelley[4] expresses this point when he says:

> In order for a person to be fully functioning, when he looks at his self, as he must, he must see that it is enough—enough to perform the task at hand. He must like what he sees, at least well enough for it to be operational.
>
> An inadequate concept of self, so common in our culture, is crippling to the individual. Our psychological selves may become crippled in much the same way as our physical selves may be crippled by disease or by an accident. They are the same, in effect, because each limits what we can do. When we see ourselves as inadequate, we lose our "can-ness."

Teachers *can* make mistakes, and even have unsuccessful lessons! Good teaching doesn't imply perfection. In teaching, there are many temporary defeats, but they must be looked on as *just that*. It should be realized that mistakes are inherent in the processes of teaching. They should merely serve as the signals for steering a more direct course to target. The route to teaching success is not a polished slide; it is more nearly a circular staircase. Some of the steps include perseverance, energy, enthusiasm, spirit, perspiration, discouragement, break-throughs, impatience, imperceptible progress, great leaps forward, and, most of all, an intense desire to teach, no matter what!

The successful teacher works at developing a high degree of ego-strength. He doesn't shatter easily. He has developed a good deal of personal courage that can see him through the most challenging of teaching situations. Self-courage is faith in oneself. Having such a faith will give action and strength to one's teaching experiences, for it is an eternal elixir which can form the bedrock for good teaching.

Dedication to Teaching Is Vital Factor

A key attitude is an intense desire to be a superb teacher. There must be the feeling inside that "this is it." Most individuals who have experienced some measure of success in teaching have looked upon it as an adventure unlike any other. Teaching is a full-time task which requires all of one's being; days off become fuel times for the next lesson. As a teacher, one must commit himself completely

Courtesy, Andre Emmerich Gallery, Inc., New York

"B/W VIII"
by Al Held, 1967
Acrylic on Canvas

—more in the manner of pouring oneself into the experience, rather than skimming off the surface as a spectator. Teaching must always be an on-going process—one of evolving and thrusting forward to embrace the profession with an enthusiasm that comes from our inner wellspring. Good teachers possess that little extra—an intangible something that enables them to pursue further when others

Making a unique and personal statement in the art material is equally as important as the development of skills. Competent artists usually have something interesting to say through their art works.

Courtesy, Chuck Friedenmaker, Edie Summey, and Phoenix Union High School, Arizona

The excellent teacher of art understands the value of keeping abreast of past artistic creation as well as the contemporary scene.

"The Mediterranean"
by Aristide Maillol, ca. 1901
Bronze

*Courtesy, Collection, The Museum of Modern Art, New York
Gift of Stephen C. Clark*

have decided to quit. They go all the way to the goal! Harold Schultz[5] discusses teaching qualities such:

The teacher's enthusiasm for art and teaching is one of the most essential qualities. If this is lacking, students cannot be expected to respond with interest, vitality, and zeal. Because teaching art is an enterprise between people, it is necessary that the teacher not only understand human beings but enjoy their company as well. It is of special importance that the teacher be capable of identifying himself with the interests and needs of those he teaches. The capacity to empathize has a direct bearing upon the ability to select the most appropriate motivation and to encourage the most rewarding kind of art activity. As an individual, the teacher needs to have qualities of optimism, patience, and dedication. Successful teachers are often identified as being curious, imaginative, and possessed of a warm and lovely sense of humor.

Regardless of physical appearance, or personal characteristics, good teachers learn to develop their own kind of flash and sparkle. They are able to inspire and move others toward their own particular brand of greatness.

Developing Your Own Brand of Enthusiasm

Good teachers are the sum total of their own expanding potential. They have a special magnetic enthusiasm that makes one want to follow them around to discover why they are so darned enthusiastic! What is teaching enthusiasm? Can this special sparkle be encouraged in others? Enthusiasm in this sense refers to qualities of the personality. For example, good teachers:

can help a student feel that he is improving
are curious and always bubbling with information
are keenly alert and have a contagious spirit of welcome about themselves
are deeply interested in teaching the subject of art in all aspects
are interested in the joy of life with its ultimate discoveries
present their lessons dynamically
motivate students to do their very best

are honest and fair at all times

try to develop their sense of humor, and can also take jokes

are interested in things their students are involved with

respect each student for what they are

are so interested in teaching, that it rubs off on others

are confident and inspire confidence in their students

are organized and prepared, but not rigid or dogmatic

like to be challenged in their thinking and try to challenge
   students

live their life fully, and set fine examples for youth

are warm human beings who respond openly and honestly to
   students

demand respect and give respect in return

In another sense, we might compare enthusiasm for teaching with Maslow's[6] definition of creativeness. He says:

Self-actualizing creativeness is "emitted" like radio-activity and hits all of life, regardless of problems, just as a cheerful person "emits" cheerfulness without purpose or design or even consciousness. It is emitted like sunshine; it spreads all over the place; it makes some things grow (which are growable) and is wasted on rocks and other ungrowable things.

Having a Creative Spirit Is Essential

One difficulty in isolating quality in teaching is that a good teacher is uniquely special. For the most part, he is unlike his supposed counterparts. He is highly individual, both in personal factors and in teaching facility. In the purest sense of the term, he is usually a highly creative person. Creativeness as interpreted by MacKinnon[7] fits our references here:

The full and complete picturing of the creative person will require many images. But if, despite this caution, one still insists on asking what most generally characterizes the creative individual as he has revealed himself in the Berkeley studies, it is his high level of effective intelligence, his openness to experience, his freedom from crippling restraints and impoverishing inhibitions, his aesthetic sensitivity, his cognitive flexibility, his independence in thought and action, his high level of creative energy, his unquestioning commitment to creative endeavor and his unceasing striving for solutions to the ever more difficult problems that he constantly sets for himself.

We might infer that a good teacher incorporates a natural air of curiosity about himself. That is, he is to lesser teachers somewhat unpredictable because of his openness to the manner in which he structures his world. He constantly searches for and discovers heuristic possibilities for seeing and expressing in the classroom. By the same token, he will not hesitate to discard any aspect in his teaching that does not hold up under fire. He is a teacher who is continually learning with the students—able to lead magnificently, yet quick to sense the moment when a student should take the initiative and step out on his own.

Learning, whether it be creative, or otherwise, does not take place in a meaningless void. Nor is it, as Jerome Hausman[8] relates, drawn from "nothing." He states:

Teachers must be aware that creative activity in art (as in any other field) does not involve the creation of a form from "nothing." Creativity in art is not creativity in a mystical or biblical sense. The forms that are created grow out of already existing facts, ideas, and skills. To be sure, each student is unique; to some extent his drawings, paintings, and sculpture can reflect this uniqueness. However, there is a sense in which the capacity to be "creative" is related to the store of skills, images, and ideas that are provided by others. This is what Pasteur meant when he said: "Fortune favors the prepared mind." Thus, good teaching in art introduces a flux of ideas and images and then helps students to uncover, select, rearrange, combine, and synthesize ideas and images drawn from this flux.

Knowledgeability Is Fundamental to Good Teaching

Central to the development of an excellent teacher is his understanding of subject material. When a teacher is adequately informed, he can present his subject from various vantage points and in many stimulating ways. As a result, teaching moves beyond the mere transfer of information and becomes a challenge to thought. In having a thorough grasp of art down through centuries, as well as a keen eye to what is being done today, the teacher is able to present lessons that stir the imagination and fan the artistic spark. Paul Beckman[9] states:

Motivate with what's happening. Get brochures from the great New York, San Francisco, Los Angeles and Chicago openings. Have the "modern Art" magazines in the classroom at all times. Push Pop, Op, Hard Edge, Funk, and

Minimal art directions. Have a hobby of reading about art and collecting and making slides. This can be done from magazines as well as from shows. Keep this collection in a constant state of development. Encourage the students to help build a classroom collection. Finally, be an artist who teaches. Have work of your own developing in the classroom. Do not use the students class time for the work but come before school, stay after school and stay during your free period to work on your art. Organize and enter shows, big or small, from the church basement to the best city gallery.

Knowledgeability in one's subject areas is basic to effective and positive teaching. When a teacher is somewhat unsure of his subject area, he tends to rely too closely on his former notes from a college class, or leans heavily on the facts as presented in a text.

Several experienced teachers in the field speak to the importance of understanding one's subject field well. George F. Horn[10] states:

> To be effective the teacher must have a comprehensive knowledge of his subject area. For the art teacher this would mean a familiarity with the art of the past and of the present, a perceptive understanding of the basis for visual organization, and a general competency with the tools, materials, and equipment utilized by the artist. This much is essential to the teacher developing a confidence in his ability to function well in a classroom situation. For it is through an awareness of the significant aspects of his subject that the teacher acquires the necessary self-assurance to teach effectively.

Knowledgeability in art does not exist as information handling alone, taken from the context of contemporary society. Good teachers understand and encourage the grasp of humanistic relationships as they relate to the discovery of art in its multivarious forms. To paraphrase McLuhan,[11] perceptive teachers in the profession are aware of the fact that environments are not passive wrappings

"I and the Village"
by Marc Chagall, 1911
Oil on Canvas

Courtesy, Collection, The Museum of Modern Art, New York
Mrs. Simon Guggenheim Fund

but active processes. Fred Logan[12] illustrates this point when he says:

The teacher of art must see his subject, the arts, as an element of human existence which has both formed and interpreted much of the positive values of earthly existence. Art not separated from science or industry, nor divorced from political or financial affairs, but rather that activity of human beings which encompasses everything from the shape of buildings to that incredible machine, television, and from the work of the lonely painter to the group production of the live theatre—it is this the art teacher deals with. The citizen aged three to eighty can be helped to use art in all its forms, to express ideas from within and from outside the individual personality. All can be helped to see anew and discriminately things which prejudice, conformity, habit, and dead tradition would shield from their eyes and ears and hands and hearts.

Art teachers should also realize that the teaching of subject knowledge in art should not be interpreted as events which happened in another century, within some past twilight zone. They need to teach that art history is happening today, all around us, and that vast invisible environments[13] are rapidly changing our viewpoints toward everything we have experienced, or will encounter. Harold Rosenberg[14] expresses this point in the following manner:

The art teacher should have a very good knowledge of modern art, very contemporary art, and have a sense first of all, which is a thing I think we all missed in school, that art is being created *now* by people on *your* block or people in *your* neighborhood, or at least in your *country*. One thing I thought to be true when I was a kid, was that poetry was written in the 19th century, by Englishmen with beards, and that painting was done by artists such as Rembrandt. The big thing in America today is that artists are able to say, "Well here I am, art is here."

Pursuing One's Artistic Talent Is Fundamental to Good Teaching

It is essential to cultivate one's artistic talents to the highest degree possible. This means that an art teacher who strives for excellence must become proficient in at least one area, i.e., painting, sculpture, crafts, printmaking, jewelry, etc., and have a fundamental grounding and sensitivity to the entire visual sphere. For those teachers who will only teach art history in secondary schools, some competency in art skills and art experiences will be valuable to the comprehension and analysis of art historical content. For art historians at the secondary level, the development of one's analytical aesthetic eye is a necessary matter. Their skill development may be less than the art teacher who will handle studio-type classes. Many teachers, however, will be in a position to teach both skill and subject matter. In either case, a sensitive vision to the visual art form is central to excellence in art teaching.

When possible, the art teacher should exhibit his work locally and in national shows in order to maintain the highest personal growth in aesthetic performance.

Art Skills and Art Knowledge Are Often Interactive

Individual growth in artistic skill is often interactive with growth in subject awareness. This is why it is vital to introduce the art class to many realms of a given unit—art tool techniques, study of art works, historical analysis, current ramifications in the museums, personal art values for students, aesthetic considerations, and any other factors which seem pertinent to a more complete understanding of a specific art area.

Good teachers can handle artistic materials effectively enough to teach it in an exciting fashion. They are also able to generate ideas of their own rather than continually absorbing ideas that others have cultivated and merely passing it on in a routine fashion. The art teacher has to be an alert, responsive, curious person. One who comes up with not only the information, but who can interpret it in an imaginative and inventive way so that students will listen, and be encouraged to the point where they want to make similar inquiries, in order to develop their own ideas.

Putting Ideas Across

Getting ideas across in art depends largely on the enthusiasm and personal punch that one puts into the presentation of the art lessons. Personal drive is always a personal thing. For some teachers, standing on a table and shouting home a direction may be effective. For a little excellent teacher in tennis sneakers, a whisper in the ear may provoke a whole stream of ideas. The point here is to tell it like it is. Hopefully, some of the magic of your know-how will touch the students.

These students are firing clay pieces in simple, "Home-made" kilns.

"Pottery with Dark Brown Geometric Design" by Marie Z. Chino, Acoma Pueblo, New Mexico

"Swamp Fire in March" 1920-60
by Charles Burchfield
Watercolor 33' x 45"

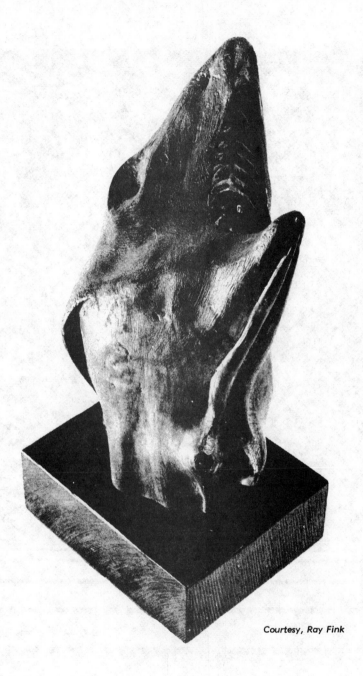

Courtesy, Ray Fink

The first important facet of driving an idea home is to preplan, i.e., to work out certain objectives beforehand. When a teacher is well prepared for his classes, whether studio or lecture sessions, he has more confidence, greater virtuosity, and generally does a better job of teaching. Preplanning eliminates needless redundancy and permits focus on key material. The choice of material used depends on the teacher, the class, and the intended objectives. The teacher must be able to select from a range of available art data the information or approach he feels is most vital to the germination of student understanding and inquiry. Once the choice of material has been decided, the *method* of presentation or approach should be determined. Good art teachers seldom follow rigid routines. Instead, they are able to inspire student pursuit by being innovative and provocative in their teaching presentations. In Whitehead's[15] terms, "The imaginative life is a way of living, and is not an article of commerce."

A good teacher will put as much variety into his visual as into his verbal presentation. He will utilize any reference, visual aid, or tool that will help him get the idea across. In a watercolor unit, for example, some of the possible approaches (and there may be hundreds more) to provide essential basic awareness include:

(1) Teacher demonstration in holding and applying brush to paper; (2) demonstration of variety of brush strokes and pressures; (3) methods of treating paper, i.e., wet, dry, glues, pastes; (4) films of artists in action; (5) introduction of pertinent books and magazines on watercolor; (6) practice on the part of students at various intervals; (7) discussion and evaluation by the students at successive points; (8) demonstration of approaches by guest artists (who could be anyone competent including college students); (9) study of watercolor painters in both historical and present art scene

The nature of the material can often suggest the idea.

"The Scream"
by Ray Fink
Wood

through slides, original works, visits to museums, galleries, artists studios; (10) complete pursuit in depth of papers, brushes, artists, and approaches. Regardless of the length of time spent on such a unit, whether three days or two months, the learning process should be intense with much student involvement. No art lesson should ever be presented once-over-lightly, where the students dawdle for a period or two and then move on to the next fuzzy objective.

Some teachers put their ideas across by working the assigned problem right along with the class, always alert, however, to the "discovery speed" of the specific class. Periodic critique sessions of student work-in-progress help to clarify and suggest directions in which the art work may proceed. It should be realized that growth in art is not always a visible, immediate experience, measurable in readily perceptible quantities. Artistic sensitivity of an intellectual nature such as art history, aesthetic analysis, or skill development often requires an indefinite gestation period. Even after artistic maturity, the artist who has worked for years in his chosen specialty needs time to bounce ideas around "inside" before they spring to the surface. California art teacher Don Herberholz[16] states what happens prior to beginning a sculptural piece:

> I can only guess at some of the ways ideas are triggered into the conscious mind from many internal and external stimuli. To be more specific, the following are some examples that I have attempted to trace back in my memory; the first source is through the material which I have collected in my studio. (This material may not bring forth an idea for as long as a year or two.) The second source is through mistakes which I have made while working on a particular piece which may suggest the next half dozen ideas.

Many good art teachers allow for outwardly crude beginnings and temporary mistakes, yet maintain a patient vigil for signs of artistic progress in their students. Often some of the more exciting

"Two Thousand Light Years"
by Peter Max, 1968
Acrylic on Canvas with Silkscreen

Courtesy, William Zierler, Inc., New York

art works in a high school or junior high class of young tyros comes after considerable practice. Good art teachers find it difficult to predict at what point a particular student will spring to life; consequently, they seek to establish conditions which can encourage such discovery. While many students will not pursue art as a career, most can increase their cultural threshold for art, and this is one purpose in teaching art skills and art history to potential consumer-appreciators, not to neglect also the personal values derived from enriching the individual.

Communicating with Students

The teacher has to be able to reach students by the approach that he takes in the presentation of art ideas. Ideas only come alive when the teacher develops a personal charisma that triggers students and starts them going. Communication may refer to the various techniques a teacher will utilize in transferring idea possibilities to students for their interpretation. Expressiveness is the key factor here. Loosely defined, it comprises the vocal mannerisms, gestures and physical actions the teacher may improvise as part of a teaching situation. At times he must speak softly, at other times, forcefully. He may be sad, happy, mysterious, humorous and intellectually exciting, all in one class period.

Physical maneuverability during a class presentation is often an important factor in the communication of ideas. If a teacher remains behind a rostrum, or sits on the corner of a desk and swings his leg for the length of a period, he reduces the power of his message considerably. For example, he may remain relatively stationary for ten minutes. To bring home a point, he may walk into the midst of the class. This gives an immediate impact to his statements, a feeling of expectancy. There is always a certain detachment behind a rostrum because of the physical distance between teacher and class. Visual variability is as important as vocal flexibilty, for it increases the quality of animation in teaching.

The good teacher often does the unexpected. He is, by example, able to inspire student inquiry by being imaginative and innovative in his teaching approaches. He leads students along a questioning path until *they* make the discoveries necessary to broaden their frontiers. Because an excellent teacher experiments, searches, explores and investigates the nature of ideas and things, his students are more likely to observe this type of spirit and therefore seek to emulate his enthusiasm.

The Art Teacher Is a Model for Art

Good art teachers have within their means the ability to inspire students to increasingly higher realms of artistic understanding. The art teacher is the only person fully qualified to teach art as skill development, as history, and as critical appreciation. As such, the art teacher serves as the primary model for all that a student can learn concerning art. If a student learns the historical aspects of art, both past and present, it is because his teacher served as a model. If a student grows in the skillful handling of art material, it is because his teacher served as a model. If a student learns to develop a critical eye toward asking the why and how of art, it is because his teacher served as a model. If a student increases his perceptual and artistic awareness to art, it is also because his teacher served as a model.

Good art teachers believe very strongly that art is a magnificent adventure. They *do not* see themselves as therapists, recreationists, hobbyists, sociologists, psychologists, or counselors. They are dedicated, hard core, often unsung, highly professional people who want to teach art and teach it well; who want to raise the standards of art in secondary schools; who want to build the image of the art teacher as one who cherishes and holds high the aims of art and the values to the individual therein. Thus, he leaves the teaching of democratic ideals to the history class, counseling to the counselor, and projective techniques to the psychologist. The models, or examples that he sets for his students are those of (1) artist, (2) art historian, (3) art critic, (4) perceptive-aware human being.

Good art teachers are deeply involved in art, in all of its aspects. They reveal this involvement by their attitudes, actions, and total behavior toward art while in the classroom, and beyond. The art teacher must constantly work at his art, whatever his choice (including that of art historian). He must be continually learning himself, for teaching is not a one way street where the student moves ahead, while the teacher remains static. The teacher must be involved in creating art, reading about it, alert to what is going on, and constantly renewing his own thinking concerning possibilities for art. Only in this manner can the teacher emphatically ignite students' thinking. Teachers are models for art, whether they want to be or not. Most of us can remember teachers in our educational background who really were an inspiration to continued learning. They had that special drive that set us on fire with their enthusiasm, love of subject, and all around respect for learning as a compelling adventure. (We can probably also remember teachers who drained confidence, and who cut down students in their tracks for the sake of their own ego.)

Environments Are also Models

Students learn from observation. They are influenced by the teacher in terms of the way he dresses. If the teacher looks square or conventional in the most rigid sense (old maidish or stiff-necked) students may accept this as their model, and act accordingly. Without suggesting how teachers should dress, they should be as sharp as possible, employing a sense of good taste in design to their appearance. This means looking sharp, and thinking sharp. The art teacher may have many images, depending on the objective. If he serves as the artist, appropriate gear should be maintained in the classroom. He should look like an artist, not a dentist. Labels are helpful to project feelings or attitudes. When serving as the art historian, it might be proper to dress to the teeth, with high button down collar, tweedy suit, (mustache applied) to provide the image of scholar as art historian. Appropriate dress for other images or objectives can also be determined. Most of all, the art teacher should be an individual: unique, unexpected, creative, unusual, intelligent, daring, mysterious, erudite, magnificent!

Classroom Environments Are Active Processes

When the student enters the art room, there should be no doubt where he is. The art classroom is in effect, an extension of the art teacher and ultimately the students who create things there. In an art room there should be things happening! The room should be

Courtesy, The Cleveland Museum of Art
Leonard C. Hanna Jr. Collection

"Race Horses"
by Edgar Degas, French, 1834-1917
Pastel on Cardboard

"The Anguish of Departure"
by Giorgio de Chirico, 1913-14
Oil on Canvas

"Six Standing Lipsticks"
by Wayne Thiebaud, 1966
Oil

visually stimulating so that a student can continually make discoveries of an aesthetic, artistic, or appreciative nature. Hanging space for news clippings, original art, reproductions, and student work, should be as extensive as possible. The art room should be carefully planned for visual readability. It is not necessary to make a circus of the room by pasting student work on the ceiling and across the windows. However, good design begins in the art room. When a student steps into the art room, it should be an aesthetic adventure, functioning to illuminate and provoke various aspects of current problems and ideas related to the art scene. Students, for the most part, will encounter *conventional seeing* throughout the remainder of the school. Many of the other teachers will be limited in their artistic and perceptual awareness, and will also look to the art teacher for inspiration.

Good teachers practice teaching art by example, in as many forms as possible. They have clearly established objectives which for the most part pertain to the teaching of art to students. As such, the art classroom does not turn into a poster factory, club announcement production class, or other peripheral business during the main hours of class session. Harold Schultz,[17] discusses various aspects of the classroom environment:

> First there is the physical environment. The atmosphere produced derives from the appearance of the studio itself. A classroom or workshop should be colorful, cheerful, and challenging to the imagination. The furniture can be varied in kind and arrangement and readily movable to meet different teaching purposes. There should be counters, shelves, and bulletin boards for the display of art objects and collections. Art materials, tools, and equipment should be within easy reach of those who need them. The total effect can encourage art activity.
>
> Stimulating as it may be, manipulation of physical conditions is not enough. Another important element is needed. This may be referred to as the emotional climate of the classroom. The nature of the emotional climate is somewhat elusive and not easily described. At the same time all successful teachers sense what it is and when it exists. It is a matter of spirit, an aura that envelops the students' activities. It is determined by the actions and responses of both the teacher and students, individually and as a group. Conditions for creativeness exist when there is a sense of "aliveness" in the classroom and when there is expression of vital interest. Students are free to move about so long as their movement is coupled with serious purpose and responsibility. There is an atmosphere of friendliness, of cooperation, and experimentation. Ideas and opinions, even though nebulous in form, are respected by pupils and teacher.

Keys to Art Teaching Success

There are some definite steps that can be taken to move in the direction of art teaching success. They include the following points:

1. Keep a teaching success notebook. Label it as such, or give it your own special twist. Within this notebook, write down all of your ideas and objectives—what you hope to accomplish within a specific period of time. Be definite in what you hope to accomplish and state such plans in your teaching success notebook. Ideas and plans that are written down are clear and immediate in our thinking, while if we fail to put ideas on paper, they remain vague and gradually disappear. Your success notebook can be a small pad that is always carried. Whenever an inspiration or idea trace comes to mind, it can be instantly recorded and saved for later evaluation, if written down. Encourage the students to do the same. An art success notebook for students could contain sketches, notes, anything related to discovering art or art ideas. The notebooks of Leonardo DaVinci are an excellent example.

2. Develop your own personal kind of brightness and alertness. Make up your mind that you are going to begin immediately to develop your awareness of the world about you, that you are going to make plans to increase your art skill, intellectual grasp, powers of observation, and sensory awareness. Begin by practicing visual observation of the natural and man-made world. Try each day to take yourself beyond the point at which you were the day before. Develop your art specialty and increase your art vocabulary. Compete against yourself, not experts who have been working at their art for years. Set *reasonable* objectives for yourself, and be sure to work hard at reaching them. Objectives can be extremely short term such as a day in which to attain them. Think of yourself as a person who is working toward self-growth in art, and remember that such growth is attainable.

3. Think of yourself as an artist who teaches. Let your students know, by your example, that you feel art is the most exciting show in town. Talk up art at every opportunity. Bring in your own art work for the class to see and evaluate. Work on your own pieces at opportune times in the classroom. Let the class see you in action as an artist who develops his ideas from generalized

threads on through to artistic completion! Exhibit your art works whenever possible and arrange for student exhibits in the community as well as the school. Encourage them to enter state and national competitions if you feel their work has reached a significant level of achievement. Get the students going in the direction of their own interests, and push them on to the very limits of what they thought possible to do! Above all, let it be known to every student they are there *to study and practice the disciplines of art*. These include (1) art skills, (2) art history and its analysis, and (3) intellectual and perceptual awareness.

4. Establish an artistic climate in the art classrooms. Indicate that here is a place where artistic endeavor is practiced. There should be definite work spaces which are planned for two or three dimensional activities, and facilities for viewing slides and films. There should also be an exhibition area where work can be subjected to critical analysis and study. The most limited of art plants can provide some form of operation in this direction. Good art teachers don't permit their subject to wither into the background of a school program. They go straight to the top and work toward building a program of which all can be proud.

5. Establish a positive attitude toward art in the school community. The reason some high school and college programs enjoy facilities and privileges not accorded to others is that some disciplines have strong spokesmen who are consistently in there pitching for more equipment, staff, and related facilities. Good art teachers are like this. They make a practice of selling the art program wherever they go. There are many ways to do this. It can be done in day-to-day casual conversation, by arranging for exhibitions in the school or community by bringing in local or nationally known figures to speak on art, by obtaining radio and television time, and most of all by carrying on the strongest possible art program. Of course, remember to keep your cool—don't exhaust yourself by over-try. Remember to keep goals on a short term basis, and keep them reachable. By your example, others will want to ride with a winner.

Most of all, develop a great respect and brotherly love for your students. They are your prime asset, your reason for being. Let them know that you like them very much, and also that you expect *only* the very best from them. Let them know that your expectations of their potential are unlimited! Try to move them far beyond what they ever thought would be possible. Don't leave room for laziness, sloppiness, or lack of commitment.

College Students Say What Qualities Good Teachers Have

Students can often provide insight or viewpoints helpful to the understanding of a situation. The following statements were selected from a college population of 200 teacher bound students over a span of two years and covering colleges in three western states. The students were asked by the author to write what they felt were qualities which define a good teacher. The following statements were selected from a larger sampling.

A good teacher,

1. is one who can explain a subject well and have patience while doing this.
2. is strict.
3. knows his material and can keep up with new things in the field.
4. can relate what he knows to students in a painless and interesting way.
5. is involved in his job and personally cares about his students because they are his job.
6. has respect for his students and expects students to have respect for him.
7. will put himself and his students on the same level intellectually and discover answers and experiences together.
8. will give the students all sides to a question, and allow them to formulate their own views.
9. commands respect and obedience through love and not through fear.

10. should go beyond the textbook.
11. is proud to be a teacher.
12. has rapport.
13. is unegotistical.
14. has enthusiasm for the subject.
15. has a sense of humor.
16. helps you when help is needed, but doesn't insult your intelligence.
17. is an interesting speaker.
18. is a happy type person.
19. sticks to the subject.
20. watches work closely and gives constructive criticism.
21. does not speak in a monotone.
22. sets high standards and expects students to comply with them.
23. has sensitivity to students as individuals.
24. can motivate you to think.
25. has a genuine interest in the students.
26. has patience and understanding.
27. has an ability to communicate.

A list of this sort could go on indefinitely. Three major aspects of good teaching, as evidenced from a study of the statements made by college students included: (1) enthusiasm for teaching, (2) comprehensive knowledge of the subject, and (3) respect and love for students as individuals. Over and over, these three characteristics were indicated by the students surveyed. Most of the characteristics related to personality traits. Apparently, from the point of view of students, these factors seem significant. It is often beneficial to listen to such voices.

Some Suggestions for Art Teachers Just Beginning Their Career

What does one say to a new art teacher just beginning his career? The following experienced art teachers offered these statements:

Jerome Hausman:[18]

The advice I would offer to a young art teacher just embarking on his career is that he maintain a continuing and deep contact with some aspect of the discipline which he is teaching. For the art teacher, this means an involvement with critical study, historical inquiry, and/or studio productivity in the arts. In addition, it would seem to me essential that the art teacher face the essential questions of becoming a more effective teacher of the arts. Necessarily, the concerns are interdisciplinary. Essentially the young teacher just embarking on his career must be prepared for a life long commitment to creative involvement in the infinite variety of problems and possibilities he will face.

Henry Hope:[19]

To a young teacher starting on his career I would say—try to avoid parading second hand the lessons you learned at school, keeping in mind that you are dealing (probably) with students inexperienced in your subject. Prepare your lessons very thoroughly at first, gaining confidence in yourself. Get a friend to attend your classes and offer constructive criticism. Avoid mannerisms of behavior and appearance. Students are quick to notice awkwardness, nervousness, tension of voice; also eccentricities of dress. Try to develop naturalness and ease of manner, but neither be condescending nor be too familiar. Humor is useful but should be relevant and discreet, i.e., you are not a comic nor an m.c. but you want to be interesting and informative—not dull, not dry, not austere, not severe.

Jack Bookbinder:[20]

Instead of describing or characterizing a good teacher by listing certain attributes or endowments, I feel inclined rather to describe what happens to a student who is privileged to be taught by such a teacher. Such a student will feel that he is in the presence of an individual whose eyes, ears and temperament are attuned to concerns of his students; whose unassuming attitude toward the known and unknown will enable him to listen and to weigh fairly the opinions and attitudes of his students; whose humility in the face of vast human problems will keep him on the level of his students whoever they may be, advantaged, disadvantaged, difficult or docile. In the presence of such a teacher, a student must feel that the information, the knowledge, the skills and the conclusions he derives are not so much imparted as shared with him. Such a student will feel that what he gains from such a teacher comes to him in an atmosphere of reverence, not for the teacher's erudition, but for the vastness of the knowledge and wisdom to which such a teacher has opened the door. If the student succeeds in the above, it does not matter much whether his teacher is short or tall, dynamic or placid; whether he or she has charm and vivacity, a good speaking voice or belongs to six professional organizations. It will not even matter whether people will say of him or her that he or she loves teaching. I suppose what I have been trying to say is that for the proof of the pudding, we should not look to the baker.

Conclusion: a Teacher's Prayer

Rather than attempt an elaborate summary of the foregoing chapter on defining the qualities of good teaching, the following poem by Harry Wood seems appropriate:

A TEACHER'S PRAYER
By HARRY WOOD[21]

May there always be more questions than answers in my classroom, more workers than drones, and enough queens to keep the hive buzzing.

May I always learn more than I teach, preferably before I teach it.

May I, their teacher, be the best student of my students. May I never hover over their shoulders, or talk over their heads. May I never gloat over nor gloss over their ignorance.

May my head and my heart serve the Blockheads and the Blackhearts as devotedly as the Einsteins and Leonardos.

May my words never put my students to sleep in body or mind, nor awaken the former without awakening the latter.

May I be incurably absent-minded when calling the roll of human mistakes.

May Laughter and Truth ring louder in my classrooms than class bells.

May I never teach classes, always People; but may I never grade People, only papers.

May I always be at home in my classroom, but let me never forget to leave my classroom at school and my home at home.

Let me be quicker to question than quote, but quicker to quip than to quibble. Let me never be Quaint in order to be Quotable.

May all my utterances participate in Truth, but never so memorably that they become Infallible Formuli. May what I say be more perfectly expressed by what I Am.

Let my Certification be this: That I shall conduct a ceaseless, lifelong Search for Meaning; but, once found, may I never champion the Meaning, only the Search.

May I nourish all Seeds, even the beautiful weeds, in whatever mind they root and be a joyful witness to their blossoming.

May I always be more eager to enter than to leave my own classroom— and my students likewise. Through the years may Monday and September be as welcome as Friday and June.

Courtesy of The Hand and the Spirit Crafts Gallery, Scottsdale, Arizona, Photograph by Glenn Short

"Eskimo Basket"
by Kuskokwim
Seal gut embrication and
beach grass

May my classroom become a favorite sanctuary for the Pet Ideas of all my students, but only an occasional roost for my own.

May I never duck a headache if it will save a student a heartache.

May I never retire from teaching, unless I have taken the precaution to quit first. May I genuinely earn my pay, my rank, and, once or twice a year, an afternoon free of a committee meeting.

May I learn to understand every Enemy (except Ignorance) as a Friend, and every Absolute (except Change) as an Enemy.

May I learn to listen, even while speaking. When I speak, may I speak well, but still better, be silent.

May those in my classes learn Love—of books, of beauty of inquiry, and of Self. Before students, colleagues, or the TV camera, may the Director of my thoughts find me a clear channel.

May I unfailingly learn to Work, Work, Work (as I am now), contriving whatever odious motivations are necessary to keep myself at it until my chores are complete, my deadlines met, my obligations to teammates fulfilled, and my Potential Contribution to society fully achieved; teach me to learn to Play, Play, Play (as I am now), contriving whatever odious motivations are necessary to keep myself at it until my games are complete, my finish lines crossed, my ultimate obligations to teammates fulfilled, and my Potential Contribution to society fully achieved; and then, may the resulting total collapse unfailingly teach me to Work, Work, Work (as I am now), contriving whatever. . . .*

Key Words Check List to a New Attitude Toward Yourself and the Way You Teach

1. New places
2. New things
3. Discovery

4. Flexibility
5. Ideas
6. Fluency

* For full effectiveness, please continue to repeat this script in a luster-creme tone of debonair cajolery, with gradually increasing echo-chamber sound-effects, until the message gets through, and you are: (1) promoted, (2) fired, (3) committed, (4) made football coach, (5) voted teacher-of-the-year, (6) nominated for Congress, (7) invited to join the Peace Corps, (8) appointed Ambassador to Ubekestan.

If none of these effects occurs, write for our follow-up Programmed Learning Course: Ten Easy Steps to a Lucrative Career as a Misunderstood Poet.

7. Innovation
8. Curiosity
9. Inquisitiveness
10. Search
11. Investigation
12. Wonderment
13. Perceiving
14. Alertness
15. Art skills
16. Art subject matter
17. Originality
18. Respect
19. Energy
20. Ambition
21. Art Practice
22. Knowledge about art
23. Art in history

24. Build a list of words which reflect your new discovery image toward art!

25. _____
26. _____
27. _____
28. _____

References

1. Harlan Hoffa, from a statement submitted to the author, 1970.
2. Ivan Johnson, from a statement submitted to the author, 1970.
3. Abraham H. Maslow, *Creativity and its Cultivation* (Anderson, Editor), New York: Harper & Row, 1959.
4. Earl C. Kelley, *Perceiving, Behaving, Becoming*, Washington, D.C.: Association for Supervision and Curriculum Development, 1962.
5. Harold Schultz, "The Teacher of Art," from the *Report of the Commission on Art Education*, Published by the National Art Education Association, Washington, D.C., 1965.
6. Abraham Maslow, *Creativity and its Cultivation*, (Anderson, Editor) New York: Harper & Row, 1959.
7. Donald W. MacKinnon, "What Makes A Person Creative?", *Saturday Review*, February 10, 1962, p. 69.
8. Jerome Hausman, "Teacher as Artist & Artist as Teacher," *Art Education*, April, 1967, Vol. 20, Number 4, pp. 13–17.
9. Paul Beckman, from a statement submitted to the author, 1970.
10. George F. Horn, from a statement submitted to the author, 1970.
11. Marshall McLuhan, *Understanding Media: The Extensions of Man*, New York: McGraw-Hill Book Company, 1964.
12. Frederick M. Logan, *Growth of Art in American Schools*, New York: Harper & Row, 1955, p. 295.
13. Marshall McLuhan, *Understanding Media: The Extensions of Man*, New York: McGraw Hill Book Company, 1964.

14. HAROLD ROSENBERG, *Seminar on Elementary and Secondary School*, Howard Conant, Editor, New York University, New York, 1965, pp. 87–88.
15. ALFRED NORTH WHITEHEAD, *The Aims of Education*, New York: Macmillan Company, 1929.
16. DONALD HEBERHOLZ, from *Invitation to Vision*, by Earl Linderman, Dubuque, Iowa: William C. Brown Company Publishers, 1967.
17. HAROLD SCHULTZ, "The Teacher of Art," *Report of the Commission on Art Education*, Published by the National Art Education Association, 1965.
18. JEROME HAUSMAN, from a statement submitted to the author, 1970.
19. HENRY HOPE, from a statement submitted to the author, 1970.
20. JACK BOOKBINDER, from a statement submitted to the author, 1970.
21. HARRY WOOD, "A Teacher's Prayer," submitted to the author.

Further References

1. BARKAN, MANUEL, *A Foundation for Art Education*, New York: Ronald Press, 1955.
2. ———, *Through Art To Creativity*, Boston: Allyn and Bacon, 1960.
3. BEARD, EVELYN, "Change, Challenge, and Art Teachers," *Art Education*, February, 1967, Vol. 20, No. 2.
4. BRITAIN, WILLIAM LAMBERT, Editor, *Creativity and Art Education*, National Art Education Association, Washington, D.C., 1964.
5. BRUNER, JEROME S., *On Knowing: Essays for the Left Hand*, New York: Atheneum, 1965.
6. CONANT, HOWARD, "The Pursuit of Excellence," an address delivered to the National Committee on Art Education at the Museum of Modern Art, May 2, 1963.
7. D'AMICO, VICTOR, *Creative Teaching in Art*, Scranton: International Textbook Company, 1955.
8. DOERTER, JAMES, "Influences of College Art Instructors Upon Their Students' Painting Styles," *Studies in Art Education*, Vol. 7, No. 2, Spring, 1966.
9. ECKER, DAVID, "Teaching Machines and Aesthetic Values," *Studies in Art Education*, 1961.
10. GAGE, N. L., Editor, *Handbook of Research on Teaching*, A project of the American Educational Research Association, Chicago: Rand McNally & Company, 1963.
11. KEILER, MANFRED, *The Art in Teaching Art*, Lincoln, Neb.: University of Nebraska Press, 1961.
12. LINDERMAN, EARL W., "Dialogue for Teaching," *Art Education*, June, 1964, Vol. 20, No. 7, pages 22–28.
13. ———, "What is a Good Teacher?" *Arts and Activities*, October, 1963, Vol. 54, No. 2.
14. LUCA, MARK, and KENT, ROBERT, *Art Education: Strategies of Teaching*, N.J.: Prentice-Hall, 1968.
15. MACKINNON, DONALD W., "Assessing Creative Persons," *The Journal of Creative Behavior*, Vol. 1, Number 3, Summer 1967, p. 291.
16. MALTZMAN, I., "On the Training of Originality," *Psychological Review*, Number 67, 1960, pp. 229-242.
17. MIEL, ALICE, Editor, *Creativity in Teaching*, San Francisco: Wadsworth Publishing Company, 1961.
18. OSBORN, A. F., Applied Imagination, New York: Scribner's, 1963.
19. PLATT, JOHN RADER, *The Step to Man*, New York: John Wiley, 1966.
20. WHITEHEAD, ALFRED NORTH, *Adventures of Ideas*, New York: Macmillan Company, 1933.
21. WILLIAMS, FRANK E., "Intellectual Creativity and the Teacher," *The Journal of Creative Behavior*, Vol. 1, Number 2, Spring, 1967.
22. YOCHIM, LOUISE D., *Perceptual Growth in Creativity*, Scranton, Pa.: International Textbook Company, 1967.

Courtesy, Edie Summey
Phoenix Union High School
Photo by Chuck Friedenmaker

Secondary students are extremely conscious of their self image.

Chapter 3

There is something antic about creating, although the enterprise be serious. And there is a matching antic spirit that goes with writing about it, for if ever there were a silent process it is the creative one. Antic and serious and silent. Yet there is good reason to inquire about creativity, a reason beyond practicality, for practicality is not a reason but a justification after the fact. The reason is the ancient search of the humanist for the excellence of man: the next creative act may bring man to a new dignity.

JEROME S. BRUNER,
On Knowing: Essays for the Left Hand,
New York: Atheneum, 1965, p. 17

Characteristics of Secondary School Students

It is generally agreed that secondary school begins at the seventh grade level and ends with the completion of grade twelve, with a vast range of differences in between this span of time. This chapter will explore some of the characteristics which distinguish students at the junior and senior high school levels.

Junior high school marks the demarcation point at which children begin to move toward adulthood. It doesn't happen overnight and often the transition is painful, particularly for the students involved. It is also rather difficult for parents and teachers of junior high students. Enthusiasm and interest is often accompanied by great physical changes and with it emotional jarrings. Most teachers who have taught eighth grade will probably agree it is a *go-go* year. This is particularly the time when good teachers must be alert to the sounds of the eighth grader— his feelings, his likes and dislikes, his attitudes, his heroes. Oftentimes he has heroes in popular music and movies. He also needs heroes in the academic world, which he usually does not have. In not having school-learned heroes, he finds his own heroes through the most direct means: television and phonograph records. However, the alert teacher can also give him some heroes in art, in the adventure of great ideas, and in the pursuit of learning. It should be remembered

Courtesy, Barbara Block and Marlene Jones, Camelback High School, Phoenix, Arizona

that children follow the examples of their teachers, and if their teachers don't give them any pathways to explore they find their own within their peer group. Junior high students need both direction and leadership demonstrated to them. Boys may pursue their interest in sports and popular music but they need also to explore art history or studio art. Cultural experiences can be moving forces in society and students need to see that these experiences are significant in one's life; that art can be extremely rewarding. There is usually only one teacher in the school that can make art come to life for students, and that's the art teacher! They've moved beyond crayons, and need more than an opportunity simply to put down ideas that are lukewarm or that were prefabricated over and over in elementary school. They need to see many high quality reproductions, innumerable slides, and they need to study original works of art. An important approach or ideal that an art teacher at both the junior and senior high level must get across to the students is that art is no game. It's serious business, and has a worthwhile place in a person's life. This idea can be demonstrated by revealing to students that art is more than drawing a picture. Art is also studying what other artists have done in art media. Most students who take art will not major in it, so the primary emphasis is not on developing artists but really on sensitizing individuals to what art can do for them in their life—the value of living an aesthetic life, something that many adults today do not have because art has not been part of their educational experience.

Drawing by Phillip Witkamp
Camelback High School Student

Gwen, High School Senior

Objectives in art have to go beyond mere creative expression. In the past when we thought about junior high and high school programs we often contrived a great range and diversity of media for presenting to the student. Every week a new media, a new project, a new "motivation." Art teachers might find it challenging to spend an entire semester on a theme such as painting or printmaking or drawing in which case great art of the past could be revealed, not in a twenty minute film showing from a rental service, but in carefully chosen, well presented, live tapes, actual interviews, artists' demonstrations so that an art subject is pursued in depth. A sensitivity to art might be reached by exploring one, two, or three units well. Art for secondary youngsters needs also to be presented as hard-core subject matter, but presented in such a way that they can grasp it, can toss it around intellectually and then digest it. They need to develop their imagination. Artists are not stupid. They are people who can express ideas in art media. They are artists because they can coordinate intelligence with superb technical mastery.

Characteristics of Junior High School Students

For our purposes, junior high begins with grade seven and ends with grade eight or nine, depending on the school system. What a beginning! First of all, each student is uniquely an individual. He is unlike any of his counterparts. Some students begin their adolescent spurt to adulthood at the very beginning of grade seven, but most enter grade seven with much of the eagerness and enthusiasm they retained from sixth grade. Notable is the newfound awareness to their own physical self, and its accompanying social manifestations. Some students remain mostly children, while others stir with a restless vigor. Many students at grade seven are still unaware of any major physical changes, although girls are probably some physical steps toward maturity.

Seventh graders are twelve years old: they are energetic, active, and on the move—interested and willing to participate in all classroom motivations. They are group conscious, identify with their peers, and usually like school very much, for its represents a great new challenge that must be met by their newly discovered abilities.

Seventh graders are eager to learn. They run to class, listen closely to the teacher, and most always do their homework assignments. They are happy to be out of the elementary classroom, and closer to their new heroes, the senior high students.

They are interested in being treated as young adults, and like the idea of discipline, rigorous work, and planned intellectual challenge. They are ready and eager to test their intellect and skills. Intermittently, they may become overly involved and exhaust themselves completely in the task at hand. Seventh graders are usually cooperative with their parents, teachers, and fellow students.

Eighth Graders

For the eighth grader adolescence is just around the corner, and with it, tumultuous changes both physically and emotionally. Maturity is coming on rapidly. Students are aware of their intellectual powers, physical skills, increases in body height, weight, and manifestations of sex characteristics that differentiate the male from female. Great contrasts in moods are evident at this stage. Students change from elation to somberness in minutes, often without warning. They want to do many things, but often neglect some ideas for spur of the moment possibilities. They often find it difficult to control their emotions. They may burst out laughing for little reason, or be sullen in the next moment. Eighth graders are active people who are doing things.

Differentiating Characteristics of Junior High Students

Generally speaking, the chief characteristics of junior high school students are categorized within (1) physical characteristics, (2) emotional traits, (3) social changes, and (4) intellectual powers.

1. **Physical Characteristics.** Students at junior high levels are different as night and day physically. No two are alike. Like adults, they manifest their individual physical differences at this period in their life. Junior high students are much like young puppies. Feet may grow much faster than the rest of the body, or various parts of the body begin to develop, while other parts do not keep pace, thus a certain awkwardness is evident. Students are often all hands and

"The Super-Who"
by Tom Jonas
Camelback High School Student
Pen and Ink

Courtesy, Camelback High School, Phoenix, Arizona

"Self-Portrait"
by Chris Schriener
Water-color

limbs, and as a result are especially self-conscious. Some students (boys or girls) experience relatively little difficulty in making the transition between childhood and adulthood, while other students have an extremely difficult crisis. Lowenfeld[1] regarded this stage of preadolescence as preparatory to the approaching crisis of adolescence. He states:

The difference between child and adult can best be seen in the diversity of their imaginative activity. This can best be observed in the different types of playing. The child plays hide-and-seek with the same unawareness as he uses a pencil, which he moves up and down while imitating the noises of an airplane. Such unawareness is characteristic of children. Quite obviously, their imagination transforms a pencil into an airplane. All children use their imagination in such an uninhibited way; if an adult would do the same he would be considered insane. For an adult, a pencil is a pencil and the pencil is for writing. The child's imaginative activity is unconscious. The adult's imaginative activity in its effect is controlled. This change in the imaginative activity from the unconscious to critical awareness, introduced by physical changes in the body, is one of the most important characteristics of the crisis of adolescence.

Courtesy, Barbara Black, Camelback High School, Phoenix, Arizona

''Easy Frog''
by Richard Robinson
Camelback High School Student
Pen and Ink

In effect, the student is moving toward a new awareness—the critical awareness of adulthood; something never experienced before. His environment is opening up before him, as revealed by his increasingly conscious visual awakening.

2. **Emotional Traits.** Junior high students have entered an extremely volatile and unstable state. New awarenesses also create new risks. Most students of this period want to be independent, but haven't learned to take this step, nor are many of them ready. All sorts of pushes and pulls are emotionally present. The student may resent adult authority, and become rebellious. He wants to be free to explore and exist independently of parents, teachers or others. This tremendous emotional struggle causes conflicts all along the line.

"Death on a Pale Horse"
by Albert Pinkham Ryder, American, 1847-1917
Oil on Canvas

The peer group has a significant effect at this stage. Style of dress, mannerisms, likes and dislikes are often determined by what the group agrees on, often more or less unconsciously—and more often than not by the powerful influence of advertising in television, movies, screen magazines, records and disc jockeys.

Junior high students are often unpredictable. How they act one day may be in deliberate contrast to the next. In many cases, the student cannot control these changes in his temperament.

3. **Social Changes.** Junior high school is a time of troublesome conflicts between adults and students. Students at this level have a great urge to be on their own, independent of parents or adults. This drive is evident in the form of rebellion. Carl Reed[2] describes this conflict:

Many students are in conflict with their parents, which carries over into school even though there may be no conflict with the teacher. Adolescents strive for independence from adults, at the same time that they are striving to become independent adults themselves. The problems of dates, lipstick, dances, automobiles, and summer camps all have to be worked out with parents, with resulting conflicts.

An increasing critical awareness of his environment leads the junior high student to react in spasmodic and often unpredictable (even to himself) ways. He is extremely sensitive to the likes and dislikes of his peers.

Students of this level may be stubborn, argumentative, overly enthusiastic, resentful, elated, or chaotic. Personality and physical changes are occurring so rapidly that the shock is felt, not only by the student, but by those around him. It is difficult for junior high students to understand why they cannot do what they plan to do when parents say no. In one sense, it is important to help students maintain their independence of judgment, and their assertiveness but without creating traumatic conflicts. These are rather stormy times for students of this age, but also exciting in many ways. Helping to weather this period with as little difficulty as possible would seem a justifiable aim.

4. **Intellectual Powers.** Junior high students have awakened to a brand new kind of world. With a coming awareness in many respects, art subject knowledge on a variety of themes holds in-

trigue for them. They are eager to explore, search, and experiment in order to find hidden meanings and gain knowledge within a specific sphere. Youth always begins with a wonderful idealism that we would desire to preserve. This is the period to challenge the thinking of youth with art media techniques and art subject information that permits him to really get his feet wet. This is an ideal period to intensify the study of art in historical context as well as bringing to the student the full and exciting world of contemporary art in today's society. He wants to be challenged in order to test his abilities to learn with the new visual awareness that has engulfed him. Although he is not an adult, he has taken giant strides in this direction. Childhood has been left far behind.

One thing that we as art teachers must do is to keep imagination alive. We need to encourage the student to continue with the inventive activity that characterized his life prior to adolescence. Often, students who are at junior high level revert to earlier forms of behavior reminiscent with later childhood. The child at this stage of the game isn't sure yet where he fits and certainly isn't sure how he should act. He doesn't know how adults act because he is not one. He is part of an inbetween world—somewhere between child and adult. At this stage transitions in thinking, emotions, and physical growth can be disturbing and difficult. As art teachers, we need to insure that the quality of our own teaching and of what we do in our classroom will be decidedly high and that the scope will be entirely broad enough to challenge students. Scope may be defined in depth as well as breadth and in some instances may be confined wholly to the developments of artistic pursuits in depth.

The following considerations should benefit the new junior high teacher.

Considerations for the Art Teacher[3]

1. Important for teacher to be fair, impartial, and consistent in her work with the student.
2. Respect the student's right to privacy—be friendly, but do not be a "buddy."
3. Provide opportunities for experiences with a wide variety of materials—encourage experimentation.
4. Provide a great number of opportunities to experience and to make judgments about his environment and himself.
5. Stress the importance of the individual's recognition and development of his interests and abilities.
6. Use self-evaluation to build self esteem.
7. Encourage students to set realistic personal goals.
8. Provide opportunities for social interaction within the peer group.
9. Do not allow the group or one of its members to negate an individual's attempts to express himself.
10. Encourage students to use art expression and technical skills in their other activities.
11. Encourage student to use his own past experiences as a "springboard" when expressing himself.
12. Maintain a healthy and productive "climate" in the classroom.
13. Allow time for planning and discussion as well as the art experience.
14. Allow adequate time for the processes involved in the experience, and for clean up afterward.
15. Social interaction should be a part of the atmosphere or climate of the classroom, but should not be the "primary function" of the class.
16. Build a sense of responsibility for materials, equipment, and projects kept within the room.
17. Do not allow one student to monopolize the teacher's time.

Characteristics of High School Students

High school in some school systems begins at grade nine, for others grade ten. Undoubtedly there is some overlap and merging with the end of junior high. Many students just entering the high school program will often relate more to their counterparts in junior high. Initially, the line between the two is often rather obscure. Marked differences occur soon thereafter, thus paving the way toward adulthood.

The senior high school student has reached a high level of intellectual attainment and concomitant potential. He is ready to pursue logical or abstract theory in detail. His intellectual potential is at its prime. He can handle foreign languages, physics, art, or whatever the program may be. At the senior high level, most students are as ready as they will ever be to learn a subject in depth. In terms of art, he needs to be pushed to the very limit of his abilities. High school students are much like adults in many respects. Yet, they lack a solid foundation in common sense or judgment as this is their rookie season toward adulthood. What they lack in wisdom (which supposedly comes with age) they make up for in spirit, enthusiasm, and energy. Most of the physical bugs of growing have more or less spent themselves by grade ten or age fifteen. Some growth is taking place, but the peak has probably already occurred, and a modified upward trend in physical growth may continue for the next few years. For the purpose of understanding what to teach high school students in art, it must be understood that they have the same potential as adults, and often with greater malleability.

As in all walks of life, there are great varieties of differences between students. High school students are individuals who are seeking their own identity. They are not yet adults. They are not yet sure of who they are. They are not even sure of what they want to look like. They experiment with their hair in an assemblage of styles contemporary with their peer group. They change their style of clothes frequently or in some cases infrequently because these are characteristic trappings which influence the sum total of their self concept. Their self identity can change from day to day. Ralph Beelke[4] describes the adolescent well when he says:

The schools assume the responsibility for giving the adolescent youth the background he will need to make his way into the world. Wishing to please, and respecting those who have a place in society, the youth adapts to his environment. He adapts in his own way. He joins a group that feels very much the way he does, and wants to act the way he feels he too wishes to act. So the period of mass teen role-playing begins and the adolescent becomes many faces. With eagerness and exuberance, he plays the roles asked of him. He screams over the Beatles, copies and imitates those his crowd takes a fancy to; and somehow seems to lose his identity. Hot rods, jackets alike, hair alike, suits alike, stockings alike, everything alike—the screaming at a game together. Dancing the Dog, the Watusi, and Mash Potato—together, yet alone. This is the teen! Wild laughter, hidden giggles, this is the teen! Defensive, super-aware of fairness and justice, loneliness, confusion, tears of happiness, tears of joy. Rebellious, searching, questioning, exploring, and reaching—this is the teen too, concerned with the role he will play in the future. Inquisitive, speculative, creative, serious, earnest, challenging; sometimes demanding—this is the teen we all know. They sometimes seem to be on a quest, looking for something. Looking for a way to cross that bridge and find the man that gives out places in society.

Students can be shaped and influenced rightly or wrongly. Art teachers need to know this. Art teachers should understand what makes high school students different from adults. They have their own cultural interests; their own peer interests, which may have been prompted by musical media, television, or other consumer systems. Students are quick to identify with an idea or a series of ideas which portray them as a distinct group.

Many high school students who elect art classes are deeply concerned with learning. Art at present is an elective subject, and as such, students take art for various reasons. The highly talented (those who are gifted) are there because they want to make art a career. Other students may be there because art is less academically trying than mathematics.

Respecting Youth as Individuals

Some high school students appear self assured while others may feel extremely insecure. As personalities have not fully developed, many students are questioning, searching and hoping to discover and give meaning to their own lives. This is where the excellent art teacher can make some giant strides. It is important to respect students. At a time when self-image is crystallizing, they need to maintain their dignity. In fact, they need to have it *underlined*. While students need to be respected, they must also learn to respect, in turn. They need to learn discipline, and to eventually discipline themselves. They must learn the discipline of working on their own, the discipline of respect for others, and the discipline of self-achievement. This does not happen in a short period of time. In some students this may require three or fours years, almost the entire length of time in high school. For others it begins almost immediately, but students, like art teachers, must begin to see themselves with a positive attitude toward what they can learn in art.

Courtesy, Edie Summey, Phoenix Union High School, Phoenix, Arizona
Photo by Chuck Friedenmaker

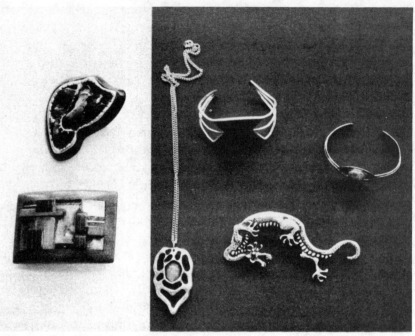

Courtesy of Robert Burkhardt, Tempe High School, Arizona.

Examples of hand built and cast
jewelry by high school students.

Those who do not plan to go on in art must see it as an important
aspect of their lives—a cultural aesthetic media that can satisfy
humanistic drives inside of them. They need to understand
what is beautiful in coming to grips with the aesthetic aspects of
life, rather than always shutting and blocking out and remaining
with the basic aspects of living as determined by an always practical
concept of society.

Thinking as Students Think

Teachers have to think in the manner that students think. They
have to catch the spirit of what is going on in young minds in the
junior high or high school level. You can't be forty, forty-five or fifty
in your thinking when kids are fourteen, fifteen or sixteen in their

Courtesy, Jack Bookbinder, Philadelphia Public Schools

thinking. You have to understand and identify with what is going on in the young, productive, and energetic mind; the old story that you are never too old to learn is very true in this case, but it takes an open attitude on the part of the teacher. You can't close your mind and say, "Well I've got the system, I've got the way, I learned it twenty years ago when I went through college." This doesn't work today. You've got to take those old foundational ideas and give them a buffing, a new polish, and make sure they fit with what is going on today. This means keeping up with current ideology, current art creations by nationally known young artists who are being accepted and reviewed in the magazines and galleries across the nation. Too often it is easy for art teachers to get out of the swing of things, to lose contact so that their world of art remains different from the world of art today.

Two major goals for both students and art teachers is to improve their understanding of art and the development of their art skill. It might be highly valuable for the art teacher to work along with the students rather than to supervise or to constantly stand over them. He may spend more time than the students on the problem. He may explore various directions or he may start the problem and come back to it at another time, thus permitting the students to observe the art teacher in action. The art teacher in this respect has to be unique, and operationally talented, if he teaches in the studio area. Also, if he teaches art history, then he should have some grounding in the particular area. He doesn't have to be an expert, but he does have to be able to fan the fires of imagination for the students.

A good teacher does not limit his pupils and does not try to decide what their limitations might be. He tries to open up the world to them, so that what he says will cause them to go farther than they would have if he had narrowly instructed them. He sets them in motion. We don't prescribe one special method of learning and one special set of formuli, because it may be in the very nature of art that there has to be some tolerance of ambiguity, mysteriousness, mystery, uniqueness, unusual situations, hunches, speculation, reflections, or imaginings. In other words, art can't be structured in the manner of a geometry class or an American history class. But this is not to imply that ideas, subjects, content, cannot be stressed. It can, but the approach is what has to be handled carefully. It might be said at this point that we are as adults what we have been taught as children; we are a composite of what we have learned in elementary school, junior high and senior high. We are a composite of our educational experiences up to the point at which we enter adulthood. This is the general pattern of what our personality is— the sum total of each "me." If we learned German, French, physics, biology, mathematics, and English in school, this is what we use in our life. And, if we did not experience art in any form or manner in school, then our life also reflects this lack.

Secondary School Art Teachers Describe Their Impressions of Students

The person best suited to know and understand the high school student would likely be the art teacher who works with his class day by day. With this idea in mind, the author approached several outstanding art teachers for their interpretations of what secondary school students are like.

Anonymous High School Teacher:

It seems to me that high school students are not too much different from each other than are adults. The thing that is outstanding about high school students is their great abiilty to act in contradiction of themselves from day to day. They can be ambitious and lazy, cooperative and hostile, serious and goofy, inquisitive and apathetic all in the same week and not think they have changed a bit. I have seen complete changes in behavior from one school year to the next. I have seen one of the nicest junior boys turn into the worst senior bum because he was elected to a high office in the class. I have seen another boy that was expelled as a freshman come back to become one of the most respected boys (by both faculty and student body) in the senior class because of his participation in school sports. Whenever possible a teacher should notice these changes and encourage the positive and eliminate (when something can be done) the negative.

Margaret Klein,[5] Chicago, Ill., high school teacher:

Teenagers come into high school looking pretty much like children. They leave looking like adults. Along the way they have amazing energy resources. They are very self-conscious about their bodies, their appearance and their sexuality. They tend to see themselves as they imagine others see them. I have found this almost impossible to change. Like all people, only more so, they love to be told how you, the teacher, see them as distinct individuals. That's why its so important how the teacher perceives and reflects back the students.

Lynda G. Brummett,[6] McKemy Jr. High, Tempe, Arizona:

Art experiences at the Junior High School level offer a unique and challenging teaching opportunity to one who is willing to accept such a challenge.

Admittedly, this period of time is not an easy one for the student. He is expected to cast off his "childish ways," and yet is still not afforded the status of young adulthood that the high school student achieves.

At this time, while clinging to the rights and privileges he enjoyed as a child, he begins to demand those afforded to an older more mature individual. Often he fails to see that, along with being allowed to do those things which he believes to be very "grown up," there are certain responsibilities which must be met according to the demands of his own particular environmental situation.

A great many permanent values are established by the student at this time; and it is important that the concept of self that is developing be a full and healthy one. He is developing attitudes about himself and of others that will be reflected in his later judgments about his world. The more opportunities he has for observations of himself—of his fellow man and the world in general, the more likely he is to be able to cope with and express himself effectively in his world.

The art situation can provide an unequaled opportunity to open up the world perceptually and creatively, if the teacher can provide those situations and experiences that stimulate the individual to grow independently; yet still allow him to become an effective part of his peer group.

To accomplish this, one must attempt to develop an understanding of the attitudes, characteristics, interests, and needs particular to the Junior High School students.

Statements by Secondary Students Regarding Art and Life

Often, what secondary students say can reveal their characteristics and personalities more accurately than any other source. What they are like in some respects is revealed by several students in their responses to the following questions:

1. *What do you think about life?*

   Sometimes it is a big bore and sometimes it is fun to be alive.

   I think it's the greatest thing that ever happened. I would like to die knowing I accomplished a lot in this life and will have a lot to show on the judgment day.

   I think life can really be beautiful if people will just let it. Some people make their life tragedy. People have too many worries and too many games with each other.

   I can take it or leave it.

   I am afraid of it. Society demands you to be one way—when actually you're another.

   Life is great. We try to live our own and someone trys to run it for you.

   It's beautifully real.

   It's too quick.

   Life, well, that's one question that lingers in practically everyone's mind. What is life about? What does life have to offer to me? Life is just a crooked road leading to nowhere with obstacles to cross and venture forth but, for what!

   Life is one big dream, or rather a nightmare.

   For the moment it's great. Cause for all I know its the only one I've got.

   Life is a trip full of fantastic scenes, vibrant sounds, extremely ranging sensations, and situations, a game of total involvement and the rules cannot be broken.

   It's a groove.

2. *What are your likes and dislikes in school?*

   I don't like the rule about having your dress a certain length or your hair (on boys) a certain length too. I think it is stupid to have a closed campus. They should trust you.

   It's a nice place to study people. Academically, forget it!

   I think a person should be able to look like he wants to.

   I dislike about everything.

3. *What does the teenager like and dislike?*

I know I like the feeling of being an individual, not just one of the crowd. I like my freedom up to a point, but I like to know my parents care where I am and what I'm doing.

The teenager (label) likes good music, art, and love with a lot of sincerity.

I cannot answer because I am only one teenager and have one mind, not millions.

I hate parents that complain that they can't talk to their kids. Some of my friends parents are that way. The thing is that when a kid has something to say the parent doesn't listen or considers them young and foolish.

He likes to be free, to not have someone telling him what to wear or how to act.

Teenagers dislike being told what they have to do.

I'm an individual. I don't know any "teenagers."

4. *How do you feel about teachers?*

They are the older generation. Very few even come close to knowing where it's at. They often preach but don't practice and even when they do preach, they don't tell it like it is.

I think most teachers have the mistaken idea that they were put here to pass along knowledge to me. No, I'm sorry. Maybe they can through some gigantic effort, help me to learn something. But they're not teaching. Most teachers are the perfect examples of the older generation.

Teachers are like most other people; there's some good and some bad.

The bad ones know it all and you can't learn enough from a good one.

I don't like the majority.

Some are groovy but others can't dig it.

They hand out knowledge to those who care enough to reach for a future.

Some are good and understand kids, others just teach.

I like a teacher who I can look up to and respect; not a pal, but not an old meanie either.

References

1. VIKTOR LOWENFELD, *Creative and Mental Growth,* New York: Macmillan Company, 3rd Edition, 7th Printing, 1963, p. 216.
2. CARL REED, *Early Adolescent Art Education,* Peoria, Illinois: Charles A. Bennett Company, 1957, pp. 46–47.
3. LYNDA G. BRUMMETT, from a statement submitted to the author, 1969.
4. RALPH BEELKE, "Means and Meaning in Art Education," *Art Education,* June, 1965, Vol. XVIII, No. 6.
5. MARGARET KLEIN, from a statement submitted to the author, 1969.
6. LYNDA G. BRUMMETT, from a statement submitted to the author, 1969.

Further References

1. BEITTEL, KENNETH R., and MATTIL, EDWARD L., "The Effect of a 'Depth' vs. a 'Breadth' Method of Art Instruction at the Ninth Grade Level," Chapter 19, from *Readings in Art Education,* edited by Elliot W. Eisner and David W. Waltham, Massachusetts: Blaisdell Publishing Company, 1966, p. 246.
2. BEITTEL, KENNETH R., *Alternatives for Art Education Research,* Dubuque, Ia.: William C. Brown Company Publishers, 1973.
3. BARKAN, MANUAL, *A Foundation for Art Education,* New York: The Ronald Press Co., 1955.
4. BURKHART, ROBERT C., *Spontaneous and Deliberate Ways of Learning,* Scranton, Pa.: International Textbook Company, 1962.
5. California State Board of Education, *Art Education Framework: California Public Schools,* Sacramento, Calif., 1971.
6. CONANT, HOWARD, "Season of Decline," in *New Ideas in Art Education,* ed. by Gregory Battcock, New York: Dutton, 1973.
7. CONANT, HOWARD, *Art Education,* Washington, D.C.: Center for Applied Research in Education, Inc., 1964.
8. GAITSKELL, CHARLES, *Art Education During Adolescence,* New York: Harcourt, Brace & World, 1954.
9. KATZ, FRANCIS ROSS, "The Longest Hour," *Art Education,* April, 1968, Vol. 21, No. 4, National Art Education Association, Washington, D.C.
10. KAUFMAN, IRVING, *Art and Education in Contemporary Culture,* New York: Macmillan Company.
11. LA MANCUSA, KATHERINE C., *We do Not Throw Rocks at the Teacher!,* Scranton, Pa., International Textbook Company, 1966.
12. LANIER, VINCENT, *Teaching Secondary Art,* Scranton, Pa.: International Textbook Company, 1964.
13. NORMAN, JEAN MARY, *Art: of Wonder & a World,* Blauvert, New York: Art Education, Inc., 1967.
14. RANNELLS, EDWARD, *Art Education in the Junior High School,* Lexington: University of Kentucky Press, 1946.
15. WANKELMAN, WILLARD, et al., *A Handbook of Arts and Crafts for Elementary and Junior High School Teachers,* Dubuque, Iowa: Wm. C. Brown Company Publishers, 1968.

"Hand Mirror"
by Tom Eckert
Walnut, Bronze, Feathers
Polished Bronze Mirror
12" long

Chapter 4

The reason that education in the creative arts can be important to even an untalented student is that such education challenges him to examine and render accurately his own vision of the world. In other subjects we pay great and proper attention to systems of acquired knowledge. To a growing mind these are seldom visions. They are rather facts: a trireme, a cathedral, a thunderbird. But in any creative art, even in the initial stages where a craft is being taught through exercises, the student's vision is demonstrably relevant.

WILLIAM MEREDITH,
"The Artist Teacher, the Poet as Troublemaker,"
from *Harvard Educational Review*,
Vol. 36, No. 4, Fall, 1966, p. 519

Organizing and Presenting Art Lessons

Motivation is the first step in the teaching-learning process. If students were self propelling in terms of ideas and imaginations, there would be little need for a stimulus from the outside, in this case the teacher. Somewhere along the academic paths, many students lose their curiosity at a rather early stage in the game. Rather than consider it lost, let's think of it as asleep, coated over with the dull wax of everyday habit and living. We can observe this by contrasting how young children experience their world. Everything within their sensory communication is open for exploration. Michael Drury has stated that nobody is born bored.[1]

However, most students begin to wrap shells around their inner and outer selves rather early, to protect themselves from the buffeting of growing. When one gets knocked down a number of times, most of us are leary of springing back up for more. In order to learn and grow, we must spring back. Motivation helps students to reopen their eyes to their own thinking and inventivities.

Generally speaking, we must consider that most students who elect to take art will have had little previous experience in either subject information, art appreciation, or skill development. Any prior experiences most likely will have consisted of limited expressive activity completed in the elementary classroom program, and usually taught by the classroom teacher.

Motivation can be defined, for art teaching purposes, as the means for getting students excited about ideas and possibilities for expressing, constructing, or appreciating some aspect or detail concerned with an art experience. Motivation is teacher ammunition to encourage ideas and intellectual pursuit in art. Motivation can serve as the trigger for developing art skills, analytical ability in comprehending art works, or expanding one's point of departure along aesthetic frames of reference. Motivation is a starting point for students, often ignited by the art teacher. Without motivation, students often resort to low level forms of art expression. They create "warmed-over" pictures from stale ideas derived from stereotypes (see chapter 1, page 6). Motivations are prods for students who are not accustomed to pursuing independent directions in art. Motivation can be considered as (1) a means of stimulating ideas for translation into graphic form, (2) as a demonstration procedure that illuminates processes, and (3) as an intellectual challenge to thought. Motivation as the sparker is intended to ignite thinking and push art learning forward.

Most students need leadership in being challenged, and strong stimuli in order to push forward in their art thinking. They must be stirred sufficiently enough to have a desire to communicate thoughts in visual terms. In this respect, the secondary student needs to develop the sensitive eyes and feelings of the artist. The artist is always full of ideas. He is able to select from his regenerative stockpile of thoughts the ideas most suitable to express or explore a specific intent. In addition, he is able to tell his ideas in original and inventive ways. The artist is both thinker, imaginer, and craftsman —able to unite art skill with idea skill into a personal technique for expressing his interpretation of some part of his world in visual form. Like the artist, we need to encourage students to plug ahead to see what happens with art media or ideas; a kind of *play the hunches* type of thinking—innovative, spontaneous, non-paralyzed and completely open and fluid. Students are full of raw, fresh vitality and we need to develop this quality. We need also to foster it in ourselves as teachers because all too often we think we've got the an-

swer, the corner on how to live. Often as teachers we can take some of our cues from youngsters. Youngsters keep us much younger in our thinking.

In the world of art, we are constantly buffeted by the ideas of change and we can face it daily by innovation in our thinking. In the central aspects of our lives as teachers and for students we need to keep the capacity for self-renewal alive. We need to retain in students the ability to weave and unweave, to remain in a state of intellectual flux, to retain a measure of flexibility, and not to fix on narrow targets for the future—targets that do not permit the creative mind to exist. For in not permitting creative possibilities to occur, the mind and the imagination can be strangled, locked in, and chained by a set of rules and routines aimed at producing functional results. The artist is not like this. He is too busy creating new worlds. The artist can make us feel, can touch us by the type of beauty that he creates. He can make us angry, too, when we do not agree with the image that he projects. It must be remembered that the artist is not a kook, quack, hippie, beatnik, or weirdo. He is a person endowed with special talents because he chose to develop such talents through his own sweat and energy.

Students, *like* artists, need to *learn* self-motivation, because source material for artistic expression does not seep through to us, osmosis style, in an aesthetic vacuum. They must learn to seek it out, examine it, and then cultivate it in their imagination.

Motivation is the means by which teachers can encourage students to increase their awareness of things in order to enrich viewpoints and ultimately seek more daring and original art forms. Motivation is a way to stoke the fire by throwing on the coals, lighting the fuse, and triggering thought. Motivation is the way in which art teachers can encourage students to search beyond the ordinary capacity to understand visual form. Above all, motivation should not be left to chance, or ignored in the secondary classroom. Jack Taylor[2] pursues motivation with the following statement:

Effective motivation is the *sine qua non* of the teaching-learning transaction. It would be difficult to design a teaching-learning model that did not include assumptions about motivation. In the past, many secondary art teachers often constructed the notion that little or no motivation was necessary or de-

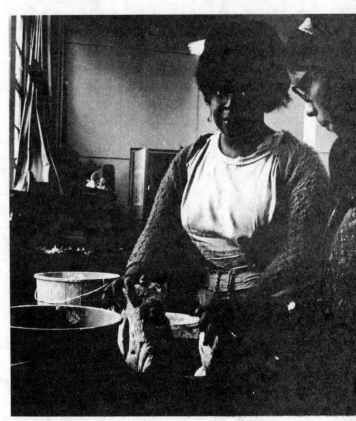

Secondary students build a kiln. Becoming involved
in an art process from beginning to end is part of
discovering what art is.

*Courtesy, Phoenix Union High School, Phoenix, Arizona
Photo by Chuck Friedenmaker*

*Courtesy of Dr. Edward L. Mattil, Chairman, Department of Art,
North Texas State University, and Dr. Leon Frankston from
Childrens Art Classes, Pennsylvania State University.*

sirable with adolescents—especially in art. Often the art teacher intuitively felt that self-directed, internalized motivation was the goal of the art program. If there was an interest in art "real" motivation would be present—buried just behind the left lung.

Motivation is a continuous process offering the potentialities for identification, involvement, confrontation and understanding—as represented by behavioral modification. Effective motivations are designed by all the learners in a particular setting, including the teacher. It is essential that motivation, individual or group, be relevant to needs, instrumental behavior and goals or consequences. Effective motivations are designed to search for and to find the "match" for each student so that he may structure his responses in art with meaning. Effective motivation can result in a commitment to action.

One of the truly exciting things about artists is that they are in tune with their own lives, inasmuch as they as a group work at understanding themselves more than many people would suspect. As a result, they are often freer and not shackled by some of the chains that society forges. Being less bound by the conventions of society, they do things that are more freeing and individually renewing to the person.

There is a real warmth and reward in being able to paint or to create something with one's own hands, something that has no purpose in the outer world but does serve very much to say: "This represents what I have been able to achieve. This is something from within me. It expresses my vision in my way." Motivation is not something that is injected into a person, although we can establish conditions which encourage motivation. When we talk about motivating students, we are talking really about getting them to do things for themselves in their way, by getting them to be ambitious, to have initiative, to want to make discoveries, to search, and explore. We need to lead students to the point where they can create their own challenges, where they can examine a situation and say, "These are the possibilities; this is what I would like to try," instead of "What shall I do? I haven't any ideas. How do you do this? Show me." The students set goals for themselves that are very much in keeping with the expectations that we as teachers look for in them. If the student feels that the teacher doesn't expect much from him, he, in turn may be inclined not to give much. As we seek the very best that is possible, we should let him know that we want his best. The teaching situation can thus be more inducive to achievement.

What we should remember as art teachers is that we don't want to establish any fixed, or rigid beliefs about art. Art is always changing, and is always interpreted in relationship to the individual. This doesn't imply that we don't have standards, but rather that we don't want to encourage narrow viewpoints in youth concerning their attitudes toward art. We need always to let the students know that the doorways of the mind can be opened to lead to greater exploration. We need to teach students to innovate on their own—to be inventive, to come up with unique solutions, to search for unusual answers, rather than always to learn what someone else innovated or invented. The mind is not a silo where informational hay is stuffed for future reference. It should be an idea trap ready to open whenever exciting challenges in art are present. The mind has a series of triggers that we can teach to fire when aesthetic possibilities occur. However, the mind only triggers itself when it is active and alert. What we need to prevent in students is *hardening of the artistries.* As teachers, we want to encourage students to try things that have never been tried before, as well as to try things that have been tried; and we want students to interpret in their own way based on leadership that comes from good teaching.

Ways to Motivate Students in Art

Verbal Discussions.   This type of motivational procedure is used most often and is usually interactive with the other types listed. Verbal discussion can be used in media presentations, or in critical-appreciative presentations in art history or art appreciation. This type of motivation incorporates as its primary vehicle, the spoken word. The spoken word might result in a carefully planned art history lecture by the art teacher or it might be a visiting artist discussing how he creates his work and the processes involved. It might be an art topic discussion between members of the class. Verbal discussions can begin anywhere, on any subject in art. Prior preparation and research by both teacher and students will help provide challenging intellectual ammunition. Verbal activity should be encouraged in the art classroom. Teaching students to be able to articulate about art in history, as well as art in contemporary thinking can help them increase their total capabilities in understanding the world of art.

Firsthand Art Experiences. This refers to on-the-spot demonstrations by artists or the teacher, of specific art media. One of the most dynamic means for bringing home artistic understanding is to make it possible for the students to observe the teacher or other artist in action. It could involve any media. Some examples for excellent first-hand experiences include welding metal, throwing on the potter's wheel, painting on canvas, casting jewelry, or drawing in pastel. There is no limitation. The teacher and students can go as far as their own imaginations and energies will take them. Firsthand art experiences can also refer to artistic discoveries away from the classroom, such as in galleries, artist studios, museums, where the students go to the source. Students may also be involved in discovering the sources for ideas, such as visiting automobile wrecking yards, antique shops, factories, the zoo, the water front, and countless other sources within each locale.[3]

Visual Art Experiences. This type of experience occurs when the teacher uses high quality films, slides, or other illustrative material to stimulate visual observation about any topic. Films can bring the subject to the student in a way that no other media can do. The camera can slow down rapid action such as birds in flight, a figure running, an explosion; or the camera can speed up the action through time sequence photography to condense a long period of time into two or three minutes. Film can also be useful as a highly creative new media to motivate for imaginative, innovative, and unique visual possibilities.

Slides are useful in the presentation of a total sequence or series of an artists' art works. Being able to see thirty or forty slides of paintings done by a single artist on a specific theme, realistic or abstract, provides an excellent opportunity to see beginning and end of media process and exploration of theme by one artist. It is difficult to know what an artist is attempting by seeing just one work. Slides can bring several works by one artist into view for evaluation and study. Slides are also invaluable in the presentation of historical art material. They are the best method of bringing history to the student without going to ancient Egypt or Rome. (See Chapter 5: Starting a Beginning Art History Program.)

Superb reproductions of artist's work are also excellent for teaching or displaying in the classroom. Visual images on display, or available in magazines can be stimulating to art students. Remember that classroom environments are highly active processes that can set the tone for further exploration. Students need to talk to the teacher, and each other, but they also need interaction with other artists and their ideas, even though it is derived from magazines, books, or reproductions. Looking at magazines that reveal what is going on in galleries today can serve as motivation sparkers. For art students to grow in art, it has to be a total process of their life, not an activity they engage in for one period a day. Thirty minutes a day spent flipping through the latest art magazine can serve to plant idea seeds in the fluid mind. Students will have much greater probabilities for increasing their artistic and intellectual awareness if they are encouraged to explore visually beyond their immediate attitudes toward art. Art growth is conditioned in many respects by the amount and extent of enriching experiences in perceiving and sensing the world. Ideas do not come from a void. There must be a mind-bank constantly searching out and storing information. This is why the process of continually looking through the art journals, visiting art galleries, and regularly discussing topics connected directly to the field of art can help students to form their own ideas regarding what they feel is art, and how they respond to it.

Art Media Experiences. This refers to investigation, search and experimentation as the student works directly with art media. In this case, the media becomes the primary source of motivation. Art media exploration may not be the most likely approach when working with a medium for the first time. Individual judgment on the teacher's part can easily determine this. If a teacher has introduced media, such as painting, there might be a value in letting the students experiment and search up to a point. Meaningless doodling would not be the intent in this case. The value in exploring the nature of a media is that often times the specific characteristics of media can suggest possibilities for further experimentation. Ideas

Two artists demonstrate to a class their paintings of a model. Experiences of this nature are direct and immediate in stimulating artistic thinking on the part of the student.

Courtesy of Dr. Edward L. Mattil, Chairman, Department of Art, North Texas State University, and Dr. Leon Frankston from Childrens Art Classes, Pennsylvania State University.

often grow from the way media is handled. Back-up motivation can combine media exploration with discussion and visual experience through films, slides, or demonstrations by other artists working in the same media.

Art Idea Experiences. In the development of a sound program of art for secondary students, it is worthwhile to build their awareness to both natural and man-made things. We need to encourage them to see the world in visual terms that are contemporary for the artist of today, and for the environment of today.

In order to build a backlog of idea information that students can draw on, the art teacher can make continual assignments in discovering details about subjects previously explored. Sources for discovery include the human form, forms from the landscape and terrain, from the sea, from observing the work of other artists, from stores, such as antique shops, wrecking yards, farms, or even magnification. For a more complete discussion on this topic, please refer to Chapter 10.

It is often puzzling to the person not engaged in art processes that the artist is able to dream up so many ideas so often and so spontaneously. However, it is not a question of pulling rabbits from a magic hat. It is rather a question of developing the creative power that one has been granted at birth. The artist has done this by building up his ability to see the world with sensitive feelers. He has learned to experience life deeply through the development of his awareness to ideas, experiences, and self-awareness. The art teacher can encourage this same approach in secondary students.

Planning Art Lessons with Care

One of the most important aspects of encouraging learning is the preparation by the teacher (or in some instances the student) of the art lesson to be presented. Organizing the lesson involves making a blueprint for action, often referred to as a lesson plan. A lesson plan doesn't have to be something recalled from an old textbook that may be limited in concept. Planning, however, always makes for a better organized, more successful teaching situation. Teachers

new to the profession will find it especially valuable to have an organized plan that carefully outlines their teaching approach to each specific lesson. As a teacher gains experience and wisdom, he may modify the manner in which he prepares a lesson, but the blueprint for action should be there on his desk when he needs it. Good teachers always prepare carefully, and this means some type of organized lesson plan. Lesson plans can be as varied as there are individual teachers. For the beginning teacher, the following sections are a basic starting point in the planning of an art lesson, and should be included in the body of a lesson plan:

1. Name of class
2. Title: studio problem, art lecture (other)
3. Objectives (see 3, below)
4. Materials (see 4, following)
5. Procedure (see 5, following)
6. Critique (see 6, following)

3. **Objectives.** It is important to understand what learning outcomes are expected from the art lesson. Planning and stating definite aims and goals helps to clarify the reason for the lesson. Also, unexpected objectives may occur that were not planned for. This is perfectly normal, and a good art lesson is fluid enough to move with the needs of a particular class. Stating sound, yet flexible, objectives gives the art teacher and students something definite to shoot for. This is quite the opposite from a "laissez-faire" approach where no one knows exactly what is going on, and only accidental outcomes may occur. Objectives can be both long range and short term. The lesson may fit within a larger learning unit intended to plan for art growth over the period of a term or year. In some instances, an art lesson has immediate goals, such as learning the use of specific media, or an art history sequence, where most of the value of the lesson will be obtained in one or two classroom periods.

Objectives are statements of goals that a teacher hopes to accomplish in the teaching of a particular art lesson. They should be clearly stated and not left in the form of generalizations, such as, to promote the growth of all children, or, to encourage free expression.

These are not definitive goals for art growth. Definitive art goals might include the following as objectives for individual art lessons:

Art Studio: (Watercolor Unit)

Learning how to use the brush in painting watercolors.

Learning how to stretch the paper on a wooden frame.

Planning the composition for painting with watercolors.

Various technical aspects in handling pigment for watercolor painting.

Matting and framing the final product.

Art History: (Related to Unit of Watercolor)

Discovering some artists in recent history who painted with watercolors, such as Winslow Homer, John Marin, Andrew Wyeth, William Blake, Charles Burchfield, Maurice Prendergast.

How their work relates to contemporary painting.

Art Appreciation and Analysis: (Sandro Botticelli)

To study the works of Botticelli, Renaissance master.

To evaluate Botticelli's works in comparison with his contemporaries, such as DaVinci, Michelangelo, Pollaiuolo.

To study how Botticelli was influenced by the Medici circle in his approach to painting.

(Pop Artists: Warhol, Rauschenberg, Oldenburg, Lichtenstein)

When did Pop art begin, and what are its major characteristics? Who coined the term?

How does the pop artist fit into the general scheme of the art world today?

How do we evaluate paintings such as "Campbell soup cans," "comic strip art"?

The establishment of criteria for evaluation of art.

Objectives can be extremely detailed if deemed necessary. A great length of time may be spent on a specific unit. The art teacher should be the sole judge of what he wants to achieve in his classroom for each specific grade. In many schools, there may be an art department of two or more art teachers. Most art teachers can arrive

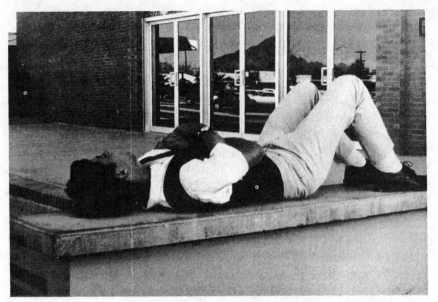

Courtesy, Coronado High School, Scottsdale Public Schools, Arizona

Courtesy, Coronado High School, Scottsdale Public Schools, Arizona

"Gumball Machine"
by Wayne Thiebaud, 1963
Oil on Canvas

Courtesy, Allan Stone Galleries, Inc., New York
Collection, Perite Levinson, New York

"Untitled"
by Philip Witkamp
Camelback High School Student
Pencil

Courtesy, Barbara Block and Marlene Jones, Camelback High School, Phoenix, Arizona

at a plan of attack for establishing major goals for identical subject areas to be covered by more than one teacher. The specific details should be up to the individual teacher.

4. **Materials.** A lesson plan should state what materials or media are to be used. Stating the materials needed helps the art teacher to know what to collect or organize in order to present the art lesson. If an art teacher leaves the organization of the media or material to spontaneity or chance, it is likely that he will overlook minor but essential materials needed to present a good art lesson. Stating the material carefully also enables the teacher to plan ahead and gather the material prior to class. There are so many little chances for things to go wrong, that it is best to be as thorough as possible. Trying to collect what is needed at the last minute, or just before class, can be disastrous as many art teachers will testify. Stating the materials also puts it concretely, and additional materials are often added if the art teacher has an opportunity to extend his thinking prior to the lesson. All material needed should be listed, including audio-visual equipment, reproductions, etc.

5. **Procedure.** The procedure includes the presentation, or a rough outline of it. It is not necessary to record every word that is to be spoken in the lesson. A step by step outline plan is helpful if the lesson involves demonstrating the use of specific media. If the lesson is in art history, the lecture can be written in a much more detailed fashion. Room should always be left for additions, subtractions, or modifications depending on the specific class. The reason for having a good outline written down is that even experienced teachers lose their sense of organization if they do not have a plan. When a lesson is presented spontaneously, much of the lesson is based on chance, and often key items are omitted simply because the teacher did not think of them. If a lesson plan were available, the key points could have been written down, and would be sure to be included. Within the procedure section should be included the number of class periods allotted to the lesson. Some lessons will be as brief as one period, while others may take two or three weeks. Length of time will depend on goals for the lesson. There is some research available to indicate that depth of instruction, or instruction concentrated

within one area over a span of time can produce learning of value to student art development. Kenneth Beittel and Edward L. Mattil[3] state:

> The study suggests that it may be well to begin earlier with students in engaging in sustained long-term projects of depth and with less yielding to their restless demands for variety. There is in fact some evidence in this and other studies by the authors that some kinds of activities that students appear to want or are insistent upon have little learning value for them, while some learning experiences that they show some real resistance to have some educational value for them.

The notion that great varieties of media and subject information must be presented over the course of a term no longer appears to be sole objectives for art in secondary schools today. Pursuing learning in art below the surface through concentrated effort along one or two units a semester might also appear to have validity.

6. **Critique.** Every art lesson should have a critique session in which the various aspects of the lesson can be analyzed with hopes of improving it the next time. The critique session is the evaluation part of the lesson or the follow up, to determine both strong and weak points. The best time to critique a lesson is right after it is over, if possible. This is when the experience is most vivid in the mind. In the critique session, the art teacher can assess not only his performance in presenting the lesson, but also the performance of the students. This evaluation period of the lesson plan enables the teacher to go over each step in relation to each student, as far as he observed, and make decisions based on what to do for the next lesson. Having a critique session helps to clarify why students act the way they do, and why they performed in a specific manner, art wise. Critiquing enables the teacher to improve his performance in teaching the art lesson.

Checkpoints in Presenting an Art Lesson

In any lesson, there are several important checkpoints that will help the art teacher turn in a much better performance in presenting the lesson. Some points to consider in presenting a lesson include:

1. Talk to the students, not to the training aid; that is, don't present your ideas to the class as you write something on the board.

Arrange the material ahead of time, write the material on the board ahead of time, or stop talking, make the adjustments, then carry on, maintaining eye contact most of the time.

2. Learn each student's name as soon as possible. This avoids having to ask the green haired boy in the third row with the live turtle to pay attention.

3. Speak clearly, and articulate each word. Avoid poor grammar, unless you are making a point.

4. Keep your lesson plan close at hand so that it is easily reachable for consultation during the presentation of the lesson.

5. When demonstrating an art media, or discussing a point, make certain that every student is paying close attention before speaking. Students moving about the room, shuffling papers, tapping pencils or fingers can be extremely distracting—not to mention their missing the point.

6. Be as thorough as possible in the presentation, but don't belabor the points.

7. Be as natural as possible, and try not to display nervous mannerisms or insecurities.

8. Make certain that every student has a good view of your table, if demonstrating a technique. Overhead projectors or other visual aids may be helpful.

9. Don't cover too much material or information in one period. Speak slowly, and allow the points to be considered. If lecturing, ask the students to save their questions by jotting them down, but to continue listening.

10. Be enthusiastic and intensely interested in the lesson that you are presenting. Students soon catch the spirit.

Considerations in Demonstrating Media

In media or studio lessons, it is usually best to demonstrate the use of the media in order to illustrate its proper uses. Films and other visual aids can be helpful in clarifying use of a tool or materials, but the best approach in explaining and presenting the proper utilization of an art tool and equipment is through teacher demonstration. The art teacher is most likely best equipped to know the needs of the class. It is possible that an advanced student in one of the art classes can assist the teacher, or demonstrate along with the teacher. However, the main demonstration should be initiated by the regular art teacher. How the fine points are worked out, including subsequent demonstrations of techniques is an individual judgment by the teacher. Demonstration assumes that the teacher has some teaching facility with the specific media. If an art teacher were completely new to the media, it would be possible to bring in an experienced artist to demonstrate, and the teacher would also be a student learning along with the rest. There may be occasions when this is the case. Ideally, the teacher is an art student who has more experience than the class. In most lessons, the art teacher will be able to demonstrate. Even in previously untried material, the art teacher can practice at home, or at school, until he has gained some control over the media. It is a great advantage for the students to see that the teacher is learning along with them.

In demonstrating media, make certain that all students can see clearly. Everyone should be paying attention to avoid needless repetition. The best method to prepare for demonstrating media is to go over the lesson ahead of time, step by step. Write down an outline so that each point will be certain to be covered. Bring in any illustrative examples of other artists' work to use as examples. The primary purpose of media demonstration is to put the idea across. A good visual firsthand demonstration can be particularly helpful in explaining the handling and use of a media to students. After the demonstration, a workable approach is to have the students dig right in and try their hand at it. Pass-out material can be valuable for helping to clarify points. Students should be encouraged to keep an art learning notebook. In the notebook can be kept notes on each demonstration, as well as ideas that may come up during art class. When a student is encouraged to keep ideas in his notebook, he will carry it with him often. It should contain not only notes and ideas, but also sketches.

When demonstrating media, it is important to cover all aspects necessary to explain the use of the media. A demonstration may have to be covered in parts until the students understand each phase. Ceramics, Printmaking, or Batik processes require many steps.

Teachers should not **avoid** a media if they have little experience in it themselves. This would represent an opportunity to dive right in and learn it. Good teachers don't limit themselves to a few ideas or approaches. They are willing to try anything!

The Importance of Working Hard in Art

Learning about art is a challenging and strenuous experience. If a student is to learn, or if a teacher is to teach well, both must set high objectives for themselves. This can be demonstrated best by action rather than words. William M. Allen,[4] President of Boeing Company, Seattle, says:

> I feel that man's objective should be opportunity for greater accomplishment and service rather than opportunity for more leisure. In my view, the greatest pleasure life has to offer is the satisfaction that flows from accomplishing or participating in the accomplishment of a difficult and constructive undertaking. We should all have leisure time and enjoy it. However, in my view, one of the principal attributes of leisure is that it enables you to develop an appreciation of the joy that hard work offers. Leisure should not be life's great objective.

This sort of philosophy in the art class could go a long way to helping a student work hard and see success in his accomplishments. This is quite the opposite attitude from that of thinking of art as a playful activity, to be engaged in after the difficult work is done. Art teachers should set especially good examples in art. Art is not therapy, or recreation, or creative permissiveness. It is plain hard work, and requires the learning of the discipline of art. There is a body of material to be learned, and media to be mastered. It will be up to the art teacher to see that the challenge is always present, and to push students as far as they are able to go in their thinking. The art class has no time for idle hands. When students enter the class, they should either be ready to listen to classroom instruction or demonstration, or begin immediately to work on the problem at hand. Piped in rock music intended to sooth the students has no place in the classroom as background filler. In most instances, it detracts from the thinking and serious students must screen it out in order to function. Students soon learn to take their cues from the example set by the teacher. If the teacher is permissive and casual, the students soon follow suit. On certain occasions, music may be appropriate to the establishment of a mood. However, in getting down to the tooth and nail of hard work in art, the conversations, music, and casual atmosphere of the lunch room or recreation room should be kept out of the art classroom. The art teacher can establish this objective at the beginning of the term. As the teacher sets the pace, the students will soon realize the excitement and adventure of art as a true challenge to artistic understanding.

Using Visual Materials with Impact

In studio lessons, strong supportive material should be utilized that clarifies the meaning behind the specific unit. The art teacher can demonstrate his approaches to media, but students need also to see how other artists interpret and express their ideas in media. For example, if a unit on designing were presented, and the emphasis was on the development of imaginative visual form, some artists in particular would stand out for their uniqueness of ideas and carry through. There are as many approaches to this unit as there are teachers, but one example would be to select artists who may be fanciful in their interpretations of unique visual form. Some artists who might be grouped along an imaginative line include Paul Klee, Joan Miro, Wassily Kandinski, Marc Chagall, and certain works of Pablo Picasso. If the visual design lesson was in a more intellectual orientation, another group of artists might be better suited to illustrate the unit. Artists having particular characteristics in common relative to more formal consideration in designing include Piet Mondrian, Josef Albers, Larry Poons, Kenneth Nolan, Ad Reinhart, and Barnett Newman. The teacher should keep as heroes artists from the right-now society to the recent past, as well as artists from any epic if they help to bring home a point relating to the specific objectives of the art lesson. Good quality reproductions, or whatever is possible to obtain, should be readily available for the students to study and learn from during the lesson. The contemporary art world today is as close as one or two art magazine subscriptions which the library can obtain. Even better, the classroom should have its own copy. It would be well worth the investment for the art teacher to subscribe to the following art journals as a means of insuring the development of learning in students:

1. ART FORUM
   Monthly
   667 Madison Ave.
   N.Y., N.Y. 10021

2. ART NEWS
   Monthly
   444 Madison Ave.
   N.Y., N.Y. 10022

3. CRAFT HORIZONS
   Bimonthly
   16 East 52nd St.
   N.Y., N.Y. 10022

These magazines, including all of the back issues, should be kept in the art room constantly; they should be organized in such a manner that the students can readily seek inspiration. Students should be given assignments to read them regularly. These magazines, and others that the art teacher may also acquire through the library, include *Art in America, Graphis, College Art Bulletin* and *Art Journal.* Students should have as a continuing assignment the search for visually exciting material from the standard periodicals usually obtained at home. Supportive visual material is not to be considered haphazardly, to be flipped through before the bell rings, and forgotten.

Space should be developed whereby much that is visually stimulating can be displayed on bulletin boards. Material of a high visual order can serve as a springboard for increased sensitivity to contemporary visual form. Films and slides are also ideal for underscoring what is being currently done in the art world, as well as revealing the art of the past. The art teacher should not be without his own carousel projector for his classroom. This should be a must for good teaching, for it serves to take the place of seeing fine original works. The best stimulation would be to get to the major galleries in metropolitan cities, but only big city schools can hope to do this. The teacher can collect good examples of major new works in slide form. These slides would also be especially appropriate for the art history lectures which are part of a good secondary classroom curriculum.

Single concept 8mm films can also be utilized in the classroom, particularly to show detailed instructions on technical art processes. The idea behind visual material is to help the teacher in getting his points across. A good library of art books on artists and art history is also a must in the art classroom for it makes art accessible to the student. Remember that students imitate their teachers. If the art teacher reads everything in sight dealing with art, the students will also pick up the idea. Art teachers, by their actions, by what they read, by what they do in art, set examples of far greater significance than most realize. The art teacher is the expert, and as such, must reveal to the students that art is the most exciting adventure ever created by man! Regular assignments should be made from the art library in the classroom. This can be supplemented by the school library offerings. The art library need not be highly expensive. Many first class paper back volumes on art are available in bookstores. One book on art, carefully selected each month, would be a worthwhile investment to good art teaching. Quite properly, the school budget should take care of this need. However, a good teacher will not wait for the yearly budgetary appropriation to do good teaching, or to make learning possible.

There will always be money funds available where there is an intense interest on the teacher's part. Funds *can* be raised. If necessary, the art club or the class can figure out some solution for acquiring good quality art books. Some teachers work with the students to perform art jobs in the school, such as poster announcements which can raise funds for the art books or subscriptions. The art class is not a poster production factory. Talents, however, can be used to improve the classroom situation. In the meantime, the art teacher can put the pressure on appropriate individuals to get a share of funds for what is essential for top learning in art. Parents or community leaders are another possible source for contributions to the art room resource material. A donation by a department store or book shop would be a community service to one's school. An art teacher has to have plenty of guts, lots of enthusiasm, and a great driving desire to help his students learn in art. He must be willing to fight hard and long to secure what he feels is of value for art learning. The art teacher must never take a back seat to anyone. If it is necessary to "crash through a brick wall" to secure an improved classroom situation, this is what the teacher should do. There is little sense in grumbling about one's lack of equipment or materials; if the art teacher is dissatisfied, then he should get in there and do something about it! Great teachers and students are made, not born!

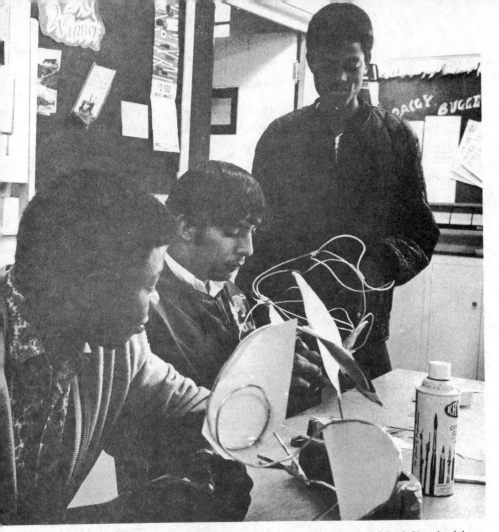

Courtesy, Edie Summey, Phoenix Union High School, Phoenix, Arizona
Photo by Chuck Friedenmaker

Establishing Criteria for Grading in Art

Evaluation at the secondary level in art is usually assessed by the application of a grade on the reporting card for each specified period of a school term. Evaluation is an extremely delicate and crucial experience that an art teacher must exercise with care. Exercise though, he must. Evaluation is the process by which the teacher assesses what the students have done up to a specific point, in art. Evaluation can be something that is cooperatively considered with the students, or it can be a subjective series of judgments on the part of the teacher. Most school systems, including college and university systems, employ a grading system that utilizes either letter grades or number grades, worth so many units, or honor points. The method utilized to arrive at a grade may be completely decided by the art teacher, or art teacher and students. The final grade, however, should be consistent with the method used by the school system in reporting grades. If grades generally follow the letter system, this should apply for all classes, including art. Art growth can be assessed just as readily as growth in any other subject. Strict attention to evaluation processes in art are a basic part of measurement between student, teacher, and parent. The grade indicates what the student appears to be doing in the class.

Some teachers may feel that the grading system is unfair, and in an attempt to improve on it, may grant blanket A's or B's to the entire class on the basis that all students are working at top capacity. Grading in this manner loses its sense of proportion, and students soon realize that the effort expanded, any amount of effort, will bring the same reward. Grading, or evaluation, has to be a personal judgment, whether teacher oriented, or student-teacher combined. Rewards given without achievement evidenced can negate a positive feeling for art. It would be marvelous if all students were concerned with their growth in art, without the extrinsic pressures for grades. However, most students are human, and have not learned the value of working for the joy to learn in art. The grade, if fairly given, is a measure of how the teacher feels the student is doing. Grades have to be given fairly and with great discernment. They must represent true effort on the part of the student.

Art teachers can develop their own systems for grading, depending on the particular class. There is no one way of evaluating student growth in art. It will be entirely up to the teacher, and if desired, the students who may or may not share in the evaluation process. The following possibilities are suggested as one system for evaluating student growth in art:

Evaluation of Student Growth in Art

1. *Media Skills*

   Handles media well
   Uses tools correctly
   Improvement
   Art product shows
      technical prowess

2. *Art as Subject*

   Understanding of art history
   Participates in discussions
   Indicates critical awareness
   Analytical-appreciative ability

3. *Creative Ability*

   Expressive qualities in
      process and product
   Uniqueness of ideas
   Original approaches
   Independent judgment
   Fluent and flexible
   Success as evidenced in
      art product
   Success as evidenced in
      classroom processes

4. *Work Habits*

   Concentrates
   Gives all out effort
   Finishes work
   Works independently
   Punctual
   Follows instructions

5. *Attitudes*

   Receptive
   Accepts criticism
   Pays attention
   Works without disturbing
      others
   Cooperative

Criteria of this sort can serve as a starting point. Each group can be considered equal, or they can be weighted as the teacher sees fit. Other criteria can be added to this list, or the teacher may decide that none of these suit a particular evaluative approach. The important thing to remember is that evaluation by the teacher (and student) is an extremely important part of the learning process. Evaluation is a means of determining at what point the student is, and what should be the next challenge. It is communication between teacher and parent.

Grading is a difficult task. Students at the extremes of any grading scale set up by the teacher will be more easily evaluated. That is, those who excel, or those who do little, will be distinctly apparent. Those on the border in between must be considered at length.

Often the students themselves have a fairly good assessment of their achievement. It may be of value to ask them what they feel they have done in terms of growth. Most students will reply honestly.

It is also important in the process of evaluating and grading for students to understand that grades are yardsticks of measurement for problems or challenges undertaken. At no time should a grade reflect on a personality or become a personal label, such as an "A" student, or a "D" student. The *work* is graded, not the student. If the work doesn't make it, it doesn't mean the student is a failure in life. The challenge here is how to evaluate so that students can see where they should improve, without losing their confidence or drive to excel. The teacher must make many individual decisions regarding evaluation that may put pressure on the student. However, the student needs to be challenged and pushed. Students are aware of their abilities, and what they have done for a particular term period. If they are granted a gift grade, without earning it, they soon use this system as their model. There may, however, be times when a strategically placed grade higher than that earned for a specific student can serve as a psychological starter. Teachers must experiment by trial and error and determine which evaluation system is workable in a fair manner for his students. The idea, ultimately, is to emphasize, not the grade, but the learning that can take place through honest endeavor in art processes.

Discipline

For teachers, it is important to remember that at all times we should try to get the best work we can from the students. If we feel that they have only given half serious effort or are not really involved in the idea dealing with the art problem, then we need to insist on higher standards. We want high standards but not at the expense of the student's concept that he may hold of himself. Students need to know where they stand in relationship to the teacher. They need to know that someone is in the leadership position, leading. In the lives of adolescents, this is a critical time. They are just learning the rules of society and are bound up with the questions that relate to, "what do I do here, how do I act in this situation,

Photo by Chuck Friedenmaker

should I smile, should I rebell?" Good discipline is necessary for good teaching. Learning does not take place when students pirate the classroom. Teachers need to work at getting the most from the students in various ways. The ultimate goal of good teaching is to lead the student to the point where he is independent of the teacher in many ways so that he can go about the job on his own, and step into the new world of ideas that he has learned as a result of searching. In the beginning, he works with others, plus the teacher, but later on, he plunges himself. He is never going to make this plunge if he has learned to defy, to shut out, and close down on what is being taught. Discipline is a basic fundamental in the classroom. Whenever there is a class of students, there must be certain rules—rules that can be flexible when the situation demands it—but firmness when firmness is needed, much in the same way that parents should be firm with their children. Teachers also need to be fair. Good planning is part of discipline. If a teacher has to hunt for this and that, gives wrong directions, fiddles with equipment, and has other minor difficulties in an actual presentation of an art lesson, all of these factors tend to dilute what is possible in a particular lesson. The teacher has to plan ahead and anticipate the pitfalls so that problems are thus "cut off at the pass" before they develop. A good teacher will let the student know she likes him, but not the act he is engaged in when she disciplines him. Discipline means also helping the student accept his capabilities as well as his limitations.

More Tips on Discipline

Speak well, and articulate. Try to use good grammar, and not to slur. There will be times when you will make mistakes. Everyone does. Just don't make a habit of it. Learn students' names as soon as possible. It is a lot easier to demand someone's attention when you can say, "What is your thinking on the subject, Jack?", rather than, "the third boy from the left with the red shirt and freckles." An excellent way to get off on the right foot in terms of meeting a particular class and preparing it to work for a term is to set down the objectives that you expect on the very first meeting of the class.

Let the students know where you stand, what you want to do in the classroom, that you do expect them to work hard, to listen, and pay attention, not to be rowdy, not to fall asleep, to come on time, to be mannerly, and to help each other. Let them know how they will be graded, and what type of effort you expect from them. More often than not this will set the pace for the rest of the term. A teacher can always let up and be a little freer and friendlier, but it is much more difficult to tighten up after a class has begun to get out of hand. I have found in my own experience if a teacher continually makes jokes the class transfers this feeling and everything is likely to become a joke. Try not to make big issues out of little issues although in some instances a series of small items can rapidly snowball into a much larger situation. Teachers have to be the judge. Sometimes little infractions here can be ways of letting off steam as long as everyone recognizes that it is an infraction and is not to be repeated habitually.

Art teachers have to know when to permit off-beat curiosity and exploration of unknowns and when to allow students to do things that are not generally approved. They need to sense when to encourage, and when to be critical. In teaching art, one has to know when to throw away the rule book and play it by ear. If we become merely academicians in teaching art, we teach systems that may work for a very few students and not for the vast majority of students we teach, or may not work at all.

There will be and there should be many directions students pursue—many avenues for inquiry. Junior and senior high school students need to develop a sense for recognizing their own power in giving shape to their ideas and feelings. They need to learn that what they do can suggest other possibilities. They need to become aware of the artistry of their vision, of the expressiveness in their lives. What the teacher needs to do is stretch the vision of the students. He needs to encourage them to reach for new goals and horizons in art. He needs to show them the important values that art has and can have in one's life. The students can only be as sensitive as the teacher and a sensitive teacher encourages students to go way beyond what even the teacher may be able to visualize and imagine.

Both Art Process and Art Product Are Important at All Secondary Levels

In the past, much emphasis was placed on the value of art processes in educating students through art. Contemporary research in art and art education suggest that both process and product are part of educating the student not only *through* art, but more significantly, *to* the wide wonderful world of art. We want to bring the student to understand that art can be a moving force in his life, that through and within art, the refinement of the sensibilities is possible —refinement indicating that a person is richer in his cultural and humanistic approach to his experiences by making art a part of his life.

Teaching High School Art

The following interview with a high school art teacher* provides insights that will be helpful to prospective art teachers.

Q: What do you feel should be the content of a high school art program?

I feel the basic art/design prerequisite is a must unless you plan to teach design concepts in the media areas. One of the major problems is that students have trouble transferring design concepts from one media to another. We try to provide a multitude of experiences within different media, working with the same design concepts. For example, we work two-dimensionally with line, and we also work three dimensionally with line, and so on. We have eliminated vague titles such as Art I, II, III, and IV, which tells us nothing. Art becomes a hodgepodge of whatever the teacher wants to do unless you have a curriculum laid out that is strong. We have designed our curriculum into media areas which is structured with jewelry, ceramics, drawing, painting, graphics, sculpture, and photography. Without this sort of planned structure, you will have a teacher presenting mosaics, for example, and when asked why, he

*Courtesy of Robert Burkhardt, Art Department Chairman, Tempe High School, Tempe, Arizona.

might say because he likes it. We're trying to put more clarity and reason for being into our program. The program is elective except for basic art/design.

Q: How do you feel a high school teacher should critique a student's work?

First of all, a ninth grader isn't very verbal, and so I have to teach them how to talk. The big comment is usually, "I don't know anything about art, but I know what I like." We begin by talking about the assignment related to the experience, and then we go into the design aspect. What was the goal? What was our criterion? How did we attempt to solve the concept through the design concept?

Q. You follow a questioning technique in your critique?

Exactly. Does the composition work? Is the work organic? Are the forms repeated? Did you achieve what you set out to do? In other words, we push thinking about the experience in relation to the product.

Q. How do you order supplies and organize the rooms?

I oversee the ordering of supplies, and each of the four classrooms is equipped to teach basic design. The specialized areas need area coordinators who handle responsibilities for each area. I buy in mass, so many gross of this and that. I shop for the best prices in the catalogs. The special coordinators handle supply needs for their area and return to me. I pass on the requisitions through channels. We have supply rooms in each specialty area, whereby volunteer students pass out materials and supplies. They receive credit for doing this.

Q: What does your program do for handicapped students?

We mainstream the physically handicapped—those in wheelchairs, crutches. The mentally handicapped are separated. They come down for supplies, etc.

Q. Do you have a program for talented students?

It's more of an academic emphasis. They take painting and a seminar. They report on artists, do research papers, make class presentations, and have tests. Every student in this class becomes a teacher, and must become "expert" in a specific area. They visit museums, galleries, and otherwise seek to excell in art history, as well as a specialized area.

Q: What would you say to a young teacher just entering a teaching system?

Take as many classes as possible in as many media as possible, and more than one class in each area. When I hire, I look for people who can teach both photography and drawing, or sculpture and ceramics. So get broad as well as deep. Learn reasons for teaching, have something to offer students, for they will be the ones who will buy and support the art of the future. We need teachers willing and able to ignite the minds of youth toward the value of art. Lesson plans are good also, because they organize your mind and give the sequence that is needed.

Q: Should an art teacher work at his own art?

Definitely. They might be in a weaving association, or in a museum program, or in a state art association. It's hard to do the art after putting in an 8-hour day. But one must find a definite period of time where the art comes first. It might be Saturday, or two hours a day. The time has to be set aside.

Q: With regard to evaluation, how do you grade?

We have five areas of evaluation: craftsmanship, skill in materials, utilization of time, success of concept, and follow-up through critique. We want them to be proud of their efforts, and not throw it into the wastebasket when they leave the room. We expect the students to develop a strong vocabulary related to the specific area. They have art every day, and this gives time for concentration.

Q: Do you relate your program to artists in the field?

Yes. Occasionally, we bring resource people in, and we encourage students to go to museums, other schools, and events related to our program. We require students to pick out articles from magazines such as *Art in America,* and *Art News,* and have them critique the articles. This is how we help to build vocabulary. They become aware of artists, which we try to reinforce in the classes.

Q. Does your program stress careers in any way?

We touch on it. We don't push it. We have a career coordinator in the district. Students in the senior year often will ask questions regarding placement.

Q: What about recruitment programs for students not in the classes? Those who go through the school system without ever taking art?

We have three days a semester in which we have students working out in the courtyard with potter's wheels, painting, etc. We put out displays at lunch time. I personally go to the junior high classes and present a slide showing of what we do in the various places. This is before the counselors get there for the freshman enrollments the coming fall. We compete with the other areas for students.

Q: How do you handle discipline?

Well, occasionally it's a problem, especially when they come in from a less structured junior high. We try to work it out with the student. Many times, a student will try to look good if you're trying to put him down in front of a class, an upmanship kind of thing. If you pull a student aside and talk to him person to person, you can often reach him. If a student is a continuous problem, you can send him to the office, and have them removed.

Q: What about problems with drugs, alcohol?

Sometimes we have this. We discuss the danger of working with tools, and to be alert. Usually students on drugs don't come to class. After 12 absences we have to justify passing a student. We

try to act long before this stage. Often we will refer the student to the nurse. With good administrative support, we have a minimum of this sort of thing.

Q: Do you do any kind of public relations in the community?

Yes, we show displays in the board of education office, in the district schools, and in the community. We put up shows in MacDonald's. The kids go over and demonstrate the potter's wheel, etc. and get all they want to eat. Everyone really likes it. You can get over-involved in outside activities. We try to get together, and choose which activities each art teacher will become involved in for the semester or the school year. With the four of us in this school, we divide up the areas of the city. One will cover displays at the state capital, and the downtown area. Another will cover the shopping centers, and so on. We really have to be selective, and assign responsibility. We each take turns on scholastic, and other competitive shows.

Q: What is the size of this school?

It's grades 9-12. There are about 1850 students, of which 425 are enrolled in the art program, and we have four art teachers here, of which I am the chairman of the department.

Q: Does your school have a range of various ethnic groups?

Yes. They are all mainstreamed in the classes. We have Indians, Chicanos, blacks, Orientals, as well as whites. We are in an older section of the city, and draw from various economic areas. We try to treat all groups equally. I show films on Indian artists, women artists, black artists. We try to show where everyone fits in. We don't make a big point of it, but do try to create more of a balance than existed in the past. We're trying, and it takes time.

Q: What about belonging to the state and national art education associations?

I do. The state art association is really at the grass roots. Everyone should contribute a little. This is where the meat is. If a district is having problems, or if strength is needed at the meeting of the legislature, the state organization can be of valuable service. At the national level, this is a broader thing, and they are trying to affect action at the national level in Washington. If one doesn't join, they can't complain if programs are cut. Young teachers, as well as experienced teachers should definitely get involved regardless of level taught. We're all in this are adventure together.

Art Curriculum for Tempe High School, Tempe, Arizona

Art Design (FA,04)   Open to Grades: 9-10-11-12

Prerequisites: None   1 Semester   1/2 Credit

Level of Difficulty: Open to students of all levels of ability.

Course Expectations: In-class projects — quizzes — tests — final exam — art fee of $7.50 — regular class attendance.

Art/Design is a prerequisite for all other art classes. The course will enable the student to become visually sensitive to the world in which he/she lives. Design is the basic foundation for art as well as everyday visual experiences. The course will develop around the basic design principles and elements which will be the basis of experiences in ceramics, drawings, fibers, graphics, jewelry, photography, painting, and sculpture. The student will also develop the ability to critically evaluate his own art work as well as the work of others.

Painting (FA,08)   Open to Grades: 10-11-12

Prerequisites: Art/Design-Drawing   1 Semester   1/2 Credit

This course may be repeated for advanced credit.

Level of Difficulty: Designed for students with average and above-average levels of ability.

Course Expectations: In-class projects — extra credit assignment — final exam — art fee of $10.00 — regular class attendance.

Painting is an exploration of paintings, ideas, and techniques, both traditional and modern. The student's own interpretation and

treatment of the subject is encouraged. Painting provides the student with an opportunity for in-depth study and the development of special interests.

Drawing (FA,09)   Open to Grades: 9-10-11-12

Prerequisites: Art/Design   1 Semester   1/2 Credit

This course may be repeated for advanced credit.
Level of Difficulty: Designed for students with average and above-average levels of ability.

Course Expectations: In-class projects — extra credit assignment — final exam — art fee of $10.00 — regular class attendance.

This course offers exposure to many drawing techniques and processes. Each student will complete a series of original drawings in media areas that include pencils, charcoal, and pastel. Subject areas include still life, perspective with landscape, face, and figure study.

During the second semester the student investigates pen and ink, watercolor, and scratchboard. The student has a greater choice in the selection of the subject.

Ceramics (FA,10)   Open to Grades: 9-10-11-12

Prerequisites: Art/Design   1 Semester   1/2 Credit

This course may be repeated for advanced credit.

Level of Difficulty: Individualized approach — open to students of all levels of ability.

Course Expectations: In-class projects — notebook — tests — final exam — art fee of $10.00 — regular class attendance.

Ceramics will appeal to the student who likes to work with his/her hands. Students will study how the natural properties of clay affect its use as an art material. A variety of methods of pottery construction will be explored in a series of projects, such as slab and coil construction, slip and drape molds, and throwing on the potter's wheel.

Sculpture (FA,11)   Open to Grades: 9-10-11-12

Prerequisites: Art/Design   1 Semester   1/2 Credit

This course may be repeated for advanced credit.

Level of Difficulty: Individualized — open to students of all levels of ability.

Course Expectations: In-class projects — notebook — tests — final exam — art fee of $10.00 — regular class attendance.

Students enrolled in Sculpture will explore three-dimensional art forms in a variety of materials such as wood, plaster, clay, wire, plastic, papier mache, rock, and metal. These raw materials will be used in the creation of expressive sculptural designs incorporating form and space and relating the three-dimensional art form to its environment.

Fibers and Fabrics (FA,12)   Open to Grades: 9-10-11-12

Prerequisites: Art/Design   1 Semester   1/2 Credit

This course may be repeated for advanced credit.

Level of Difficulty: Individualized — open to students of all levels of ability.

Course Expectations: In-class projects — extra credit assignments — art fee of $10.00 — regular class attendance.

Students in this art course will explore the use of fibers and fabrics. The course objective is the construction of creative, beautiful works of art to wear and decorate the home. Students will have the opportunity to work in a variety of different processes such as batik, tie dye, macrame, weaving, stitchery, coiling, and rugmaking. New and original applications of these techniques and processes will be studied and designed by the students. Displays of finished projects made during the semester will be exhibited.

Jewelry (FA,18)   Open to Grades: 9-10-11-12

Prerequisites: Art/Design   1 Semester   1/2 Credit

This course may be repeated for advanced credit.

Level of Difficulty: Individualized — open to students of all levels of ability.

Course Expectations: In-class projects — quizzes — tests — final exam — art fee of $10.00 — regular class attendance.

The Jewelry course will enable the student to learn the fundamentals of jewelry-making, covering hand-formed methods, including cutting, shaping, forging, soldering and various casting, enameling techniques. Advanced levels of this course will incorporate hand-formed methods, inlay, casting, copper enameling, and lapidary techniques. Each student will be encouraged to develop a personal approach to his jewelry design.

Art Seminar (FA,22)   Open to Grades: 9-10-11-12

Prerequisites: Art/Design — Approval of Instructor — Placement by Special Services   1 Semester   1/2 Credit

This course may be repeated for advanced credit.

Level of Difficulty: Academically challenging — designed for students with a high interest level in art and above average talent.

Course Expectations: In-class art projects — term paper — written reports — oral reports — field trips — art fee of $10.00 — regular class attendance.

The Art Seminar is designed to give the gifted and talented student an in-depth experience into the visual arts. This student will have developed the basic concepts, vocabulary, and skills of a given media of art from previous art classes. Each student will have an individual program of study which will be developed jointly by the student and teacher to meet the needs and interest of the student. The program of study will be extended beyond the student's regular class. The class will participate in field trips, listen to guest speakers, and complete weekly reading and writing assignments. Each student will also give an oral presentation on a comparison of an art style, period of time, or artist of his/her choice. These activities are designed to broaden and enrich his/her art awareness and understanding.

Graphic Arts (FA,23)   Open to Grades: 9-10-11-12

Prerequisites: Art/Design   1 Semester   1/2 Credit

This course may be repeated for advanced credit.

Level of Difficulty: Individualized — open to students of all levels of ability.

Course Expectations: In-class projects — tests — final exam — art fee of $10.00 — regular class attendance.

Students taking this art course will have the opportunity to investigate a variety of printing processes used in reproducing original pieces of art work. Woodcut, etching, silk screen, lithography, monotype, and linoleum printing are examples of types of creative processes explored. This course would appeal to the student who enjoys drawing. An advanced investigation in printmaking may be selected by the student. Commercial aspects such as product design and advertising layout are available to the advanced graphics student.

Photography 1-2 (FA,27)   Open to Grades: 10-11-12

Prerequisites: None   1 Semester   1/2 Credit

Level of Difficulty: Introductory course — designed for students with average and above-average levels of ability.

Course Expectations: Written and performance tests — written and performance final exam — laboratory assignments — in-class projects — notebook — textbook — materials costing student money — regular class attendance.

The course is designed to teach the student to use a camera, to process film, and to make black-and-white prints. The student will also learn basic photograpic theory to include the function of vari-

ous parts of the camera, the structure of film and how it works, light and its effect on photography, and photographic composition. Basic darkroom techniques are included.

Advanced Photography (FA,28)   Open to Grades: 10-11-12

Prerequisites: Photography 1-2 — B final grade   1 Semester
                    1/2 Credit

This course may be repeated for advanced credit.

Level of Difficulty: Individualized — advanced skills — technical skills — designed for students with average and above-average levels of ability.

Course Expectations: Written and performance tests — written and performance final exam — laboratory assignments — in-class projects — out-of-class assignments — materials costing student money — regular class attendance.

This course has been developed to teach advanced photo skills including exposing and processing of both color slides and color prints. Initial nine weeks advanced black-and-white work; second nine weeks basic color work. Other semesters student may take are individualized work covering portraiture, scenic, macro, copying, slide-tape presentations. Emphasis throughout all semesters is on photojournalism.

Teaching Junior High School Art

The following interview with a junior high school art teacher[*] will help provide insights.

Q: How long have you been teaching junior high school art?

Well let's see, it's been three years here in the valley, and three years overseas in Australia.

[*]Courtesy of Joe Wilczeuski, Junior High Art Teacher, Estrella Junior High, Phoeniz, Arizona

Q: How do you present art lessons?

The average junior high student would be extremely interested in getting down to their projects. Developing listening skills is one of the prime things I have to work with. As far as getting them interested in too many projects, no hassle, but getting them to listen so that meaningful concepts go into their head, that's a different thing. I use quick demonstrations that point out the highlights, salt the lesson with a little art appreciation, and then get them started. Then I can come around and help them in their visual skills. You can't stand there for two or three hours, as in high school or college, and talk to them. They're very high key, and you would soon have chaos. Ten or fifteen minutes of discussion with examples, and then I have the students go to work. Every teacher will be different. I like to point out things when they're doing the project.

Q: What do you feel should be the content of a junior high school art program?

I base my program on a lot of things that are very similar to the college classes. I think the program should have a studio class exposure as far as two-dimensional and three-dimensional experiences are concerned. We're on a 9-week rotational basis, so I try to get specific tool skills going with different classes. I do conte crayon, pastel with one class, and do painting with another. Then I try to rotate it around. Even if the students don't work with all the media, they see it around, and discuss it. I don't want the classes to be just project oriented where all they do is just come in and do art work, and never understand why they are doing it. I use artifacts, audio visual material that shows artists, and the history behind the media or the project, I mix this with the studio aspect. I don't do art history every Friday. It depends more on the flow of the project, and I work it in as an integrated segment so that it has more meaning and isn't isolated. I also teach them how to verbalize about their work. I have them get up and explain something they've seen at an exhibit that we went to, or the class will look at each other's work, and describe it descriptively. Concentration is very short at this age. You aren't going to get a kid to come up and talk for an hour, but at least you can get them to talk about shape and color, etc. and it might take all of 17 seconds, but its a beginning. It's so easy at this level to help a few kids and let the others go, especially when you have 30 students in a class. But I make sure that each student finishes their project.

Q: Are you able to get around to every student?

Yes, I've got a grade book system. Not that I'm harsh on them, but they know I'm aware of what they're doing. I rotate through the room about once a week, and we look at their folders which they keep their work in. We check their work on the shelves where they store it. It takes an entire period, and we discuss evaluation, and its really worth it to the student, and to me.

Q: Do you have a sequence to your program?

In the nine-week program, I start each class on a different project, then rotate around. In my first year of teaching, I made the mistake of starting all classes with the same media, such as wet painting, or wet plaster; and it gets difficult to store, or to work. Especially with 150 wet paintings around the room. I follow units, but all the classes don't do the same units. But the students come in, and see the work from the various classes, and want to do that. Plus we have pretty good rapport with the other departments.

Q: Do you have one art room in your building?

Yes, one huge art room, about 40 feet by 45 feet. We have good storage as far as cabinets and lock up for tools, and supplies. We have a kiln that stands 4 or 5 feet high, two ceramic wheels. Lots of kids at this age want to do clay, and they come in all excited about it. I've got a real good unit worked out as far as hand built pottery. I have one special class that works on the potter's wheel for the whole year, and we find out who really wants to get that out of their system, or who really enjoys it. So what it amounts to, is that I give all the students exposure on how the potter's wheel is used, and then some students concentrate in that area. In a week's time, we can work on various clay methods such as drape, slab, coil. We have filmstrips, discuss balance. Sometimes everyone does a coil pot. They understand the limitations of space, equipment, and so forth.

Q: How many students are enrolled in your school?

We have about 960. So in one day, I have 6 classes, and they average about 28 to 30 in a class. That's 180 kids a day. This includes grades 7 and 8.

Q: Do you feel that you should keep your own art going?

I really do. Drawing is my specialty. But I work on a variety of things so that the students can benefit. When we work on clay, I'll spend a few periods working on something. I don't want them to copy me, but they regard me as an artist who teaches. They sure do.

Q: How do you grade?

The things I look for when I'm grading include first of all, how well they handle materials; how creative they are on an assignment. One assignment I use is, I say "You're a kite, and looking down on a field, what can you do in relation to perspective, and being so high up." If work is excellent, I tell the kids. If a student doesn't complete a project, I grade him unsatisfactory. I want the kids to have a good success rate, but at the same time, you can't candy coat it.

Q: Are students required to take art in your school?

It's part of the elective program. This includes art, music, spanish, industrial art, and home economics. Theoretically, a student in junior high who stays at our school will get four choices that he is involved in. It's possible they wouldn't get any art, but I find that my area and industrial arts is heavily hit, and with a mixture of boys and girls.

Q. How about discipline? How do you handle it?

I jump on them right when it happens. I'll just stop whatever I'm doing and talk to them in a normal tone of voice. If necessary, I talk to them after class. If things aren't ironed out, they come to see me after school. Very seldom do I bring the principal in. I don't send the kid up to the office. That's an easy way for the student to sit down for a period up there.

Q: Are you in an economically diverse school district?

I would say we are lower middle class. We also have the air force base here and these students are here 10 to 22 weeks and then they're gone. We're predominately white, but there is quite a large Chicano population, and the blacks are in a minority, as far as numbers.

Q: Do you meet with other art teachers in your district?

There are 3 junior highs in the district, and 13 elementary schools, and all of the art teachers of these schools meet once a month. We discuss problems, plan ways to work together on events, go over classroom lessons, problems, etc. We have a really far out art consultant who has been in the district twelve years. We also push public relations. We discuss entering fairs, showing works of our students, and also our own.

Q. Do you belong to professional organizations?

I belong to the union, and to the art organization. I'm not a placard waving type, but I'm aware of my professional growth, and what the organizations can do to help. There are several teachers who complain about things but don't belong to either organization. They still want all sorts of professional days paychecks, etc. I don't go to every hearing or greviance, but I try to give input in order to grow professionally.

Q: Do you do lesson plans?

Yes, I really do. I was not one to ever think they were worthwhile. But now, I can see the value. They help me to organize my thinking.

Q: What would you say to a new teacher just beginning?

Work with your colleagues. Keep your eyes wide open. Don't give up. Forget what salary you're earning, that can come later. Learn to teach. And its important to love kids. You have to jell with them and understand them, and be patient.

Art Curriculum for Boulder Valley Public Schools*
Boulder, Colorado

Art I

Art I is the basic art-studio orientation course utilizing the elements and principles of art and artistic awareness under laboratory conditions. All art experiences are based on the art elements of space, line, shape-form, texture, and color; and the related principles of limitation, dominance, balance, rhythm, and unity. Students become acquainted with a number of different media and are encouraged to experience, invent and transfer learning from one medium to another. The specific program content includes drawing, architectonics, extensive color study, perspective, structure and composition, art vocabulary, art history, painting, design and three-dimensional experiences.

Art II

Drawing and Painting—tenth, eleventh, or twelfth grade,
> Elective
> 1 or 2 semester = ½ or 1 credit.
> Prerequisite: Art I

This course offers a wide variety of drawing and painting experiences with emphasis placed on art structure utilizing colored slides. Drawing experiences include: contour (blind and controlled), gesture, outline, mass, memory timed pose, modeled, analytical, ink and watercolor wash, positive and negative, visual-verbal descriptive, threading of black and white, and an ant's eye view. Tactile experiences will be emphasized in the study of painting. These will include glazing and scumbling techniques, collage techniques, watercolor, tempera and acrylics. Application of conceptual color usage is utilized.

Art III

Printmaking—tenth, eleventh or twelfth grade,
> Elective
> 1 or 2 semester = ½ or 1 credit.
> Prerequisite: Art I

This course offers experiences in relief, intaglio and silk screen processes. A great amount of emphasis will be placed on drawing and design as related to the expression of printmaking. Students will work

*Courtesy of Verle Mickish

with woodcuts, linoleum, plastic, etching, engraving, dry-point, color-graphs and serigraph.

Art IV

Applied Arts—tenth, eleventh or twelfth grade,
> Elective
> 1 or 2 semester = ½ or 1 credit.
> Prerequisite: Art I

Applied art is a beginning commercial art course that studies lettering, graphics, layout, interior design, advertising, packaging, and illustration. As the student progresses in levels of achievement, a more intensive use of new and contemporary methods of color and design will be expected. The advanced Applied Arts course will enable some students to enter a vocation in art.

Art V

Sculpture—tenth, eleventh or twelfth grade,
> Elective
> 1 or 2 semester = ½ or 1 credit.
> Prerequisite: Art I

This course will begin with basic experiences in three-dimensional form. As students progress, emphasis will shift to conceptual sculpture involving multi-media. Creative experiences are offered in: wood, plaster, wire, metal, clay, casting and welding. Students will learn modeling, carving and construction techniques is sculpture. Exploration and creative color, sound and movement as related to sculpture will be offered at advanced levels.

Art VI

Pottery—tenth, eleventh or twelfth grade,
> Elective
> 1 or 2 semester = ½ or 1 credit.
> Prerequisite: Art I

The pottery course will include the basic techniques and understanding of clay as an art medium. Experiences will be given in: coil, slab, and other hand-building techniques. Advanced students will have the opportunity to work a potters wheel. The students will also become knowledgeable in glazing and firing techniques of stoneware and raku. Glazing formulation is available.

Art VII

Applied Design—tenth, eleventh, twelfth grade,
        Elective
        1 or 2 semester = ½ or 1 credit.
        Prerequisite: Art I

The Applied Design course emphasizes the design and construction of original jewelry in all media. All construction techniques are explored including hand-wrought and centrifugal casting, lost wax process, silver, brass, copper, pewter, bronze, leather, wood, stone, bone, and others. Creative experimentation is encouraged. The areas of enameling and weaving place emphasis upon the basic techniques and creative application of the design elements and principles.

Environmental Art—tenth, eleventh or twelfth grade,
        Elective
        1 or 2 semester = ½ or 1 credit.
        No Prerequisite

This course is divided into two sections: Section A is academically oriented while Section B is activity oriented. Environmental Art is a contemporary involvement course that includes all the multi aspects of art in society, "Megalopolis" concept, audio and visual pollution, art history and appreciation. Audio and film media are incorporated.

Two-dimensional Art II, III, and IV, is a combination of the two-dimensional art experiences. Included in this course will be common experiences as described in the above course descriptions for Drawing, Painting, Printmaking and Applied Arts.

Three-dimensional Art V, VI, and VII, is a combination of the three-dimensional art experiences. Included in this course will be common experiences as described in the above course descriptions for Sculpture, Pottery and Applied Design.

° For One and Two Art Instructor Departments—Secondary Level Only.

Herbert Read's[5] statement on the senses seems appropriate here:

It must be understood from the beginning that what I have in mind is not merely 'art education' as such, which should more properly be called visual or plastic education: the theory to be put forward embraces all modes of self-expression, literary and poetic (verbal) no less than musical or aural, and forms an integral approach to reality which should be called aesthetic education—the education of those senses upon which consciousness, and ultimately the intelligence and judgment of the human individual, are based.

Through art, the student is capable of seeing the world with visual sensitivity. Through art, the student can develop a critical-appreciative awareness to environmental forms, man made forms, and artistic aesthetic forms in art.

Process in art can refer to perception in understanding visual form, or understanding and comprehension in interpreting visual form that is evident in great art down through the ages. Comprehension of product can refer to the student's own work, or to the work of professional artists, or other students. The product represents the ultimate achievement of the artist. Within it is represented the sum total of the artist's effort in art media. The process refers to what happens to the student when he either works in art media himself, or his comprehension of art works through the development of his critical-appreciative experiences in interpreting art works.

Ordering Art Supplies

The new art teacher will find that ordering art supplies is an essential aspect of a new position. Unless art has never been taught before within the school system, chances are there will be some basic inventory, especially if a previous art teacher has ordered supplies and equipment. One can never rely on this, and must wait and see regarding what existing supplies are available. The first order of business in ordering supplies is to take an inventory. This can be done by examining whatever is on hand, including any items of capital equipment. Capital equipment is usually thought of as items that will be used over a period of time, such as kilns, easels, potter's wheels, or other more permanent tools. The simplest method of checking out supplies on hand is to write down the exact description and amount of each item. Step two is to determine if there is a set budget allocated for the art program. In many school systems, depending on their business manager, budgets are allocated to departmental areas sometime prior to the beginning of the school year. Amounts can vary from practically nothing per pupil to completely adequate appropriations. Obviously, a school in a lower income

"Beso de Amor"
by Rip Woods
Oil on Canvas

Courtesy, Rip Woods

Courtesy, Randy Schmidt

"Untitled"
by Randy Schmidt
Ceramic

Courtesy of the Artist

"Birds of Prey"
by Marlene Linderman

Courtesy of The Hand and the Spirit Crafts Gallery,
Scottsdale, Arizona, Photograph by Glenn Short

"Cherokee River Cane Basket"
with walnut blood wool dyes
by Edmund Youngbird, Cherokee Indian

neighborhood may have greater difficulties in maintaining an adequate budget for art. Budgets are often subjective decisions on the part of administration, so make certain that you are in there plugging for the art program. Great programs in art can be carried on with extremely low budgets, but it's a heck of a lot more challenging and satisfying if the teacher has some budgetary support from within the system. Assuming that an art budget would be practically non-existent, it would take a highly ingenious art teacher with a good deal of driving energy to secure supplies from scrap piles, art stores, or kindly merchants.

Once the amount of budget is determined, the art teacher must now decide what supplies or equipment are needed to carry on the coming year's program. If current catalogs and advertising brochures listing items and processes are not available, the art teacher should write to local school supply houses for such recent catalogs. Most school supply companies are more than happy to have their salesman call, in addition to sending available catalogs.

The next step involves the planning of the yearly art program, at least on a tentative basis, so that some decisions can be made regarding supplies that must be ordered prior to school. Most school districts probably allow certain inexpensive supplies to be purchased during the school year. Many school districts have their own supply warehouses whereby the school system purchases in bulk quantities, thus reducing operating costs. This is usually the case in metropolitan systems which have many secondary schools within the system.

When consulting the catalogs, certain terms may be unfamiliar. Understanding some of the more frequently indicated supply terms will assist in ordering. The following examples are typical in ordering supplies:

1. Quire—usually 24 or 25 sheets of paper, or other materials.
2. Ream—500 sheets.
3. Package—usually 100 or 150 or 50 sheets.
4. Gross—144 sheets, or 12 dozen.
5. Oak tag—cream colored, smooth, lightweight cardboard.
6. Bogus—gray paper, inexpensive, for pastel work.

7. Poster paper—thin construction type paper which comes in standard assorted colors. Color selections are limited and must be supplemented by gift papers, and other scrap papers obtained through one's ingenuity.
8. Tissue papers—are good quality, with varied assortments of beautiful colors.
9. Raffia—long strands of dyed grass, good for weaving some things.
10. Stomps—pointed, rolled cardboard pencils for blending pastels or charcoal.

The art teacher will soon become savvy in the ordering of supplies. Experienced art teachers can often be of invaluable assistance. Each locale will have its sources for specific materials. In order to make funds go further, it is best to get reasonably priced yet good quality papers and other materials. The same rule applies for poster paint and water color trays. Tempera paints should be thick enough to be opaque, and watercolor trays should be semi moist. Machine scoring pencils make perfect drawing instruments because the graphite is especially soft, providing a dark black surface. Many discount stores also offer imported art supplies that can serve very well. The art teacher has to be careful in ordering, in order to make fullest use of the funds available.

Once supplies are ordered, they must be stored carefully, and a continuing inventory kept in order to protect the supplies and to replenish any basic materials that are depleted. Carelessness in attending to these matters will result in improper care of tools and materials, and ultimate loss of valuable equipment through neglect. Good habits in taking care of supplies and tools must start with the teacher.

The Art Room as an Active Environment

In reference to the facilities of an art room, they are whatever exists in the school at the time the new art teacher arrives. In some instances it consists of three, four, or more rooms together, in a unit. In others, there is one small room, twenty by thirty feet, sometimes even smaller. In some instances, art is taught in a regular classroom where supplies have to be brought in for each class. But regardless of what the room is like, the art teacher starts at the point when he arrives on the scene. If the room is lacking in table space, then he discovers a way in which to bring in more tables. If no tables are available, teachers and students work on the floor, or the wall, or they make their own tables. If supplies are deficient, then he discovers a method for securing supplies. Initiative is the key. Supplies can be obtained by going directly to the principal, to the superintendent, to the board of education, to the community, to the merchants, to second hand stores, or to paint stores, or scrap metal yards, or wherever it is possible to obtain supplies. In some instances, the supplies will dictate the art products. In other instances, the product will determine the supplies to be obtained. The top-notch, first-rate teacher doesn't have a stereotype in his mind of what an art room should be like. He knows there should be certain basic equipment. He needs at the very least a surface upon which the student can work. Pottery wheels, jewelry tools, and woodworking tools are necessary in the secondary art program. These and all other materials can be obtained. There is one thing that new teachers as well as experienced teachers should keep in mind. The word *no* does not exist in most instances. When *no* does exist, it is important to find out how much yes is present in the *no*. Art teachers have to have a solidly based image of their own potential for the tide of public and administrative opinion will swing positively toward sincerely oriented teachers. A good teacher of art can move an entire community to art where even the most apprehensive doubting Thomases will engage in and support the art program. Usually they have to be shown!

Career Possibilities in Art

Art teachers should spend some well chosen moments discussing with their students future possibilities for art as a career when they graduate from high school. In today's society, there are many types of possibilities for art careers that are particularly challenging and individually satisfying. The following are suggested as definite possibilities:

1. **Art Teachers for Public Schools and Colleges.** There is a growing demand for teachers of art at all educational levels. Teachers can specialize in studio skills such as painting, printmaking, interior design, graphic design, photography, or sculpture, or in subject matter fields such as art history. One of the most sought after college teachers in the field today is the art historian. This would be an excellent career field for a student highly interested in the aesthetic and historical aspects of art, but not specially talented in studio skills.

2. **Museum Curators.** Art museums and galleries offer many challenges to specialists who become knowledgeable in historical aspects of art, and how to care for art and arrange for exhibits in museums and galleries. This is a rapidly growing field of endeavor for a person who might desire to study museum procedures.

3. **Industrial Designers.** Industrial designers are in strong demand within a field that is expanding rapidly. An art school education is necessary here. Artists of this type design everything from refrigerators to automobiles.

4. **Commercial Art.** The new term for this field is graphic designer. Many possibilities exist in the advertising world for highly talented designers and illustrators. An art school or college art preparation is a must.

5. Other possibilities include television, cartooning, illustrating, stage designing, textile designing, weaving, jewelry, or other crafts within one's own studio and environmental design. All of the careers indicated require a college degree in art. For students who may be interested in going into one of the art fields either as artist or historian, it is important to encourage them to attend a professional art school or college art program. Specialities in art will determine which type of college or art school the student should attend. For the talented student who wishes to pursue a career in art, every effort should be made to have the student continue his art studies. Many avenues exist whereby the poor student can attend college.

Many students work their way through with various sorts of odd jobs.

The following list outlines several career possibilities in art:

Archaeology	*Architecture*	*Art Director*	*Crafts Teacher*
Photographer	Draftsman	Book and	Public School
Illustrator	Designer	Magazine	College
Historian	Architect	Publishing	Art School
Author		Television	Private School
Art Researcher		Advertising	Overseas
		Agency	Teaching
		Newspaper	

Photography	*Designer*	*Crafts*	*Industrial Design*
Commercial	Film	Ceramist	Automotive
Portrait	Fashion	Leathersmith	Record Cover
Newspaper	Textile	Metalsmith	Appliance
Television	Graphic	Wrought Iron	Machinery
Fine Arts	Furniture	Glassblower	Journalistic
Filmmaker	Interior	Weaver	Furniture
	Environmental	Woodworker	Parks
	Stage	Jeweler	Playgrounds
	Costume	Sculptor	Shopping
	Historical	Stone Worker	Centers
		Gravestones	

Museums	*Artists*	*Historians*	*Publishing*
Curator	Police	Antiques	Book Author
Director	Illustrator	Search Service	Magazine
Educational	Courtroom	Treasure	Reviewer
Director	Artist	Hunter	Art Critic
Business	Television	Stage and	Art Consultant
Director	Comic Books	Film	Art Book
Administrative	Magazines		Dealer
Guard	Outdoor signs		Archivist
	Murals		
	Fine Artists		
	Landscape		
	Seascape		
	Portrait		

Museums	*Special Fields*	*Community Fields*
Restorer	Occupational	Art Center
Historian for	Therapy	Teacher
Ancient Crafts	Art Therapy	Parks and
	Special	Recreation
	Education	Community Arts
	Art Alliance	Civic Club
	Director	Art Teacher
		Retirement
		Center Crafts
		Teacher

Printing

Silkscreen
Woodcut
Etching
Lithography

Responsibilities for Art Teachers outside the Classroom

There are many activities outside the classroom instructional program that can be of considerable value to the art teacher. They require that the art teacher become involved in some of the following:

1. Public relations — art teachers can help to promote their programs by becoming involved in public relations. This could mean speaking about art to P.T.A., museums, retirement centers, and other groups that can provide feedback to administrators and boards of education.

2. Help fellow faculty — the art teacher can be of special service to colleagues. Often, little aids such as posters, signs, and illustrations can be handled on a volunteer basis, or provided for by the school art club. Keep in mind, that it is important to give of oneself, if one is to grow professionally, but giving has to be within reason.

3. Role of professional organizations — the art teacher should become a member of the National Art Education Association, and also whatever state organizations exist in the field. In membership there is strength, as well as assistance. To join means to become part of a larger team that has comparable goals, and links your school program to the greater picture. Annual meetings of the national organization enable teachers to share common problems and work toward solutions.

4. Administration — it is vital for the art teacher to explain the art program to both principal and board of education. By developing a sympathetic ear to art needs, improved programs can be the result.

5. Communicate with parents — the art teacher should make a considerable effort to meet and know as many parents as possible. In this way, the parents will be able to share in the concerns of the art program, and will also support their children. In this age of ID numbers, personal contact is very important. Art teachers can go far toward illuminating the value of exciting art programs.

References

1. MICHAEL DRURY, "The Secret of Enthusiasm," *Glamour*, July, 1960, 420 Lexington Avenue, New York, N.Y. 10017.
2. JACK TAYLOR, from a statement submitted to the author, 1970.
3. EDWARD L. MATTIL, "The Effects of a 'Depth' vs. a 'Breadth' Method of Art Instruction at the Ninth Grade Level," *Studies in Art Education*, III, I, Fall, 1961, National Art Education Association, Washington, D.C., pp. 75–87.
4. WILLIAM M. ALLEN, President of Boeing Company, from *Nation's Business*, August, 1967, Washington, D.C.: 1615 H Street, N.W.
5. HERBERT READ, *Education Through Art*, New York: Pantheon Books Inc., 1958, p. 7.

Further References

1. BARKAN, MANUAL, *A Foundation for Art Education*, New York: The Ronald Press Company, 1955.
2. BELLACK, ARNO A., editor, *What Shall the High Schools Teach?* 1956 Yearbook. Washington, D.C.: Association for Supervision and Curriculum Development, 1956.
3. BRUNER, JEROME, *On Knowing*, New York: Antheneum Press, 1965.
4. BRUNER, JEROME, *The Process of Education*, Cambridge, Massachusetts: Harvard University Press, 1960.
5. CONANT, HOWARD and RANDELL, ARNE, *Art in Education*, Peoria, Ill.: Charles A. Bennett Company, 1959.
6. CONANT, HOWARD, *Art Education*, Washington, D.C.: Center for Applied Research in Education, 1964.
7. FRANCESCO, ITALO DE, *Art Education: Means and Ends*, Scranton, Pa.: International Harper and Brothers, New York: 1958.

8. FRAZIER, ALEXANDER, *New Insights and the Curriculum*, Association for Supervision and Curriculum Development, Washington, D.C., 1963.

9. FOSHAY, ARTHUR, "Discipline-Centered Curriculum," *Curriculum Crossroads*, A. Harry Passow, editor, New York: Bureau of Publications, Teachers College, Columbia University, 1962.

10. GODFRY, MARY E., "Grading and Pupil Evaluation," *Art Education*, March, 1964, Vol. XVII, No. 3, pp. 17–20.

11. HUBBARD, GUY, *Art in the High School*, Belmont, California: Wadsworth Publishing Company, 1967.

12. KAUFMAN, IRVING, *Art and Education in Contemporary Culture*, New York: Macmillan Company, 1966.

13. KELLY, EARL C. and ROSEY, MARIE I., *Education and the Nature of Man*, New York: Harper & Brothers, 1953.

14. LANIER, VINCENT, *Teaching Secondary Art*, Scranton, Pa: International Textbook Company, 1964.

15. LANSING, KENNETH, *Arts, Artists, and Art Education,* Dubuque, Ia.: Kendall-Hunt, 1977.

16. LOWENFELD, VIKTOR, and BRITTAIN, WILLIAM LAMBERT, *Creative and Mental Growth,* Macmillan Company, 1963, 3rd Edition.

17. MATTIL, EDWARD L., Project Director, *A Seminar in Art Education for Research and Curriculum Development*, The Pennsylvania State University, University Park, Pa., 1966.

18. McLUHAN, MARSHALL, *The Gutenberg Galaxy,* Toronto, Canada: University of Toronto Press, 1962.

19. National Art Education Association, *Art Education in the Junior High School,* Washington, D.C.: edited by John A. Michael, 1964.

"Cross"
Master of the Grandmont Alter, French, Limousin, ca. 1189
Champlevé Enamel and Gilt Copper

Chapter 5

A work of art is immersed in the whirlpool of time; and it belongs to eternity. A work of art is specific, local, individual; and it is our brightest token of universality. A work of art rises proudly above any interpretation we may see to give it; and, although it serves to illustrate history, man, and the world itself, it goes further than this; it creates man, creates the world, and sets up within history an immutable order.[1]

HENRI FOCILLON,
"The Life of Forms in Art,"
George W. Henborn, Inc., New York, N.Y., p. 1

Discovering Art History for Youth

Starting a Beginning Art History Program

The preceding quote by Henri Focillon expresses so well the magnificent, timeless beauty of the aesthetic product, regardless of the type of media utilized, or the time in history from whence it came. The invisible thread of art was picked up by man when he held a stone ax in one hand and a charred ember in the other. His marks on the walls of life have been going on ever since, and the beat gets louder, more resonant as man in culture looks both backward and forward at his aesthetic humanity.

Art history is a relatively new and developing field. The study of art in history began little over two hundred years ago with the publication of J. J. Winckelmann's *Geschichte der Kunst des Altertums* (*History of the Art of Ancient Times*) in 1764.[2] Thus, in the field of art history generally, there isn't a strong pattern to follow or emulate.

Defining Art History

What is art history? Essentially, it is the study of how man as artist has interpreted and expressed his culture in graphic form. Countless research by dedicated scholars has provided the groundwork for the enlightenment of contemporary man through the study of artifacts and monuments uncovered and available to all in museums, and through reproductions in books and journals. Thus, for the art teacher at the junior and senior high level, the beautiful story of art as it happened down through the ages and across centuries, can be illuminated in the classroom for the benefit of students and teacher. We are thinking here of teaching art history in the school program, not as an accessory to the beginning of a studio unit, but as a direct and basic corollary to a total art curriculum at the secondary level.

Studying Art as a Part of History

Art as history, as fact and emotion, is an exciting adventure that teachers need to bring into the art classroom. In no way or manner does it lessen the studio aspects of the art program. In the past some art teachers may have seen a conflict between art as subject, and art as expressive vehicle. The following statement by Howard Collins[3] underscores the often held viewpoint:

In the minds of many art educators, the very expression (*of art history*) reeks of mustiness, an apparition of the past, a reversional specter exhumed to harass the status quo and enfetter the creative impulse. This picture of the study of art history as an asphyxiate is as unfortunate as it is inaccurate. The systematic study of the wellsprings of historic styles can no more act as a depressant on the creative mind than the study of history can ensnare the adventurous spirit of the political scientist, or a cognizance of past literary styles can enfeeble the efforts of the living poet.

"Winged Genie"
Mesopotamia, Assyrian Period, 9th Century B.C.
Gypseous Alabaster

Courtesy, The Cleveland Museum of Art
Purchase from the J. H. Wade Fund

Fortunately, this attitude is diminishing before the flood of evidence to indicate that a great surge to understand art as subject awareness and critical-appreciative matter is becoming the backbone of a combined studio-historical-appreciative curriculum at the secondary level. Structuring a curriculum of art awareness based on this triad of options has gained increasing acceptance by art teachers across the country.[4] The significance of studying art in historical context rather than as antecedent to studio programs, is substantiated by the writings in the field. James Schinneller[5] defines art history in the following manner:

What can art tell us? It can tell us of the aspirations and deeds of past civilizations. It can relate the grandeur of man long before the march of Roman warriors into Gaul. Twenty-one centuries before the Santa Maria, Pinta, and Nina sailed westward from Palos or before Nicolaus Copernicus looked toward the sky, Greeks searched for and found a universal beauty within stone. Fragments of their works provide insight into their skills, accomplishments, and dreams. The Grecian concern for richness through idealized proportions and serenity has given both seeds and fruit to nourish innumerable men in succeeding centuries. Art provides a civilization with the means of achieving immortality; for through the future unfolding of its products, its period and contribution live once again in the mind of man.

Manual Barkan[6] sees art as a subject for study. He states:

For effective teaching in art, a teacher must perceive the field of art as a subject for study. Only then can he translate fundamental qualities and characteristics of the field into activities that can lead learners to realize and understand the nature and meaning of art. A curriculum for learning does no more than translate the essential characteristics of a field into learning experiences. The teaching of art requires understanding of the subject matter of art both from the points of view of making works and analyzing them. Strictly speaking, the field of art can be studied through these two interrelated yet different processes.

Allan S. Weller[7] sees as basic ingredients for education in art, the following:

Sufficient knowledge about the history and theory of art to give perspective for making or assessing judgments about works of art. One does not expect students to make learned or brilliant judgments, but it should be possible to give them the kind of training which will keep them from complete lack of understanding of the role of serious art which is widespread.

Familiarity with great works of art, both of the past and the present. A few significant works, studied in some depth, will be more useful in establishing useful avenues of approach than discursive contact with large numbers of works, no matter how significant.

Where the Art Teacher Can Begin

The study of art as history can begin at any point in time or space, anywhere. For many new teachers of art, the study of art history may seem a vast, almost unmanageable assortment of facts, figures, and dates, merged into one unwieldy, frightening mass called the history of art. Where to begin? The art teacher, before trying to present subject material, should plan and organize a system by which the information to be presented has some continuity and order. A logical starting point is to gather all available books on the specific art history topic. One's personal library could be a starting point. If nothing is available from this standpoint, the school library, or the public library would be the next step. Perhaps a friend has a good book in the area of interest. In the beginning, the first few art history lessons do not have to be that extensive. Having as objectives, some carefully organized key points about a specific art subject will be a starter. The lesson might be twenty minutes, or the total length of one class period.

With books, magazines, and other resource material at hand pertaining to a specific topic, the next step concerns the availability of visual material necessary to illustrate the art lecture. Obviously, some interaction between book or literary and illustrative source must be considered at the time of topic selection. The best resource material would be to bring in the original paintings, pottery, jewelry, or the like. In the absence of original material to clarify a lecture, reproductions of high quality in the form of slides, commercial reproductions, or book illustrations can serve as visual documentation and reference points. Mounting illustrative material pinpoints it for presentation.

Some excellent beginning reference sources for researching an art history topic include:

1. The McGraw-Hill Encyclopedia of World Art is a reference set of volumes that many community libraries have available. Articles are written by noted specialists in various fields of art his-

"Christ Carrying His Cross"
by Martin Schongauer, German, before 1440-1491
Engraving, Lehrs V. 69.9, only state

tory. This is a good beginning source for obtaining information quickly.

2. The Art Index is published periodically and has many valuable reference sources to specific topics of interest in art history.

3. For that matter, The Encyclopaedia Brittanica, or Americana has exceptionally strong articles pertaining to the art of different periods. These publications would be available in rural school districts also.

4. Time-Life, Inc., National Geographic, and other publishers have put out volume series of various cultures in art history. These publications are relatively inexpensive, and permit the retrieval of general information suitable to the introduction of an art historical period.

5. The College Outline Series is another basic beginning source for attaining an introduction to a period.

When visual and subject material are available in sufficient quantity, the preparation of the lesson can be initiated. It will be necessary to do some reading and investigation in order to grasp the feeling for the topic. One should never present any subject if he is not sufficiently well read in order to comprehend it. An evening well spent in reading up on the topic can provide the art teacher with plenty of stimulating and informative information for presentation. If a formal art lecture has never been given before, there will be many rough spots. The idea, of course, is not to worry unduly about this. One's own spirit and enthusiasm for getting something of value across to the class will serve in good stead. Taking the time to prepare thoroughly will lighten the load immeasurably. The teacher will find that his own vistas will begin to open up before his investigation. When the art teacher learns art as history, he strengthens his entire concepts regarding what art is, or can be.

In reading through the literary material, the main points can be noted. The planned lesson can be pre-written, but should not be read verbatim as this becomes rather monotonous. Learning the material, and outlining it for presentation will keep the lecture more flexible. If the lesson is to be strictly subject information, it should be planned accordingly. Subject information can be considered from any point in history. Interesting topics include the following.

Contemporary Art from 1945 to the Present
Black Artists Working Today
Chicano Artists Working Today
Oriental Artists Working Today
Renaissance Art in Northern Europe
Renaissance Art in Italy
Picasso and Cubism
The Art of Mexico
African Art
Oriental Art
Jan Van Eck, Inventor of Oil Painting
Artists of Colonial America
Ten Artists Painting Today: Their Works and Interpretations
French Impressionism
Matisse: Master of Color

In glancing at the preceding list, it suggests that selecting a subject area from which to present an art history lecture is entirely up to the immediate interests of the teacher. In considering the selection of a topic for presentation, the following points should be considered:

1. There should be visual material available to support the lecture.
2. The lecture should be planned to stimulate intellectual thought at the secondary level.
3. The material should lend itself to organization for presentation.
4. The material should be presented in terms of relationships for today.
5. Background information should be available in reference to the culture from which the material comes.

When it is determined that a subject area can be organized and presented at a level that will challenge secondary thinking, the art teacher is then ready to pull out from the larger body of subject material that he has examined, those points of significance that will provide meaning and feeling in relation to the historical area in question. What is significant as subject information is always a personal, subjective judgment by the teacher. The main objective in studying art in historical context is that a feeling for the time, the manner in

"Wild Horse"
by Eugene Delacroix, French, 1798-1863
Lithograph, Del. 78, state I/II

which the works were created, should be related to an understanding of man's achievement within our own culture. If a teacher can impart to his students a lasting and sincere feeling toward the great value that art in history has, he will have accomplished much in his class. To understand art history, one must be able to identify with it in terms of when it was created. Rudy Turk[8] explains it in the following manner:

We need to make the student aware that man's senses have developed through the years. For example, the renaissance individual looking at a Giotto painting—Vassari tells us that people walked into his paintings because they were so realistic! We look at these paintings and none of us could be deluded into walking into one of them. They're too awkward, and the sense of space is not strong enough. Vassari wasn't telling us a lie, for the artist is often working for illusions. But man's sense of what is illusionistically possible has varied through the ages. For the renaissance person, Giotto's paintings were realistic, or the same as real space. What is real? Man's concept of real changes from age to age. We also have to be aware that a renaissance man coming into our environment wouldn't understand it. For real is always a changing thing, relative to one's conceptions and experiences. For example, in our own time, most of us over 35 years are old enough to remember the cylinder records, on the old phonograph, and remember "happy days are here again," and grandpa and grandma may even have thought this sounded real. Then we got flat records, and that sounded real and the other stuff sounded phony. Then we got hi-fi equipment. And today you may walk into a room and think that the train is charging right at you. Maybe our grandchildren are going to look at our art in the twentieth century and say "how incredible!" How could those people ever mistake that for reality? "Reality" is a conceptual thing.

In other words, as teachers and students we need to think of the art works in terms of the times in which they were created. We must not expect a Roman sculpture created 2,000 years ago to have the same meaning as a sculpture created yesterday. Teachers have to reveal to students that Roman thought and emotion was based on concepts valid for the day. The judgment of such work must then be based on the criteria contemporary to Roman times. If we understand art works in such a context, we are then able to transfer such understandings to present day concepts for comparison and evaluation. History is really a recognition of the difference between various cultures and a study of them in relation to our present culture.

When a tentative subject area is decided upon, the art teacher should examine his visual material. It might be slides, reproductions that are mounted, or illustrations in books or magazines. What-

ever can be drawn out from an examination of the visual material should be noted down. Does the work evoke moods or feeling? Is there literary content? Is there a feeling for harmonious organization of the works? What was the artist attempting to say? Is there a visual message apart from subject content? Is the artist speaking in terms we can understand today? These questions, and many others will serve as a beginning basis for interpreting the works on an individual basis. One's own feelings and interpretations will often contrast with what other individuals or teachers will say. Next, it is often pertinent to see what the books say about the same art works, or same artists. Is there any agreement between yourself and the authors? How are you different in your thinking? In this way, the art teacher has a starting point for preparing an art lesson dealing with historical aspects or critical-appreciative aspects of art as subject.

Another good approach to understanding art as history is to approach it from a viewpoint other than art. Rudy Turk[9] says:

There is a little pocket book I recommend to students who come to me in art history. It's called *Rats, Lice and History*, by Hans Zinsser. It shows that the history of disease which is never recorded in your basic history books, has been a tremendous influence on the development of culture and society in history. When you can break away from the pure political concept of history, with its kingdoms, and the reigns, and examine the social side, the aesthetic side, the medical side, it gives you more freedom to relate art to its culture, and to understand it. For example, I can't conceive of anyone ever teaching the Italian renaissance of medieval art without first reading the Apocalypse. El Greco is not understood until you have read that. You have to know other parts of the specific culture. In the thirteenth century, an Englishman by the name of Blanket started selling wool coverings, and blanket becomes a word that we use in vocabulary to this day. When a student realizes that people had blankets in the thirteenth century and used them, he becomes more aware of what an art object can mean to that society, too. The student can realize that people were people at all times in history. In this sense, art has a reality also, for the specific time.

Understanding the Limitations in Using Slides and Reproductions

Colored slides representing the works from history past, or illustrating examples of what is currently taking place in the galleries can be an extremely valuable method of getting visual information before the student. A well made, carefully taken slide of the original art work is a most interesting substitute for the actual art work. However, there are certain limitations that art teacher and students should be aware of, in order to compensate for any deviation from the actual. First, the concept of size is lost completely. A slide is two by two inches in actual measurement. It may be any size up to eight or ten feet square when projected on a screen, depending on the distance of the projector from lens to screen. In most instances, the slide will be from four to eight feet in viewing focus. The projection, however, does not tell us the actual size of the art work. Some art works which are actually miniatures are thrust completely out of proportion. The same applies to surface feel or texture. The slide presents a flat illusion of the photograph from which it came. The scale of the original is thus completely out of kilter. It is important for the art teacher to make this distinction almost immediately. Probably the best approach in illustrating the relationship of slide to original art work is to bring in an original art

"Columbus Tripped Out"
by William Wiley, 1967
Dyptych

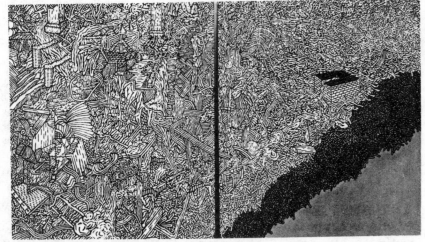

Courtesy, The Hansen Gallery, San Francisco, California

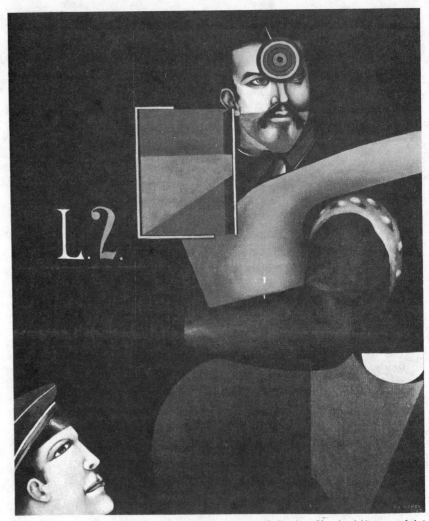

Courtesy, Contemporary Collection, Cleveland Museum of Art

"Louis II"
by Richard Lindner, American (b. Germany), 1901
Oil on Canvas

work, and slides taken of it. The students can examine the actual piece in terms of texture, scale, color relation, proportion, and all of the properties indigenous to the art work. Once the students have a clear picture of the actual piece, the representative slides can be shown, and the differences can be realized. It is not necessary to acquire a Picasso or Rembrandt to illustrate this point (although if one is handy, that's a horse of another color). A fine example by the art teacher, or even the student will serve the purpose. A good approach here might be to bring in examples of different types of art, such as pottery, oil painting, wood carving, watercolor, and sculpture. Each media can be compared to its counterpart in slide form by instructing the students to note the differences or variations from the original.

Reproductions found in magazines, art journals, or commercially produced examples also have specific limitations. Although size dimensions and some description is usually typed on the mount the same problems of loss of scale, texture, and color are involved, and the teacher must be careful to point out the differences. Reproductions or slides in black and white are even further removed from the original art works. With these limitations noted, however, there is still much to be said for such visual supportive material. In many instances within public school programs, these are the only means of bringing artistic greatness and understanding to the student. Eventually, when the student is able to see some selected originals, hopefully he will make the necessary transference from slide to original, and crystalize his understanding and critical awareness to art.

Also, every effort should be made to plan a trip to a local gallery, or artist's studio. This would provide students with the means for comparing original forms of art work to printed illustrations.

Bringing in Guest Lecturers in Art History

An excellent method of strengthening an art history program is to plan for the inclusion of guest lecturers. Most art teachers would have some difficulty in booking a major museum curator, or learned scholars of high magnitude. However, a guest lecturer for the art class can be defined to include many types of scholars. These include (1) museum or gallery curators, (2) college instructors of art history, (3) artists interested in discussing their art, (4) other art teachers, from a college or high school who are known to the teacher, (5) interested art history buffs of the local community, (6) college students majoring in art or art education, and (7) scholars from another discipline. Any of these individual types would be entirely suitable as a "guest lecturer." The person need have only a great interest in art from a specific viewpoint. Close relationships are always found with anthropology, archaeology, architecture, and history in general. In exploring the possibility of obtaining guest speakers who can come into the art classroom, some investigation on the art teacher's part will often turn up community members, or even parents of students who are versatile in certain areas relative to what is being studied. Some initiative and early planning will be necessary. Local colleges are always prime sources for seeking out speakers. Remember, that a good art teacher doesn't let anything stand in his way! For example, another possibility for solving the guest lecturer problem in a small rural community (also to be considered in accessible districts) is to send out a tape to a potential scholar, with planned instructions. A tape recording would make the entire United States accessible to the smallest, most isolated rural school system. It will take pre-planning and some effort. There will undoubtedly be some disappointments such as being turned down by scholars. Just having a teacher from down the hall discuss his viewpoints in the class can be a beginning. To be remembered is that guest lecturers are a part of the larger art history sequence, which in turn, is part of the art program, in general.

What Is an Art Historian?

If we clarify what an art historian is, or does, we lay the groundwork for better understanding of the subject of art history. In the field of art, there are specialists, or scholars who teach the subject of art history. These individuals are most often found in college art departments. They may also be found in public schools at the secondary level, or at museums and galleries. They are individuals who have established as their chief goal in life, the study and interpretation of some aspect of our art heritage. Some of the requirements to become an experienced art historian involve a good deal of visual observation of one's world, and considerable reading. The bona fide art historian lives the art historical life. It is his approach to experiencing the world. The making of an art historian (or an artist for that matter), is a slow, disciplined, challenging, and difficult process. It is a matter of much experience in museum visiting, recording, assessing, judging art works, and consistent comparisons with previous visits in other places. It is a matter of being interested in many aspects and facets of life. The art historian interprets or records what artists have left behind. Essentially, without the artist, we would never have an art historian. The art historian is a sensitive, highly specialized individual who has a finely tuned grasp of certain aspects of the contemporary or past portions of the art world.

For the person who will teach some art history at the secondary level, the foregoing description of the art historian can provide cues in approaching historical material for interpretation and presentation to his classes. Some points to consider in thinking along the lines of the art historian are:

1. Attend as many art shows in galleries and museums as possible. If living in a rural community, take a trip at least once a year in order to visit galleries and museums to be right on top of both historical material, and idea material for one's studio classes.

2. Think and observe aesthetically. Prepare your mind to see the world of man and nature with aesthetic vision. Search out the beauty that is there, remembering that beauty is a perceptual experience, dependent on one's insights into visual form. Keep in mind that the more one searches within the arts, the wider is his reach and grasp.

3. Purchase a 35mm camera and start one's own slide collection. Add to this by acquiring slides from museums of their most significant works. Become a collector of fine, original art works by both young students and known artists.

4. Read all that you can on various subjects. Read intensively in the fields of your interest, but also remember that art teachers are the sum total of all they read and experience in many fields.

5. Understand that we are moving from a print oriented culture into an age of simultaneity and immediacy, a world of electronics, cinema, and television. Books will continue to be with us, as will the spoken word. Be flexible enough to interpret many ways to one's own historical or studio growth. Immerse yourself in as much humanity through the ages as possible.

Art History as a Basis for Living Today

The art teacher as art historian needs also to help his students to understand why we are interested in any period of artistic endeavor, or styles of the past. For example, we should not study a past style, or the art of a past period merely for the sake of doing it. Phillip Kennedy[10] states:

This approach where we study a past period just to learn about a past period is known as antiquarianism. Antiquarianism can be a very meaningless approach to the study of history. The attitude, for example, that we study the history of an ancient Chinese civilization, merely to become expert, to become well informed so that we can tell other people what ancient Chinese art was all about seems rather dubious an enterprise.

What we want to do, it seems to me, is to look at past periods in the history of art, design, architecture, in order to be able to look at the work from that past period and be able to ask the question of how it relates for us, today. What it can tell us about life, and living, the victories of a particular civilization or culture of the past. What were its aesthetic victories? What were the great aspects of the civilization? What was civilizing or humanizing about the works? What do these works say to us as human beings of the 20th century? Art History is a means of better understanding ourselves today, to determine where we are heading both artistically and culturally speaking. Also as a means of determining what we are as individuals. We need to see ourselves as part of the continuum of history.

In studying particular ages, or epics from the past, we can see directions to both present and future. Much of western civilization (from European man) was and is influenced by the Greek past. In studying the history and art of ancient Greek culture, we can understand **our present beliefs, Kennedy**[11] states:

"Kokoschka Drama Komoedie"
by Oskar Kokoschka, 1907
Lithograph

In the classical past, in the plastic arts, in literature, in mythology, we have over and over again the act of hybris (pronounced hewbris). This act of hybris is the act of man going against the gods; man daring to fight the gods on Mt. Olympus; man daring to build a high temple on a very high hill, on the Acropolis. This temple is man imposing himself against the sky, against nature. This is man daring to be rational and creative; man daring to change his environment. Man daring to think and to build and be what he jolly well desires to be. This idea of hybris recurs through history. In medieval German literary tradition, we have the Faustian man. Here man will actually sell his soul in order to know all, and learn all. In the eighteenth century, the German poet Goethe picked up this theme and wrote his famous work, *Faust*, based on the western man who has dared to question, in order to think and ultimately change his environment.

By contrast, Eastern man was opposed to committing hybris. He has been the opposite of the Faustian man. He has been willing to listen to nature, in order to learn about himself and his environment. The term is *Tao*. It means the way, or the path; to go the way of nature, not to fight it.

Understanding past cultures from Western man, and past cultures from Eastern man, we can assess our relationship or focal distance. In teaching such philosophies as *hybris*, or *tao*, we provide students with the basis for understanding all of art history. The idea of man fighting nature, can be interpreted all through history. During the eighteenth century, European man was a revolutionary, a natural counterpart to this attitude of man fighting for his beliefs.

Today in art, many of the old boundaries or barriers are breaking away. The artificial walls between the arts and sciences are eroding before man's quest for insight. Today we realize that the scientist is both creative and scientific and that the artist is scientifically oriented and artistic. Even within the visual arts, the distinction between what is painting, or sculpture, or design, is a rather thin line. It is becoming difficult to pigeonhole certain art works as sculptural or as paintings. Tradition is constantly changing; and for some periods of time, such as the present, the changes are occurring so rapidly, it is difficult to know what is happening. Living through or in the midst of such changes is extremely disquieting for those so involved. We have a great tendency to look backward at the past, which seems so serene and established. Even the immediate past seems clear and in focus compared to the immediate present.

Learning the Art of Today Can be a Springboard for Understanding the Past

One approach to the introduction of art history is to begin with the present and gradually work backwards. The more applicable we can make art history to the present, the more successful we will be. We can best understand the past if we relate it to our present time. The art teacher needs to show to the student that the artist of today isn't much different from the artist of the near or distant past. In fact, this in itself is a valid reason for the study of art and artists from the past, any past. Man can see what man has done in various epics. Relationships as well as differences can be evaluated in the light of what contemporary attitudes are toward art and life in general. The value in approaching art history from the standpoint of what is being created today is that students will have a focal point. They can best relate to their own immediate experiences. They are aware of their twentieth century as they have experienced it. The secondary high teacher can begin with the present, and then point out that all the paleolithic cave painters, in some ways, were not much different from painters today. Unlike some theories of thought, the cave man was likely to have been a highly intelligent individual, but whose attitudes were conditioned by *his* society and experiences. Human beings have probably been human beings all through the course of history.

Learning Dates, but Getting a Feeling for Art Periods Also

Committing some highly significant dates to memory can be valuable to one's comprehension and handling of art history. The art teacher need not focus *all* attention on the need to memorize the life and death of every key artist from every cultural epic in art history. Probably much more significant to student growth and insight is to encourage the student to catch the feelings for a certain art period, or particular style. Some of the greats from each era, with perhaps some key examples, would be suitable to memorization. The art teacher should strive to achieve a good balance between fact and feeling for a period. There would, of course, be little value to memorization for the sake of memorization. With meaning, in context to the philosophical and cultural frames of reference to a period, information of a specific sort can be enlightening for the student, and provide a greater depth. The art teacher should encourage the students to learn as much as they can about a period under study. Encouraging students to undertake independent research in art history, to be shared with the class can bring meaning to student understanding. Once again, teacher enthusiasm for the subject will serve as a prime motivator in many instances. Students stand a much greater chance of becoming sensitive to an art period, if the teacher projects this type of attitude!

References

1. HENRI FOCILLON, *The Life of Forms in Art*, New Haven: Yale University Press, 1952, translation by Charles Beecher Hogan.
2. JOHN IVES SEWALL, *A History of Western Art*, New York: Holt, Rinehart & Winston, 1961, p. 32.
3. HOWARD F. COLLINS, "Art History/High School," *Art Education*, National Art Education Association, Washington, D.C.: Vol. 16, No. 5, May 1963, p. 6.
4. JEROME J. HAUSMAN, editor, *Report of the Commission on Art Education*, Washington, D.C.: National Art Education Association, 1965.
5. JAMES SCHINNELLER, *Art: Search and Self-Discovery*, Scranton, Pa.: International Textbook Company, 1968, revised edition, p. 9.
6. MANUEL BARKAN, "Curriculum and the Teaching of Art," from *Report of The Commission on Art Education*, Washington, D.C.: National Art Education Association, 1965.
7. ALLEN S. WELLER, "Art, Artist, Teacher and Critic," *Art Education*, Washington, D.C.: National Art Education Association, January, 1965, Vol. 18, No. 1, p. 8.
8. RUDY TURK, Curator, Arizona State University Collections, from an interview with Mr. Turk, February, 1969.
9. *Ibid*.
10. PHILLIP C. KENNEDY, Professor of Art History, Arizona State University, Tempe, from an interview on March 2, 1969.
    Iowa, 4th ed., 1979.
11. *Ibid*.

SOURCES FOR OBTAINING SLIDES, FILMS AND FILM STRIPS ON ART HISTORY°

American Library Color Slide
  Company, Inc.
305 East 45th Street
New York, New York 10017

Producciones Ancora
Consejo de Ciento
160 (Edificio Creta)
Barcelona 15, Spain

ESM Documentations
Box 709
New York, New York 10009

Imago Color Slides
Box 811
Chapel Hill, North Carolina 27514

Prothmann Associates, Inc.
2795 Milburn Avenue
Baldwin, Long Island,
    New York 11510

Frederick Teuscher, Inc.
P.O. 146, Planetarium Station
New York, New York 10024

Reinhold Visuals
Van Nostrand Reinhold Company
450 West 33rd Street
New York, New York 10001

Walden Film Corporation
    (Super 8mm Film Loops)
153 Waverly Place
New York, New York 10014

° With the purchase of a 35mm camera, the art teacher would be able to make many of his own slides by taking photographs from selected books on art. This method is considerably cheaper than commercial purchasing.

An Outline Chronology of the Great Achievements and Artists through the Ages

The following chronology is intended to be a resource foundation for stimulating further investigation. The events and items listed in each period are excellent points of reference for introducing students to a study of the specific period. This chronology aims to provoke curiosity and interest regarding outstanding contributions made by civilizations through the ages.

Ancient World

The Old Stone Age (about 150 centuries B.C.)

Cave painting, Altamira
    (15,000 B.C.)
Cave painting, Lascaux
    (15,000 B.C.)

Venus of Willendorf
    (15,000 B.C.)
Stonehenge (18,000 B.C.)

Primitive Art (any century)

Stone images, Easter Island
    (17th century)

Guardian figure, Africa
    (19th century)

"Woman and Child" (Maternity Group)
Africa, Ivory Coast, Korhogo District, Senufo Tribe
Wood

Egyptian Art (Old Kingdom, 27–25 centuries B.C.)

    Step pyramid (2650 B.C.)   Sphinx (2530 B.C.)
    Papyrus half-columns   Seated Scribe (2400 B.C.)
    Cheops pyramid (2750 B.C.)

Egyptian Art (Middle and New Kingdoms, 14th century B.C.)

    Tutankhamen (1360 B.C.)   Akhenaton (1365 B.C.)
    Temple of Hatshepsut (1480 B.C.)   Queen Nefertiti (1365 B.C.)

Sumerian Art (36–18 centuries B.C.)

    White Temple (3500 B.C.)   Gudea (2150 B.C.)
    Head of Akkadian Ruler   Law Code of Hammurabi
      (2300 B.C.)   (1760 B.C.)
    Victory stele of Naram-Sin
      (2300 B.C.)

Assyrian Art (8–6 centuries B.C.)

    Palace of Sargon II (742 B.C.)   Dying Lioness (650 B.C.)
    Winged-Bull Gate (742 B.C.)   Ishtar Gate, Babylon (575 B.C.)
    Ashurnasirpal II Killing Lions
      (850 B.C.)

Persian Art (6–3 centuries B.C.)

    Persepolis (500 B.C.)   Palace of Shapur I
    Bull capital, Persepolis   (262 A.D.)
      (500 B.C.)

Aegean Art (16 centuries B.C.)

Minoan Art (17–14 centuries B.C.)

    Snake Goddess (1600 B.C.)   Treasury of Atreus, Mycenae
    Octopus vase (1500 B.C.)   (1300 B.C.)
    Harvester vase (1500 B.C.)   Bull-leapers (1500 B.C.)

Mycenaean Art (16–13 centuries B.C.)   The Lion Gate, Mycenae
    Vapphio cups (1500 B.C.)   (1250 B.C.)

Greek Art (8–4 centuries B.C.)

    Geometric vase (8th century B.C.)   Theater at Epidaurus (350 B.C.)
    Black figure vase (525 B.C.)   Standing Youth (480 B.C.)
    Red figure vase (490 B.C.)   Polyclitus, sculptor, (450 B.C.)
    Kore (maiden) figure (650 B.C.)   Charioteer (c. 470 B.C.)
    Kouros (youth) figure (600 B.C.)   Apollo (c. 460 B.C.)
    Calf-bearer (570 B.C.)   Poseidon (c. 450 B.C.)
    Rampin Head (560 B.C.)   Discobolus (Discus Thrower),
    Hera (570 B.C.)   by Myron (c. 450 B.C.)
    Treasure, Delphi (530 B.C.)   Dying Niobid (c. 450 B.C.)
    Herakles (490 B.C.)   Three Goddesses (c. 438–432 B.C.)

Dying Warrior (490 B.C.)   Phidias, sculptor, Parthenon
Basilica at Phestum (550 B.C.)   sculptures carved under his
Temple of Poseidon (460 B.C.)   direction, (490–432 B.C.)
Parthenon (448–432 B.C.)   Mausoleum at Halicarnassus,
Propylaea (437–432 B.C.)   built 359 B.C.
Erechtheum (421–405 B.C.)

Greek Hellenistic Art (4–2 centuries B.C.)

    Mausolus (359–351 B.C.)   Scraper, by Lysippus (c. 330 B.C.)
    Aphrodite by Praxiteles   Dying Gaul (c. 230–220 B.C.)
      (c. 330 B.C.)   Pergamum (180 B.C.)
    Hermes by Praxiteles   Winged Victory of Samothrace
      (c. 330–320 B.C.)   (c. 200 B.C.)
    The Apollo Belvedere   Laocoon (late 2nd century B.C.)
      (late 4th or 1st century B.C.)   Veiled Dancer (c. 200 B.C.)

Etruscan Art (6 century B.C.)

    Apollo (c. 510 B.C.)   She-wolf (c. 500 B.C.)

Roman Art (1 century B.C.–4 century A.D.)

    Temple of Fortuna Virilis   (13–9 B.C.)
      (late 2nd century B.C.)   Arch of Titus, Spoils from the
    Sanctuary at Praeneste   Temple (81 A.D.)
      (1st century B.C.)   Column of Trajan (106–113 A.D.)
    Pont du Gard (1st century A.D.)   Vespasian (c. 75 A.D.)
    The Colosseum (80 A.D.)   Philippus the Arab (244 A.D.)
    Pantheon (118 A.D.)   Plotinus (3rd century A.D.)
    Basilica of Constantine   Arch of Constantine (312 A.D.)
      (c. 310 A.D.)   Constantine (4th century A.D.)
    Roman Patrician (c. 310 A.D.)   House of the Vettii (79 A.D.)
    Ara Pacis (Altar of Peace)   Garden, wall painting (c. 20 B.C.)

Early Christian and Byzantine Art (5–16 centuries A.D.)

    Portrait of Eutropios (c. 450 A.D.)   St. Basil (1554–1560)
    S. Vitale (547 A.D.)   Sant' Apollinare in Classe
    Santa Sophia (537 A.D.)   (533–549 A.D.)
    Interior St. Mark's (begun 1603)

The Middle Ages

Islamic Art (14–17 centuries A.D.)

    Alhambra (1354–1391)   Blue mosque (1609–1616)
    Taj Mahal (1630–1648)

Early Medieval Art (8–10 centuries A.D.)

    Palace chapel of Charlemagne   St. Pantalmon (980)
      (792–805)

Romanesque Art (11–13 centuries A.D.)

St. Sernin (1080–1120)
St. Etienne

Pisa (1053–1272)
Baptistery, Pisa (c. 1060–1150)

Gothic Art (12–16 centuries A.D.)

Church of St. Denis (1140–1144)
Notre-Dame (1163–1200)
Rheims (c. 1225–1299)
St. Maclou (1434)
Salisbury Cathedral (1220–1270)
Gloucester Cathedral
   (1332–1357)
Chapel of Henry VII
   (1503–1519)
Abbey Church (1208)
Florence Cathedral, dome by
   Brunelleschi (1420–1436)
Orvieto Cathedral (c. 1310)
Milan Cathedral (begun 1386)

Palazzo Vecchio (begun 1298)
Ca' d'Oro (1422–c. 1440)
Jamb statue, Chartres Cathedral
   (c. 1145–1470)
Annunciation and Visitation
   (c. 1223–1245)
The Virgin of Paris
   (early 14th century)
Marble pulpit, Baptistery at
   Pisa, by Pisano (1259–1260)
Cimabue (c. 1240–1302)
Duccio (1255–1319)
Giotto (c. 1276–1337)

Late Gothic

Master of Flemalle (c. 1440)
Van Eyck Brothers
   (Jan.: c. 1390–1441)

Van der Weyden (1399–1464)
Van der Goes (1440–1482)
Bosch (c. 1460–1516)

Renaissance

Early Renaissance (15th century A.D.)

Donatello (1386–1466)
Ghiberti (1378–1455)
Masaccio (1401–1428)
Filippo Lippi (c. 1406–1469)
Piero della Francesca (1416–1492)
Pollaiuolo (1429–1498)
Verocchio (1435–1488)

Mantegna (1431–1506)
Bellini (c. 1431–1516)
Botticelli (1445–1510)
Ghirlandaio (1449–1494)
Perugino (1446–1523)
Signorelli (1441–1523)

High Renaissance (16th century A.D.)

Da Vinci (1452–1519)
Michelangelo (1475–1564)

Raphael (1483–1520)
Titian (1477–1576)

Mannerism (16th century A.D.)

Giorgione (1478–1511)
Tintoretto (1518–1594)
El Greco (c. 1542–1614)
Gorreggio (1494–1534)

Veronese (1528–1588)
Cellini (1500–1571)
Carracci Brothers (c. 1557–1609)

Renaissance in the North (16th century A.D.)

Grunewald (1485–1530)
Durer (1471–1528)
Cranach (1472–1553)

Holbein (1497–1543)
Clouet (1486–1541)
Bruegel (1525–1569)

Baroque

Italy (17th century A.D.)

Bernini (1598–1680)

Flemish (17th century A.D.)

Rubens (1577–1640)
Van Dyck (1599–1641)
Frans Hals (1580–1666)

Jan Steen (1626–1679)
Rembrandt (1606–1669)
Vermeer (1632–1675)

Spain (17th century A.D.)

Ribera (1588–1652)
Zurbaran (1598–1664)

Velazquez (1599–1660)

France (17th century A.D.)

De la Tour (1593–1652)
Le Nain (1593–1648)

Poussin (1594–1665)
Lorraine (1600–1682)

England (17th century A.D.)

Hogarth (1697–1770)
Gainsborough (1727–1788)

Reynolds (1723–1792)

Rococo

(18th century A.D.)

Tiepolo (1696–1770)
Watteau (1684–1721)

Boucher (1703–1770)

Neoclassic

(19th century A.D.)

David (1748–1825)

Ingres (1780–1867)

Romantic (18th–19th centuries A.D.)

West (1738–1820)
Copley (1738–1815)
Blake (1757–1827)
Cozzens (1717–1786)
Constable (1776–1837)
Turner (1775–1851)

Goya (1746–1828)
Gericault (1791–1824)
Delacroix (1798–1863)
Daumier (1808–1879)
Millet (1814–1875)
Corot (1796–1875)

Realism (19th century A.D.)

Courbet (1819–1877)
Homer (1836–1910)
Eakins (1844–1916)

Post-Impressionism (19th century A.D.)

Cezanne (1839–1906)
Seurat (1859–1891)
Van Gogh (1853–1890)
Gauguin (1848–1903)
Toulouse-Lautrec (1864–1901)

Munch (1863–1944)
Rousseau (1844–1910)
Maillol (1861–1944)
Barlach (1870–1938)
Lehmbruck (1881–1919)

Impressionism (19th century A.D.)

Manet (1832–1883)	Monet (1840–1926)
Renoir (1841–1919)	Whistler (1834–1902)
Degas (1834–1917)	Rodin (1840–1917)

Expressionism (20th century A.D.)

Fauvism	Roualt (1871–1958)
Matisse (1869–1954)	Beckman (1884–1950)

PRONUNCIATION GUIDE

Altamira	al ta MEER a
Arezzo	ah RET so
Arnolfini, Giovanni	ar nol FEE nee, joe VAHN nee
Bauhaus	BOUGH house
Bellelli	bel LEL lee
Bellini, Gentile, Giovanni,	bel LEE nee, jen TEE lay,
Jacopo	joe VAHN nee, YAH co po
Böcklin, Arnold	BUCK lin, arnold
Borgo San Sepolcro	BORE go san say POLE cro
Bosch, Hieronymus	bos, here ON i mus
Boscoreale	bos co ray AH lay
Botticelli, Sandro	bot tee CHEL lee, SAN dro
Boucher, François	boo shay, fron swah
Brancacci	brahn COT chee
Braque, Georges	brock, zhorzh
Brera	BRARE a
Bruant, Aristide	brew ahn, a rees teed
Bruegel, Pieter	BROO gul, peter
Caprichos	ca PREACH os
Caravaggio, Michelangelo	car a VOD jo, michael AN jel o
Cenami, Giovanna	chay NAH mee, joe VAHN na
Cézanne, Paul	say zan, paul
Chagall, Marc	shah GAHL, mark
Champs Élysées	shahns ay lee zay
Chardin, Jean Baptiste	shar dan, zhon bah teest
Charivari, La	shar ee var ee, la
chiaroscuro	key AH ro SKOO ro
Chirico, Giorgio de	KEE ree co, GEORGE o day
Cot, Pierre	ko, pyair
Crivelli, Carlo	cree VEL lee, CAR lo
Daedalus	DED a lus, DEED a lus
Dali, Salvador	DAH *lee*, salvador
Daumier, Honoré	dome yay, on o ray
David, Jacques Louis	dah veed, zhock loo ee
Degas, Edgar	d'gah, edgar
Delacroix, Eugène	del a crwah, uh zhen
Demoiselles d'Avignon, Les	de mwah zell dav in yon, lay
diablerie	dyah bler ee
diptych	DIP tick
Douanier	dwahn yay
Dufy, Raoul	dew fee, rah ool
Dürer, Albrecht	DURE er, AL brekt
Eremitani	air ay mee TAH nee
d'Évreux, Jeanne	day vruh, zhonn
Eyck, Jan van	IKE, yon van
fauve, fauvism	fove, fove ism
Fontainebleau	fon ten blow
Fragonard, Jean Honoré	frag o nar, zohn on o ray
gaufrage	go frazh
Gauguin, Paul	go gan, paul
genre	ZHON ruh
Géricault, Jean Louis	zhay ree co, zhon loo ee
Gérôme, Jean Léon	zhay rome, zhon lay on
gesso	JESS o
Ghirlandaio, Domenico	gear lon DIE o, doe MEN ee co
Giorgione	george o nay
Giotto di Bondone	JOT toe dee bon DOE nay
Giulio Romano	JOO lee o ro MAH no
Gogh, Vincent van	GO, vincent van
gouache	gwahsh
Goya, Francisco de	GOY a, francisco, frahn THEES co day
Gozzoli, Benozzo	GOT so lee, beh NOT so
Grande Jatte, La	grahnd zhot, la
Greco, El	GRECK o, el
Gris, Juan	greece, whahn
Grosz, George	gross, george
Guernica	GWARE nee ca
Harunobu, Suzuki	ha roo NO boo, soo ZOO kee
Heem, Jan de	HAME, yon de

Holbein, Hans	HOLE bine, hans
Huys, Pieter	hoyss, peter
Icarus	IK a rus
Ingres	ang'r
Kandinsky, Wassily	can DIN skee, va SILL ee
Kirchner, Ernst Ludwig	KEERSH ner, airnst LOOD vig
Kiyonobu	kee yo NO boo
Kiyotada	kee yo TAH da
Klee, Paul	clay, paul
Kokoschka, Oskar	ko KOSH ka, oscar
Kollwitz, Käthe	CALL vits, katy
Lascaux	lass ko
Leblanc, Mme.	le blahng, madame
Leonardo da Vinci	lay o NAR doe da VIN chee
Lyons	lee awn
Madrileño	mah dree LANE yo
Manet, Édouard	mah nay, aid wahr
Mantegna, Andrea	mon TANE ya, AN dray a
Marmion, Simon	mar mee awn, see mawn
Masaccio	ma SOTCH o
Matisse, Henri	ma teess, on ree
Medici	MAY dee chee
Medici, Giuliano de'	MAY dee chee, jool YAH no day
Michelangelo Buonarotti	michael AN jel o bwoe na ROT tee
Millet, Jean François	mee lay, zhon fron swah
Mona Lisa	MO na LEE za
Mondrian, Piet	MON dree ahn, pete
Montefeltro, Federigo da	mon tay FELL tro, fay day REE go da
Mont Sainte-Victoire	mawn sant veek twah
Moulin Rouge	moo lan roozh
Nemours	n'moor
Perugino, Pietro	pay roo JEE no, PYAY tro
Phocion	FO shun
Picasso, Pablo	pea CASS o, PAB lo
Piero della Francesca	PYAIR o della fran CHESS ca
Pietà	pea ay TAH
Pollaiuolo, Antonio	paul eye WOE lo, an TONE ee o
Poussin, Nicolas	poo san, nicholas
Primavera, La	pree ma VAIR a, la
Raphael (Raffaello Sanzio)	RAF ee ul, RAFE ee ul (raf fah EL lo san zee o)
Redon, Odilon	r'dawn, o dee lawn
Renoir, Pierre	r'n wahr, pyair
Rivera, Diego	ree VAIR a, dee AY go
Rouault, Georges	roo oh, zhorzh
Rousseau, Henri	roo SO, on ree
Rue des Moulins	rew day moo lan
Rue Transnonain	rew trahns no nan
Ruisdael, Jakob van	RISE dale, YAH cub, jacob van
Sabine	SAY bine
Sassetta	sas SET ta
Sassetti, Francesco, Teodoro	sas SET tee, fran CHESS co, tay o DORE o
Savonarola	SAV o na ROLL a
Seurat, Georges	sir ah, zhorzh
Simone Martini	see MO nay mar TEE nee
Stanza della Segnatura	STON za della sane ya TOO ra
Titian (Tiziano Vecelli)	TISH'n (tee SYAH no VAN CHEL ee)
Tommaso da Modena	toe MAH so da MOD en a
Toulouse-Lautrec, Henri de	too looze lo trek, on ree de
Treviso	tray VEE zo
triptych	TRIP tick
Uffizi	oo FEET see
Velazquez, Diego	ve LASS kess, ve LATH keth, dee AY go
Vermeer, Jan	ver MARE, yon
Watteau, Jean Antoine	wah toe, zhon on twon

BOOK-OF-THE-MONTH CLUB, INC., 345 Hudson Street, New York, N. Y.

"Flying Eagle"
Woodcarving by an anonymous folk sculptor, 19th Century

Courtesy, Rudy Turk, University Art Collections, Arizona State University
Purchase, The American Art Heritage Fund

Chapter 6

America was an experiment. When it began, five nations of Europe were passing none too smoothly from the stabilities of feudalism to the new beliefs, discoveries, and motivations of the modern age. In France, Spain, Portugal, Holland, and England, the power of the church-state, and with it the power of wealth, title, and property over the lives of men, was being challenged. The man of middle station was to be the prime mover in the new age; his jostling for elbow room in society was to be called individualism.[1]

OLIVER W. LARKIN,
"Art and Life in America,"
New York: Holt, Rinehart & Winston, rev. ed. 1960, p. 5

The Growth of American Art

As we stated in the preceding chapter, probably one of the best ways to introduce secondary students to the study of art in history is to begin with the subject closer to home, notably art in America. This covers a relatively short span of approximately 200 years. It represents the art of the colonies, territories, and the United States. In beginning with American art, we provide the student with some frame of reference as a basis for challenge and discovery. In this approach, we deal with a familiar culture, and with native attitudes and habits, including a common language. Once the idea of studying art in historical context is understood, it can be united with studio, or kept as separate units of the art program. Both approaches are recommended. In providing an approach to the study of art history through the study of American artists, points of departure into the past art of foreign countries will be more easily instituted. It should be remembered that building a cultural level in secondary students is a difficult but challenging enterprise. There is no American tradition of the arts for the student to compare.

Most of the general public is ignorant of art or art history. For many, they live in a 19th century situation as far as art is concerned. The general public has a dichotomy of beliefs, in which their comprehension of art and their comprehension of science are completely at odds.

Twentieth Century Artist: Unorthodox or Traditionalist

It may help secondary level students to be able to see the distinction between artists who have chosen to create in a style that is acceptable to many through its reliance on well established, well accepted modes of expression, and the unorthodox type of artist who invents his own approach to art. The artist who works in a well accepted mode, we refer to as a traditionalist. He may paint in an impressionistic vein, or in a style similar to that used by the Flemish school, or in the Renaissance style. An artist who works in such a literary style which contains subject that is clearly recognizable is usually thought of as a traditional painter. Working in a traditional style is a perfectly acceptable method of working. Many, many artists work this way. In fact, it may well be the most direct means of working for young students in order to learn how to draw and paint.

On the other hand, there are rapidly emerging approaches to artistic expression that utilize unorthodox methods for expressing ideas—unorthodoxy in terms of media and ideas. An unorthodox approach is uniquely a part of an individual artist's experience. He chooses to express his artistic ideas in unique and unusual ways. Unorthodox approaches remain enigmatic or independent for the unsophisticated as they are not comparable to any known tradition. Time has not exonerated their works and made their styles acceptable to the average taste. The unorthodox artist of today is more likely to be at the forefront of discovery. His approaches may signal modifications to come in the world of art. Because of the uniqueness of his vision, and his way of working, his approach may appear completely foreign and isolated to someone used to viewing traditional landscapes, portraits, or scenes of the pastoral countryside. Over a period of years, with repeated showings of an artist's work, a certain respectability often results. Some artists are able to transcend boundaries of acceptance regardless of how individual and unique their work is. Such an example is Pablo Picasso who has remained a unique individualist his entire life, yet his work is acceptable but not understood by the average man. An example of an artist who is acceptable to the average man as well as the artist is Andrew Wyeth, painter of New England scenes. Wyeth is accept-

"Portrait of Ann"
by George Bellows, ca. 1913 (1882-1925)
Oil on Canvas

Courtesy, University Art Collections, Arizona State University
Gift of Oliver B. James

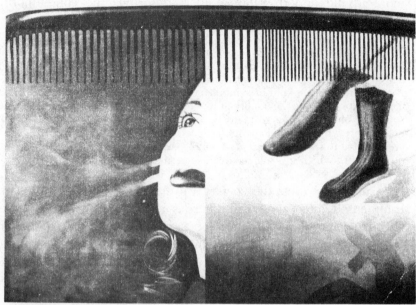

"The Light That Won't Fail I"
by James Rosenquist, 1961
Oil on Canvas

Courtesy, Leo Castelli Gallery, New York
Collection: Joseph H. Hirshhorn

The artist of today may follow some past tradition or style, or he may seek entirely new directions which have no tradition. Both approaches require uniqueness of idea, and skillful technique.

Courtesy, Albright-Knox Art Gallery, Buffalo, New York
Gift of Seymour H. Knox

"100 Cans"
by Andy Warhol, 1962
Oil on Canvas

able to the artist for his painterly know-how and compositional draftsmanship, both sought after goals of the artist. He is acceptable to the man on the street for his literary style, and his ability to recreate the New England countryside in an acceptable nineteenth century mode of romantic remembrance. He has tremendous nostalgic pull.

For art to grow, however, there have to be artists who have a vision that is unlike the commonplace, the tried. Many artists of today are setting trends for the future. They are breaking down the old rules for what art is or is not. One of the unique things about an artist is that once the general critics or lay public have just about established what their definition of modern art is, the artist is off on a new tack creating new criteria for defining art. The artist, as an antenna of society encourages us to see a life of visual forms in new ways. All of life is this way. They scoffed at the Wright brothers. Airplanes, rockets, computers, automobiles, refrigerators, electricity, and many other valuable aspects of our society would not have been possible without men of vision. For the artist of today, new vision is his cup of tea. He is transforming the entire concept of how art is approached. Often, it is completely impossible to predict what the contemporary artist will try next. His art is highly individualized and personal, and as such he tempts us with his imaginative vision. He has stepped forcefully into the twentieth century, while the viewer often remains in nineteenth century viewing perspective. Contrast the fixed point of view type of painting of the renaissance artist (Leonardo, Bottecelli) with artists today who, break every conceivable rule regarding what an art work should be. As illustration, art today is composed of plastics, foam rubber, nails, knives, soil, rocks, found objects, and whatever else is captured by the artist and considered an art form. One of the values of art is that it permits man as artist or student to recreate his world or any part of it. In addition, it also enables him to create new worlds never before seen! This is one of the most exciting aspects of the art experience. It enables one to go beyond the real world, the existing world, toward a new order of visual form that is created by the student or artist. In the twentieth century, man as artist has moved faster and faster toward new worlds of his creation. Often there is fragmenta-

tion and cloudiness. The old, past world of romantic lyricism no longer exists, except as we view it in paintings completed during a more idyllic period. Allan Weller[2] describes the contemporary artist:

It is one of the many paradoxes of contemporary art that at the same time that some aspect of artistic creation seems to proliferate at an ever increasing tempo, the deliberate obscurity of much of the art so produced also increases. A peculiarly private kind of symbolism and exploitation of uniquely individualistic expressions is the quality of much of the work by the strongest creative spirits of our time. We seem to welcome the mysterious, the unclear, the uncertainty which we feel about all aspects of the world situation of which we are a part. It seems to find its counterpart in the deliberate pleasure we take in work which in itself seems in some measure unresolved.

Like much of present day society, the artist interprets the world in a fragmented, alienated sense. There is a searching process going on within each artist, just as contemporary society also explores means for solving the complex problems concomitant with a computer oriented culture.

Today is one of the most exciting times for art, for the emphasis is not only on newer media, but also on twenty-first century ideas to challenge the uniqueness discovered in working with new media. Both uniqueness of idea and media are merging through experimentation in the artist's studio; and it can happen in the classroom! The art teacher serves as the interpreter. He has to translate what the artist is doing into terms that can be utilized to teach art to students. Interpretations and definitions, however, are always to be considered relative to ways of thinking about art, and not to be considered absolutes. Victor D'Amico[3] states:

If you define art for any artist, he is going to change it. The minute you define art precisely, the artist is "dead"; he is not even listening to your definition. He is, instead, thinking of how he is going to change your definition, and get out of it.

The artist today is more involved in his society, and his work reflects this feeling. Although today's artist, for the most part, does not mirror objective realities per se, he is interpreting the times in an individual and personal manner. For the most part, he may be giant strides into the future as far as his imaginative expression goes. This of course establishes conditions that involve risk for the viewer. Images strange to one's vision are often startling, and upsetting.

Man of today in the twentieth century has his eyes fixed firmly on the future—a future that is unclear, except in the knowledge that man is hurtling toward it faster than at any other time in history. By contrast, man has also brushed the dust off his distant past. The spades of the historian have plunged deep into the art-bearing strata of buried civilizations. Each new excavation makes a mark in the epic of human art history extending or correcting the images presently held.

Art in Colonial America

In the morning of America's development, European settlers of some means brought various artists to the new land. Their assignment was to record the new frontier, and to take it back for Europeans to see. These early artists, often totally unkown to us by name, are referred to in the literature as *limners*. The first portraits were handled rather flatly with considerable linear detail and with subdued color. It is doubtful if the early settlers in America would have put up with any of the frills, lace or romanticism of a style that was not rough-hewn and in character with the Indian frontier.

Artists came from England as well as from Holland and many of the Dutch settlers in upper New York state and Pennsylvania were portrayed by artists who painted more or less in the Dutch tradition. More sophisticated painting and portraiture did not begin until the eighteenth century and is referred to as the American School. One of the first artists to arrive in America included Robert Feke (1705–1752), a portrait painter who recorded many of the families of the day. With the full blossoming of the colonies, the painter John Singleton Copley (1738–1815) painted the colonial scene, thus preserving it for contemporary Americans to see. Copley was a native American, born in Boston, whose stepfather was also an artist. He spent the latter part of his life in England where he continued to paint and earned enormous sums for his great talent. Copley was undoubtedly influenced by Benjamin West (an Ameri-

can in London), and Joshua Reynolds. Copley was but one of many American artists who felt the need to study abroad, for the academies in England and France were well-established and acceptable among the educated. Many American art students of the day included Charles Willson Peale, Gilbert Stuart, Ralph Earl, and John Trumbull. These men eventually brought back standards of painting from Europe and consequently influenced the beginnings of an artistic heritage in America.

"Untitled"
by Donald Judd, 1968
Anodized Aluminum and Plexiglas

Courtesy, Leo Castelli Gallery, New York
Collection: Mr. and Mrs. Giovanni Agnelli

The artist most responsible for influencing the growth of American painting was Benjamin West. Born in Philadelphia, he was a great talent who was sent abroad to study with the intention of returning in order to bring artistic glory to America. West was influenced by David and the French neoclassicists of the period. His subject matter therefore was from historical themes and based on heroic acts in history. In his pictures he included great events indigenous to America at the time, such as Indians, and settlers making treaties with the Indians. His artistic interpretations of the Revolutionary War and various aspects of colonial life are treated in a neoclassical style, with a certain monumental epic approach, much in the manner of David and Ingres. West spent many of his years in London and painted for the aristocracy. In fact, he became so admired that the ultimate student ambition for a young artist from

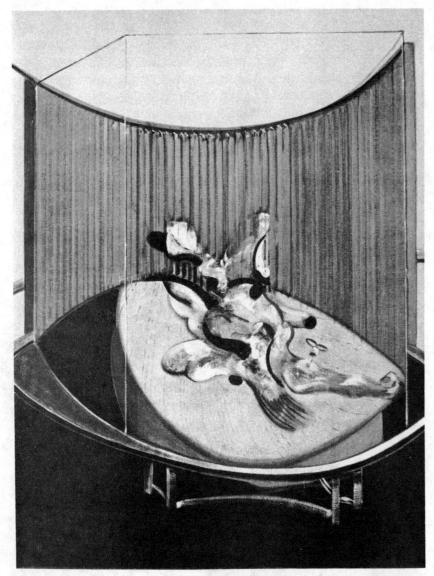

Courtesy, Marlborough Gerson Gallery, Inc., New York

"Lying Figure with Hypodermic Syringe" (2nd Version)
by Francis Bacon, 1968
Oil on Canvas

Courtesy, Leo Castelli Gallery, New York
Collection: Phillip Johnson

"Untitled"
by Morris, 1968
Asphalt, Mirror, Threads, Copper Tubing, Steel, Cable, Wood, Felt, Lead

Artists of today are in the process of breaking traditional rules in art. They seek new media appropriate to the contemporary age.

Courtesy, Allan Stone Galleries, Inc., New York

"Caloma Ridge"
by Wayne Thiebaud, 1968
Acrylic

America was to travel to England and study or receive advice from Benjamin West. Such great American artists as Charles Willson Peale, Gilbert Stuart, Ralph Earl, and John Trumbull were all inspired by Benjamin West.

Another early artist of note was Gilbert Stuart, a truly remarkable portrait painter. He is probably best known for his paintings of George Washington and is remembered most for his unfinished portrait of Washington known as the Atheneum portrait.

Following Gilbert Stuart was Charles Willson Peale, another outstanding portrait artist. His brother James Peale, was a painter of still lifes. In fact, several members of the family were involved in painting. Charles Willson Peale had a son whom he named Raphaelle Peale and Raphaelle also became a talented painter. Charles the father outlived the son by two years. He had another son, Rembrandt Peale, who became an excellent portraitist. All of these men painted for the most part under the influence of the classical style, with the possible exception of Rembrandt Peale who foreshadowed the romantic movement in America.

Thomas Sully was a contemporary with Raphaelle and Rembrandt Peale. He lived in Philadelphia and was the leading portrait painter of his day. One of his best historical scenes is "The Passage of the Delaware," a painting of George Washington that is exhibited in the Museum of Fine Arts in Boston.

It is of considerable value for the art teacher to remind the student or teacher-to-be that experiences in visiting galleries can reveal qualities of the esthetic experience not available in books, in movies, or in other visual experiences. For a person to grow in understanding art, he has to experience it firsthand in the museums. At first there may be a strange feeling of being in a place that one has not visited often. One often hears comments that museums are cold, dark, dingy, and totally dusted over with the residue of history. But museums contain thousands of treasures just waiting to be discovered by a student, teacher, or class. Many American museums contain the history of America recorded by these artists. Visiting an art museum should not be a one time, once a year experience. Returning again and again brings new discoveries with each visit. One has to be imbued with some feeling for the search, for nothing of value in life comes easily, whether it be in art, poetry, history, or business. Whatever is of value in one's life is earned through search and perseverance.

It should be mentioned also that while there were learned painters, such as the Peales, Sully, Morse, West, Stuart, and Copley there were also folk-artists painting who had no formal training, but painted more in the manner of Grandma Moses. Artists of this type did woodcarving, ironwork, roosters, weathervanes, decorative gunstocks, and garden tools. Some of these implements are among the finest recorded instances of native artistic talent. Folk artists normally painted for pleasure and not for livelihood. Folk artists can be found in all countries in all stages of history. It was an art that revealed the expressive qualities of the common citizen. Many of these artists may have read a book on the subject of art yet lacked formal preparation in an art school.

John Trumbull, another American painter contemporary with Charles Willson Peale, studied with Benjamin West in London. He returned a year later and was commissioned to paint the rotunda of the capitol in Washington. This was an interesting assignment in lieu of the fact that his father was governor of Connecticut. It seems that contacts even in those days were of importance for the artist. It should be mentioned that he was interested in historical paintings, and the Republic was interested in recording some of its finest moments in the early history of its development.

Nineteenth Century Artists in America

Several artists stand out in the nineteenth century. While France was busy with the neoclassical revival, America was involved in a romantic landscape style influenced by European tastes. One of the best known artists of the time was Thomas Cole who painted the Hudson River, the Catskills and upper New York state. He was one of many artists who were referred to as the Hudson River School painters. Many of the Hudson River painters were not concerned with epical paintings, but intimate little landscapes which revealed the realistic beauty of nature. They were not impressionists, but recorded what they saw in a personal, naturalistic

"Still Life: Balsam Apple and Vegetables"
by James Peale

Courtesy, University Art Collections, Arizona State University
Oliver B. James Collection of American Art

"Osprey, Otter, and Salmon"
by John James Audubon, 1844 (1785-1851)

Courtesy, University Art Collections, Arizona State University
Gift of Oliver B. James

way more in the nature of Courbet or Chardin. Other artists of the Hudson River School include Thomas Doughty (1793–1856), John F. Kensett (1816–1872), and George H. Durrie. He is probably best known for his many illustrations and paintings which were popularized through the Currier and Ives prints.

The frontier was also painted. One of the first men to paint it was George C. Bingham (1811–1879). The frontier at this time was the Mississippi. Bingham was influenced by Benjamin West, Thomas Sully, and Washington Allston. One of his best known works is "Fur Traders Descending the Missouri" about 1845. Another frontier artist was George Catlin (1796–1872). He painted Indians during the move West. An artist who was outstanding for his understanding of wild life and birds but who was also an accomplished painter was James John Audubon (1785–1851). One of his teachers during his art school days was David. Few Americans knew him as a painter but as a naturalist and researcher on birds. His book titled *Birds of America* which contained 435 plates illustrating 1065 birds was published between 1827–1838.

"The Skater"
by Louis Eilshemius, American, 1912 (1864-1941)
Oil on Masonite

"The MacKenzies of Brooklyn"
by an Anonymous Folk Artist, 1850
Oil

Folk artists were part of the American Scene. Largely unschooled in the formal sense, many anonymous artists created beautiful art works of the times in which they lived.

Courtesy, University Art Collections, Arizona State University
Gift of Oliver B. James

"Pioneer and the Indian"
by Frederic Remington, American, 1961-1909
Oil on Canvas

Courtesy, University Art Collections, Arizona State University
Oliver B. James Collection of American Art

"Portrait of Woman"
by Thomas Eakins

Another lesser known but interesting folk painter was Edward Hicks (1780–1849). He was a deeply religious man who mixed religious idea with a charming personal expression. His painting "The Peaceable Kingdom" done in 1848 is a masterpiece of charm.

Shortly after the Civil War several artists of note painted in America and made lasting contributions. One of these was Thomas Eakins. Eakins was born in Philadelphia and painted there most of his life. He taught at the famous Pennsylvania Academy of Fine Arts and was the first artist to introduce live models to student classes. One of his paintings that is particularly well-known is "Max Schmidt in a Single Scull." James McNeil Whistler, another American (1834–1903), spent much of his time in Paris. Whistler was influenced by Manet and the Impressionists. Whistler also painted

"The Pool"
by James McNeil Whistler, American, 1859
Etching

many scenes in London. His most famous painting is the "Portrait of His Mother." John Singer Sargent was also a contemporary of Whistler and painted portraits and women of high fashion in a fresh approach. Artists such as Albert Bierstadt (1830–1902) painted the Far West in a spectacular technique. Other artists also deserving of mention are George Inness (1824–1894) who painted romantic landscapes. Along with Inness was Albert Pinkham Ryder (1847–1917) who painted mystically. Ryder was the type of artist who painted the solitude of the sea, and night. He was probably preoccupied with depression, death, loneliness, and solitude.

A marvelous still life painter in the last half of the nineteenth century was William H. Harnett. Harnett grew up in Philadelphia and possessed an unusual ability to draw. He was the type of artist who delighted in making a photographic-like image and is reminiscent of Charles Willson Peale and other high visual types. His painting "After the Hunt" is a typical illustration. Much of his painting was intended to deceive the viewer by creating an illusion of reality. Letters look as though they can be picked from a tack board. Hinges, and guns have a lifelike character. He was a powerful draftsman and could control his paint exceedingly well. There were very few artists who painted like Harnett, probably because very few artists can paint this well. The interesting thing about artists is that they are different personalities and as such they paint in different ways. Some artists paint portraits best, while other are designers.

Another artist who was particularly exciting both from the standpoint of literal content, as well as drawing and compositional ability was Winslow Homer. He painted in the latter half of the nineteenth and the beginning of the twentieth century. He was an illustrator by trade, working for *Harper's Weekly*, but his heart was probably closer to painting. He painted the world naturally with a fresh vision, and his painting style remains unique today. He would be a marvelous example for students to study today. His compositional know-how was superb. One of his best known works is the "Gulfstream." Homer traveled a good deal and therefore extended the periphery of idea possibilities to paint. He traveled to the Caribbean Islands, the Adirondacks, Canada, and as a result had a base from which to draw substance. On the other hand, many artists never go anywhere, never leave their hometowns; Thomas Eakins seldom traveled and spent most of his life in Philadelphia. It is not so much where one goes, but what one does with what he has while he is in a location. What makes Homer's drawings, paintings, and prints so exciting is the fact that he had several basic qualities necessary for a great artist. He had imagination which he explored endlessly; he had great enthusiasm and driving interest to put something down on paper and an excellent sense of design.

Different regions of the country also produced great artists. The West can lay claim to a fine artist: Frederick Remington (1861–1909). He painted cowboys, Indians, soldiers, and the wild frontier. He painted the entire West, whatever was there. The frontier is easy to identify with Remington's works; one becomes a cowboy, or an Indian on the great desert plains eyeing the buffalo herd.

In the early days of the country, very few women became artists, for it was felt that their place was in the home. One of the few great women painters was Mary Cassatt (1845–1926). Her themes were mostly figurative and she dealt extensively with mother and child. She explored mother and child as a theme almost as extensively as Georges Braque explored the cubistic still life. Her teacher was Degas and one can see the influence. Many of her pictures are created as though the viewer was looking down from above, with the eye level always above the figures. Her drawings are naturalistic. Her success lies in the fact that she was truly a great draftsman. For anyone wishing to grow in art, this is a prime necessity. One must be able to organize a picture and one must be able to draw.

In 1900 a group of artists in New York, led by Robert Henri (1865–1929), a magnetic teacher and highly gifted painter, broke with tradition in terms of what was pleasing and secure in painting. Instead of painting pleasing little landscapes or idyllic figurative works Henri and seven others including Sloan, Glackens, Luks, Shinn, Prendergast, Davies, and Lawson vigorously painted the turbulence and energy of New York City. The critics and the public at large did not like their works and dubbed them the Ashcan School because of their unorthodox techniques, and subject matter drawn from the poorer sections of New York City's backyards, alleys, and otherwise less genteel subjects of the city. The significance of these

"Roof Gossips"
by John Sloan, American, 1871-1951
Oil

"Stag at Sharkey's"
by George Bellows, 1882-1925
Oil on Canvas

men was that they brought a new attitude to art concerning what painting should be. Not only did they paint in dynamic new ways, but in ways that were more natural and individual to an artist in contrast to the old style academy approach. Their scenes are reminiscent of Hogarth, and Bruegel in earlier history. These artists, known as "the Eight" also arranged for the Armory Show of 1913. This was a show of avant-garde work from France and parts of Europe in which cubism, expressionism, German expressionism, and Fauvism were introduced to the American public. The show was truly unique in terms of expressing what was currently going on in Europe, at the time, although the American public or critics had not seen anything like it. Most of the public and the critics laughed out loud. However, this show marked the beginning of a new attitude, a new approach towards painting, and art.

References

1. OLIVER W. LARKIN, *Art and Life in America,* New York: Holt, Rinehart & Winston, rev. Ed., 1960, p. 5.
2. ALLEN WELLER, from an address presented at Arizona State University, in March 1968.
3. VICTOR D'AMICO, from *Education in the Visual Arts,* Cooperative Research Project No. V-003, Edited by Howard Conant, New York University Printing Office, 1965, p. 137.

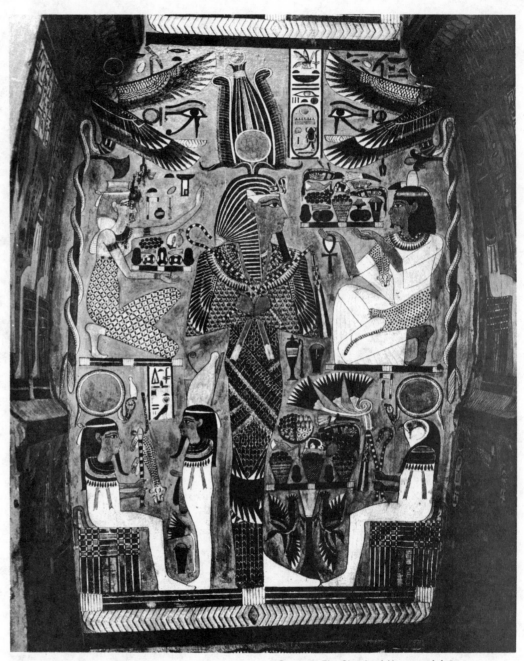

"Detail from Coffin Case of the Priest of Amon-re, Bekenmut"
Egypt, Thebes(?), Dynasty XXII
Paint on Gesso over Wood

Chapter 7

History is not always a matter of dates nor wisdom a matter of age. Since the beginnings of the era of exploration, modern man has constantly encountered cultures out of the past. Many of these cultures have long been dead, and now exist only in relics but many are still alive today in the people and their objects of art. An ever-astonishing fact is the simultaneous existence of races on different levels of civilization and sometimes with the same country.

BERNARD S. MYERS,
Art and Civilization,
New York: McGraw-Hill, 1967, p. 9

Old World Art

The Ancients

Where does the story of art begin? Man, as artist, has used artistic forms of expression as symbols to help him insure a successful hunt, drive evil spirits from his shelter, or to assist in his after death journey to the world beyond. As far as researchers can ascertain, man started creating art works approximately 20,000 B.C. This would put man, as artist, in the latter stages of the Paleolithic or Old Stone Age. Animals and figures painted on the walls of caves in France and Spain indicate a refinement of form that surely must have started long before visible evidence such as these cave paintings in Altamira and Lascaux, France, would indicate. Deep within these caves appear beautiful animals and figures depicted and preserved down through centuries and across the ages. In this ancient world of art, smaller figurines and animals have also been uncovered, to reveal that Stone Age man felt some inner need to express in stone, bone or horn the most striking images about him. In some parts of the world today evidence of primitive man still exists, such as the bushmen of South Africa and the Australian aborigines. What brought Paleolithic man into decline? No one really knows. One supposition is the domestication of animals. Of course, life did not change over night. It took many thousands of years for man to move from the caves and hunting phase to farms and man-made shelters. The New Stone Age or Neolithic period, was a period of man evolving as farmer and controller of his own food supply. Although stone was still primarily the basic material for tools and weapons during the Neolithic period, crafts also developed such as pottery, weaving and certain basic methods of architectural construction.

Man continued to live in tribal villages until a few hundred years before the birth of Christ. Some evidence of Neolithic man's attempts at constructing are evident in the megalithic monuments that he built. Their purpose was probably religious rather than functional or civic. They constructed tombs known as *dolmens*. Others known as *cromlechs* served a religious function. One such excellent example is to be found at Stonehenge in southern England. Stonehenge is architectural in scope although it was probably not intended for living within. We can never be sure and this is the beauty and challenge of art in history. We always wonder what purpose early man intended for the remains we have uncovered. What civilizations, what type of person was able to construct with a bare minimum of tools such gigantic works as Stonehenge? Primitive man did not have written records and thus little awareness of his own history. Ultimately, he had no inner drive for expansion or change. In fact, change would be regarded as suspicious, just as outsiders are regarded suspiciously.

Another example of Neolithic man's sculptural talents can be found on Easter Island where large heads have been carved from volcanic rock. One wonders about these megalithic monuments.

"Amenemhat III" (1842-1797 B.C.)
Egypt, Middle Kingdom, Dynasty XII (1991-1786 B.C.)
Black Aswan Granite

*Courtesy, The Cleveland Museum of Art
Purchase from the J. H. Wade Fund*

Who created them? Other examples of primitive art have been uncovered in various parts of the world. Neolithic survivors still exist in the world today and include tribes in Africa, Australia and in the islands of the South Pacific and the Americas. Striking analogies may be ascertained by studying the art of these primitive societies and comparing this information with that of evidence unearthed concerning Neolithic times.

A strong unifying force in primitive society was religious worship. Primitive societies were deeply concerned with their ancestors and the worship of them. They employed geometric designs in much of their art, in an attempt to create forms in abstraction from everyday appearance, that would be more in keeping with the other-worldliness of the ancestor or spirit world. Earlier Paleolithic man did not use his art as only symbolism. The pictures he painted on the walls of the caves in southern France and northern Spain and in other regions in the area were intended to represent forms as realistically as possible in order to insure a good hunt, the idea here being that the more closely the animal depicted is to the real object the greater the possibilities of obtaining the real animal. In Neolithic art which immediately follows the Paleolithic period, art takes on a more symbolic or spiritual essence in keeping with religious rituals that Neolithic tribes and societies depend on as a cohesive force in the development of their culture. Ancient man used pigments derived from natural sources, primarily earth colors: browns, reddish hues, ochres, yellows, and charcoal for blacks and for darkening the red and yellow earth colors.

Man slowly evolved from the use of tribal magic to the worship of gods within his religion. Gods replaced voodoo magic as a means of communicating with unknowns. As man progressed from thinking in terms of strict naturalization and reality during the Old Stone Age, he moved more toward symbolism in which he placed a greater emphasis on ideas and emotions, so that fact was replaced with symbol and as such naturalistic art forms were replaced by symbolic art forms such as masks, totem poles, idols and other forms of primitive art utilized to represent important aspects of a tribe's religion and its needs. In the Southwest, Hopi Indians create Kachina dolls to represent their gods.

The use of symbols seems to imply a move toward the civilization of man in which his ideas predominate over what he sees and experiences. In many respects this is the way artistic man thinks today. He deals with symbols in his art. He interprets his experiences rather than always attempting to illustrate exactly. It might be said that contemporary art is probably much more symbolically utilized or expressed than art in a naturalistic vein. Australian aborigines are probably among the least developed of the primitive peoples. When they were first discovered in Australia they knew nothing of pottery or of houses in any conventional sense and often lived in caves just as Stone Age man did. They have a very interesting art form in which they portray X-ray pictures on bark in which naturalistic type animal, figure and fish forms are depicted in outline form.

Art itself is a product of man's urge to express his ideas and his experiences. Man has been creating for as long as he has existed. Through art, man's confrontation with his philosophies, psychologies, and spiritual needs find expression. The arts of man down through time serve as a means of communication and as a record that ties all of the ages in a common bond of art. Art is a cultural expression of all humanity, both living and deceased. A study of art history itself, depends for its validity upon a solid framework of uncovered factual information. In ancient times, and often today, art works have been produced for a utilitarian purpose and the attitude toward any type of art—painting, sculpture, or architecture—was considered for function first and for design as a more or less secondary objective in the creation of the art work or architectural form. However the thought remains that something beyond function must have existed in the minds of artistic people of long ago, for art has persisted down through the ages. Utilitarian function could have been an outward decision to create, but being able to give birth to artistic form in a material must have had some significance for those artists who did create in ancient times.

Most of the early works, such as those that were done on the walls of the caves in France and Spain were done in order to perform some magic that would enable the hunter through spearing his prey in a drawing to do the same during the hunt, so that magic and religious ritual became the function in very early times and even today in some areas of the world this type of tribal ritual still remains.

The term primitive art is somewhat misleading, for when we look at the tremendous and often astonishing skill involved as represented by the works of ancient times, we realize that these craftsmen—gold craftsmen, basketweavers, leather craftsmen—had highly refined sensibilities to artistic creation.

Prehistoric or pre-history refers to that evolution of man in his world before written records. It includes the Stone Age period. The main epochs of the evolution of man are as follows: the beginning of man as far as we can ascertain was during the Eolithic or beginning of the Stone Age, and dates between 1,000,000 to 500,000 B.C. Evidence is found in Java and Peking men. The next stage is Paleolithic or Old Stone Age, which ranges from 500,000 to 20,000 B.C. Evidence is found in Piltdown and Heidelberg man. The next epoch is Mezolithic or Transitional Stone Age from 20,000 to 12,000 B.C. Next comes Neolithic or New Stone Age, 12,000 to 3,000 B.C. Next comes the Bronze Age, 3,000 to 1,000 B.C. And next comes the Iron Age 1,000 B.C. to A.D. All these are epochs in the evolution of man and within these stages of man comes his first beginnings toward art or toward expressing form in a media.

The artist began to simplify the form, retaining basic geometric resemblances, but otherwise creating a "shorthand" of the original version. In contemporary art the artist does much the same thing. An artist who has drawn the figure hundreds of times often tries various exaggerations and reductions through abstract means. Abstraction also lends itself well to a decorative treatment and design.

Egyptian Art

Egyptian art began roughly 5,000 years ago and it may be said to have centered around the influences of the Pharaoh (king) who was both supreme ruler and god. As supreme ruler his word transcended all others and his wants, desires, and power determined what was created in Egypt during the Old Kingdom and the dynasties. The various periods of history in Egypt (as in the Orient) are referred to as *dynasties*. What records we do have of Egyptian art have been found in the tombs which they created. We have little evidence of their society and civilization, but the tombs were built to last forever. Much of the art remaining is to be found on the walls of the tombs—created to insure an environment for the dead Pharaoh or other important personage to accompany him on his trip to the other world. Some interesting characteristics of Egyptian art include the repetition of a bull's tail which hangs from Pharonic ceremonial garb.

This type of symbolic expression was evident in Egyptian artistic expression for a period of approximately 3,000 years. Another interesting characteristic of Egyptian art has to do with the depiction of the figures, particularly of Pharaohs, in which the torso shows a front view with head in profile. This style seems to have been created in order to convey the otherworldliness, or supreme godliness, of the Pharaohs and apparently originated with the artists who worked within the royal court. The method of representing the figure is head and legs in profile with eyes, shoulders and torso in frontal view. This method of representing the divinity of the Pharaohs survived unchanged for at least 2,500 years.

The pyramids were created by the Egyptians to serve as eternal tombs for the Pharaohs, and as such, many buildings were constructed surrounding the pyramids in order to accommodate great religious celebrations during the Pharaoh's lifetime. The pyramids reached their developmental climax during the fourth dynasty in which the famous pyramids at Giza were created. These pyramids formed the shelter for the tombs of which the three gigantic pyramids at Giza were the largest ever created. The reserve heads found in the tombs at Giza, the Narmer Palette, and assorted other sculptural figures, including the gigantic Sphinx, are fine examples of Egyptian artistry. The head of the Sphinx towers some sixty-five feet in the air. The Sphinx itself was another tomb for a divine ruler thought to be Chefren, although damage has obscured the details of the face. The Pharaohs believed their divine power came from the god Amun whose identity was fused with Ra, the sun god. Many of the ancient tombs had been ravished, as graverobbing was a constant practice in ancient Egypt.

Here are some terms that are worth remembering: *Pharaoh* was the king or the ruler during ancient Egyptian times who was god-like in stature. He in turn appointed nobles who became the ruling elite and helped him rule his kingdom. Their god was *Ra*, sun god, and *Ka* is a force that is counter to one's body which accompanied the body through life and also travelled with it after death. It might be somewhat in the order of a soul, a counter-force. A *serdab* is a minuscule, secret chamber built deep in the side of a tomb that is called a *mastaba*. The desire to create such tombs and pyramids during the Old Kingdom was actually to provide a safe place for the dead. The pyramids are royal tombs and represent the climax of this type of belief, particularly the pyramids of Giza. Within the tombs, murals were painted on the walls depicting everyday life of the ancient Egyptians. Pictures include the raising of cattle, grain, harvesting, warriors, wars, and various figurative subjects depicting the nobles and the Pharaohs of the time. The largest of the pyramids ever built is that of Khufu. Of the three, Khafre is somewhat smaller. The larger the pyramid, the greater the power of the Pharaoh. The Egyptian artist was an artist of high capabilities. The different types of artists included sculptors who worked in stone, goldsmiths, potters, and painters. Some of the stones that the sculptors used to create the giant statues and other magnificent works included porphyry, diorite, and hematite. These stones are much harder than granite. It should be remembered that man had been working with stone from the beginning of the Stone Age. In the beginning he shaped his tools and later on his feeling for form extended to sculpture and the depiction of rulers and Pharaohs for their tombs.

Greek Art

Greek art is one of the most illustrious periods of artistic development in the history of civilization, yet there are several great difficulties in gaining knowledge and insight regarding the Greek achievement. For example, the Greeks were among the first people in history to write at length about their artists. However we only have such information as was handed down to us from Roman records. Another difficulty that we have in relation to deciphering Greek art is that much of what has been found in terms of written records, via Roman interpretation has no tangible visible evidence in existence. On the other hand, there are other works which do survive and which are considered masterpieces of their time but are not mentioned at all in the written records; so the reconciliation of literary evidence with that of original monuments that have been found, plus the weaving of strands of Roman art that was copied from the Greek, gives us a puzzle that is confusing yet extremely exciting. For the larger measure, the Greeks are little known to us today. Of the records we do have, we know that various Greek-speaking tribes invaded the peninsula around 1100 B.C. and during the next succeeding centuries created the civilization that spawned greatness. Of the tribes, two main groups are outstanding. They include the Dorians who settled on the mainland and the Ionians who settled the Aegean Islands and the nearby coast of Asia Minor. The Greek civilization in its formative years spans roughly the period from 1100 to 700 B.C. We have very little evidence of what the Greeks accomplished during this time. The earliest known dates to which we have some evidence appears to center from 776 B.C., the point at which the Olympic games were counted, and as far as we can determine, the starting point of Greek chronology.

One of the oldest Greek styles in the fine arts is known as the *geometric style*, evidenced in painted pottery and small-scale sculpture. Larger monumental sculpture and architecture did not originate until much later. In the beginning, Greek pottery was decorated with abstract designs consisting of triangles, circles, and angular forms. Gradually human and animal figures began to appear within such geometric frameworks. If we are interpreting correctly, we may suppose that this first geometric style found on pottery has a somewhat primitive quality, a Neolithic feeling that would be quite in keeping with tribal customs which were in existence in the early years of Greek development. Primitive is here again interpreted to describe a way of working that is different from contemporary Western attitude for Greek pottery design was by no means rudimentary. It was a highly sophisticated expression of an intelligent people. Geometric pottery has been discovered not only in

Greece, but also in some countries of the Near East and Italy, thus establishing that Greek traders plied their wares across the European continent. The Phoenician alphabet is also in evidence on these vases. During the period of time in which *geometric* vases were first created two Homeric epics were apparently being lived, the Iliad and the Odyssey. While the geometric style predominated up to the end of the eighth century B.C., the seventh century introduced a new form known as the *Orientalizing style*. The Orientalizing style introduced many influences brought in from the Near East and other parts of the Eastern world. In the Orientalizing style human figures are evident as well as curvilinear motifs, spirals, rosettes, and interlaced bands of decoration. The geometric designs still remain, but in a subdued quantity. They appear for the most part only on the lips, shoulders, and handles of pottery. Major areas of this type of pottery are dominated by narrative illustrations. Orientalizing vases fall into groups, the first of which is known as *proto-Attic* so-named because it was developed in Attica near Athens. A second group of Orientalizing vases is known as *proto-Corinthian* pottery, that was made in Corinth. A third style of vase work which had a far greater range and lasted a longer period of time than the geometric and the *Orientalizing* was the *Archaic* which lasted from the latter part of the seventh century to roughly 480 B.C. The *Archaic* period is fine evidence of vase painting which also coincides with much that is monumental in the architecture and sculpture of Greece.

The idea of working in stone for sculpture and for building did not take place until the middle of the seventh century B.C. This idea occurred during the Orientalizing period. Before this time, buildings and objects had been made of wood. Only the foundations of a few buildings have survived and it is not possible to reconstruct their appearance. Archaic pottery reveals to us scenes from mythology as well as scenes from everyday life with an extremely high evidence of artistic accomplishment, particularly in the Athenian vases. Many of the finest vases frequently bear the signatures of the artists who made them, revealing that even artists of ancient times took pride in their work and were known in their day for their tal-

"Roundel" Segmentum from a Tunic
Egypt, Byzantine Period, 5-6th Century
Tapestry Weave. Silk and Wool

Courtesy, The Cleveland Museum of Art
Purchase from the J. H. Wade Fund

ents in art. In some instances Archaic vase painters can be recognized by the style of their works. We are fortunate to have many examples by a single artist and are able to see what an artist did over a period of a number of works of so long ago. Even in ancient Greece a particular artist was an individual who expressed ideas uniquely in his own way quite apart from his colleagues. Archaic Greek painting was not confined to vases. It also has been discovered in murals and panels although we have very little of these. We have some evidence, however, of Archaic painting from Etruscan tombs of the same period. A question often asked is whether there was a relationship between the murals and the vase paintings. Greek painting is essentially drawing in outline with a brush and filled in with solid flat color. The figures are often highly spirited and lifelike with a certain stylization that is characteristically Greek or classical in expression. The black figure styles of many Attic vase painters replaced previous approaches to the figure evidenced in the Orientalizing style. Exekias is usually thought of as the great master of black figure ware.

The Archaic period in Greek art lasted roughly 200 years. Attic pottery, or the pottery of Athens and neighboring environs was the focal point of ancient Greek pottery. Athens became the most significant focal point because of the findings which verify that Greek people lived there from Hellenic to classical times.

While Egyptian culture grew almost imperceptibly over many thousands of years the development of the high point of Greek culture occurred quite rapidly, and covers less than 1,000 years. Greek culture might be said to have begun around the time of the first Olympic games which took place in 776 B.C. In the geometric period, sculptures were made from terra cotta, a type of clay and were produced on a prolific scale. Other media including stone, metals, bone and wood were also utilized in making sculptured figurines. The geometric style which began approximately 1100 B.C. permeated both small-scale sculpture, pottery and jewelry. The various phases of geometric pottery making include proto-geometric, the early geometric, severe geometric, ripe, and late geometric to 700 B.C. The geometric period was supplanted by the Archaic period

which spanned roughly 250 years and is noted as a time of transformation. The Archaic period spanned roughly 725 to 480 B.C., involved the earliest traces of architecture and includes also black figure pottery which occurred during the middle Archaic period 625 to 525 B.C. and early red figure pottery which is notable roughly from 525 to 480 B.C.

Greece was considered the seat of civilization at this time, for outside of the Greek-speaking cultures existed the barbarians. In addition to the great art forms that have come to us from Greece during the Archaic period, coinage was invented. The alphabet was adapted from the Phoenicians, and the Greeks made great advances in industry and commerce. They traded with many countries including the Near East.

Many of the mysteries of Greece have never been answered, such as why they built great temples when in fact their own homes were modest, and devoid of grandeur or regality. This is all the more amazing when we consider that the earlier periods of Greek art are evidenced in small-scale pottery and sculpture whereas in the later periods, monumentality became the focus. The Greek artist throughout the periods of greatness always displayed an exceptional sense of proportion, whether in pottery, temples, or in sculpture. Although there might be individual differences peculiar to specific locales, there was an overall Greek concept of idealized form. This idealized concept permeated pottery, architecture and sculpture. While the temples remained geometric, the human figure moved from the geometric form toward naturalism. Human scale was omnipresent. Emphasis in the earlier forms tended to be symbolic and not naturalistic with an emphasis on simplicity, geometry, and orderliness. In the beginning, wood and other less permanent materials were used in the temples and the buildings. This was later replaced by marble and limestone. Cast bronze was also produced prior to 500 B.C. Certain Egyptian influences in sculpture include the left foot forward, and the front view of the torso.

In Greek culture the ideal was the perfect human. Man, therefore, was the focus of life. Even the Greek gods were personified as idealized humans. This attitude reflects for the first time, rational man. Life was no longer determined by some predestiny or other worldly control. Tribal man was diminishing in place of Western or intellectual man.

Greek Architecture: Crowning Achievement

The Greek culture reached its zenith during the fifth century B.C., led by Athens which moved to great heights in terms of its architectural achievements. During the fifth century the Parthenon (447–438 B.C.), the temple of Zeus at Olympia, and the temple of Athena Nike were constructed. Under the leadership of Pericles, the political leader of Athens, a majestic architectural building program was initiated and carried on until the end of the century. The Parthenon is referred to as the crown of the Acropolis—the crown not only of the Acropolis, but of all Western architecture. Indeed, we still see its duplication—shabby in some instances—in many cities across Europe and the United States. It is evident in our libraries, museums, and our public buildings. It was designed by Iktinos and Kallicrates. The Parthenon and other buildings similar to it were used as temples in religious ceremonies, and not for living. The temples had no windows, only a doorway; thus, positioning in the direction of the sun was most important in order to permit light to enter in the most dramatic manner.

"Head of a Foreign Warrior"
Greek, 3rd Century B.C.
Marble

Courtesy, The Cleveland Museum of Art
Purchase from the J. H. Wade Fund

Most sculptures were life scale. Sculptures were often utilized as part of the architectural design. They formed pediments for the temples and often depicted gods and legendary epics of Greek mythology. One of the best known of Greek sculptors was Myron who created his works during the fifth century. He is best noted for his *"Youth Throwing a Discus."* Other sculptors of the fifth century included Polykleitos and Phidias. As far as legend will tell us Phidias was commanded by Pericles to rebuild the temples on the Acropolis which included the sculpture of the Parthenon and the other buildings. Among his creations was the cult statue of Athena that stood forty feet high. Each side of the Parthenon had various figures created by Phidias.

Great painters of ancient Greece first made their appearance in the fifth century including Nikon and Polygnotos, Apollodoros, and Parrhaisos. Techniques that we use today, particularly pioneer advances in perspective, have often been attributed to these men. Again these attributions are based on literary indications, for we do not have any remains of their paintings.

During the fourth century a period of reconstruction and renovation took place. Old temples were rebuilt, including the temple of Apollo at Delphi, the theatre of Dionysus at Athens, and the temple of Artemis at Ephesus.

Sculptors of the fourth century included Skopas, Timotheon, Bryaxis, and Praxiteles, who is best known for his well-preserved Hermes found at Olympia, and his Aphrodite of Kindos. Skopas did the pedimental sculpture of the temple of Athena. Lysippos, who made bronze statues of athletes, was another well known sculptor of the day. Probably the six greatest sculptors of antiquity included Myron, Phidias, Polyclitus, Praxiteles, Skopas, and Lysippos. One of the main difficulties in describing the sculpture of the period is that we have very little that is original from their hands, with the exception of the Hermes by Praxiteles. We must rely upon the literary evidence and the fragments from temple pediments, which tell us little. Myron was a sculptor of athletes as well as a sculptor of animals.

Pericles, the political leader of Athens, was responsible for four notable buildings: the Parthenon (447–438), the Propylaea (437–432), the temple of Athena Nike (430's), and the Erechtheum (begun sometime after 438 and finished approximately 404). Periclean architecture is unchallenged for the quality of its work. The architect-sculptor most responsible for the excellence of this work was Phidias. The buildings and temples on the Acropolis had stood almost undamaged for nearly 1,000 years. Systematic spoilation began in roughly the fifth century A.D., when after the decline of Greece the Parthenon was used for various purposes including its function as a Christian church. Finally, in 1687 it was used as a storage chamber for powder for the Turks. A portion of the temple was blown to pieces by a direct hit from a cannon ball. In 1801 Lord Elgin removed to London most of the remaining sculptures of the Parthenon. They are visible today in the British Museum.

Art of the Middle Ages: Medieval Art

Medieval art is often considered the art that centered around the Christian ideology. In the early stages of the Christian movement, there was little visual art. Evidence in museums will bear this out. In many ways, medieval art was an art of mood, feeling, and symbolism. It called for forms that were more in keeping with the new religious movement—art forms that could convey the symbolism of a religion apart from the natural reality of the immediate environment of the time. The earliest records of Christian art have been found in the catacombs or tunnels that formed vast passageways outside the walls of Rome, passageways that were used by the Roman community as burial chambers. In these early catacomb paintings, mythology is intermixed with Biblical stories with God predominating. These paintings were coincident with the end of the Roman state and the rise of the early Christian church with its attendant movement. Gradually, the Roman Empire became thinned by division within, and with it the power of the Roman state weakened. On the other hand, the power of the Christian church increased, while many of the same people who were Roman citizens turned to Christianity. Much of the art that is in evidence from the early phases of the medieval ages had to do with Christian stories from the Old Testament recorded in mosaic form in the churches of Rome and other cities of the declining Empire. The mosaics lent themselves extremely well to the religious imagery of the Christian church. In the glitter and color of the mosaic stones it was possible to create an image that was flattened and somewhat patterned, thus more "God-like," and much different from the naturalism of the marble sculpture of Grecian antiquity.

During the course of the first 500 years A.D., Rome was subject to successive sacking, warring and fighting. As a result population decreased and it ceased to be a center of artistic achievement. Gradually other cities such as Ravenna and Constantinople became centers for Christian ideology. Also influential in the decline of Rome was the decision of the ruler Constantine to move the capital to a location at the other end of the Mediterranean, to Constantinople.

The first major flowering of Byzantine art as part of the Christian epoch is generally considered to have begun during the reign of Justinian 527–565 A.D. Two major works survive from Justinian's reign. They include the church of Hagia Sophia in Constantinople and the church of San Vitale in Ravenna. Both housed significant mosaics that were constructed as part of the wall surface in the days of Justinian. The idea of a central church appears to have originated in the fourth century and roughly parallels the basilica, a city building, deriving from Roman conception.

During the period of the medieval ages when early Christian art was predominant, it was altogether logical that the art of the time be found in the churches. The churches thus became important centers for the carrying on of artistic tradition.

During the Middle Ages there was a constant pulling and tugging situation between the Empire and the Church. Each saw itself as all-knowing and all-powerful. The head of the Church could use threats of cutting a citizen off from his salvation.

Other evidence of artistic activity during the early stages of medieval art include manuscripts, jewelry and brooches all considered minor art in their time just as they are considered minor today, although certainly valid forms of aesthetic expression. Prob-

ably the earliest manuscript that we have on view from the Roman world is a copy of Vergil's Aeneid in the Vatican Library in Rome. Book illustration was common in both Greece and Rome, although we have very few examples or fragments to verify this. There are some fragments from the fourth, fifth and sixth centuries. Another magnificent example of Christian artistic endeavor is the Book of Kells, a copy of the Gospels, now contained in the library of Trinity College in Dublin. It is illustrated with an intricate decorative treatment of the stories of the Testament. It should be remembered that most of the population of the West was illiterate at the time, thus reading was probably imbued with special religious meaning per se, particularly since the language being read, such as Latin or Greek, was different from the native tongue.

When historians first began to study the art of the Middle Ages, they thought of the 1,000 years between 300 and 1300 A.D. as an age of darkness, an empty vacuum with little substance of cultural or esthetic value. At the beginning of this continuum was the glorious antiquity of Greece; at the other end was the rebirth of classical antiquity in the form of the Renaissance, and in between a black silent void. History has verified that this is no longer true.

In the beginning of early medieval art is a style of art referred to as barbaric or animal style. It is typified by highly stylized, imaginatively formed animals on purses, belts, pendants, jewelry and other wearing apparel and tools. Strong echoes of this influence can be observed in the angular, aggressively hostile-appearing design of the great cathedrals with their sharp, barbed spires that shoot into the air like so many spears. During medieval times this so-called barbarian style usually consisted of metal work, but also extended into wood and into manuscript illumination. The influence of the barbarian style was most evident in Scandinavia. Ordinarily when we think of barbarians the first thing that comes to mind are Germanic invaders or Vikings. During the period of 600–800 A.D. when Germanic tribes, Vikings, and other aggressive warrior-people were stomping through Europe, Ireland produced some of the finest art masterpieces ever recorded. The art consisted of the illumination of Bibles and other Christian books. These were developed in workshops known as scriptoria (scriptoriums) and some of these illuminated manuscripts have a visual beauty that is unsurpassed even today. Several pages from the Lindesfarne Gospels and Book of Kells are excellent examples. The idea in decorating these manuscripts so beautifully was to reflect the word of God, for the manuscript was a sacred object containing the holy message. Contrast the pagan warriors of Europe with these beautiful works coming from artistic scriptoria workshops in Irish monasteries. Much of the influence of the outside world however was felt by the monks in the monasteries and they saw fit to include monsters in their pictures, monsters however, that were under control and checked by the influence of a divine force as depicted and interpreted by artistic monks.

Christianity grew in importance, with its hope of redemption offering shelter and understanding in a barbaric world torn by war and confusion. With the growth of the Christian church came books and a book-making industry which helped to spread the word of the Christian church. With the spread of the Christian ideologies came also the spread of art in the form of illustrations for the books. This is significant when we realize that during the decline of antiquity and with the advent of the Dark Ages, art was preserved in this form. Scratching out an existence for most of the population was primary. Probably one of the greatest medieval manuscripts ever produced during the Christain development was a Book of Psalms known as the *Utrecht Psalter*.

Much of Christian art has a flatness and lack of environmental clues, probably in some part due to the influence of Oriental art. This is significant when we remember Constantine moved the Roman empire to Constantinople where Near Eastern influence was predominant. What resulted was manuscripts that were illustrated during the early Christian epoch in a combination of Greek style and Oriental, a seemingly dichotymous combination, whereas in classic Greece the emphasis was on the naturalism and idealism of the human figure. Greek art was associated with paganism and therefore was discarded eventually as not relating to Christian beliefs, or its symbols were absorbed. Early Christian symbolism was used in many reliefs on sarcophagi, in church constructions, as well as manuscripts.

Carolingian Art

The Carolingian period began with the reign of Charles the Great (771–814 A.D.). After his death the Carolingian movement continued in France and Germany. From the Carolingian age we have a collection of illuminated manuscripts, several statuettes, jewelry, and certain examples of architecture. The most outstanding example of any type of cultural heritage from the Carolingian age are the manuscripts which were illuminated and were the main preoccupation of the learned scholars of the time. Many of the illuminated manuscripts are considered artistically inferior, for the function of the copyist was not to be original but to reproduce the message of the book. Although, there are several exceptions where manuscripts excell in beauty. One such highly significant illuminated manuscript is the *Utrecht Psalter*, mentioned earlier. The *Utrecht Psalter* consists of 108 vellum leaves and the minuscule illustrations are line drawings executed in brown ink. Another important art piece from the Carolingian era is the Bayeux tapestry. It is embroidered in eight colors and contains roughly seventy-two scenes. The width is 20 inches with the length being 231 feet and there are over 600 human figures, more than 500 animals, and many ships and other indications of environment. The Bayeux tapestry stands apart from the ordinary miniature manuscripts, illustrations and other art produced during the Carolingian era.

Gothic Art

Gothic art derives from cultured Italians who considered the architecture barbaric and uncultivated (just as the Goths were considered barbarians). In later periods the word lost its hostility and was accepted as a period in architectural history that attained its peak in the thirteenth century. Gothic art is reflected mainly in the great cathedrals that were created in various parts of Europe. The Dark Ages was characteristically also an age of brutality in which war, oppression, hatred, and vehemence were at the surface of life. The great cathedrals that were constructed in the twelfth and thirteenth centuries were aimed at unifying the population, building up the primacy of the Christian church, and for displaying the importance of the church in the affairs of the populace. The Gothic cathedrals were the largest architectural constructions ever erected since the pyramids. Some of the main cathedrals include:

the Cathedral of Amiens, 1220–1269
the Cathedral of Chartres, about 1145
the Cathedral of Notre Dame, 1163–1235
the Cathedral of Salisbury, 1220–1258
the Cathedral of Florence, 1296
the Cathedral of Orvieto, 1290–1310

Gothic art usually dates from the beginning of the twelfth century. It is primarily an art of architecture and all the great cathedrals were constructed during this period. Gothic art was particularly visible around the original location of Paris: the cathedrals of Chartres, Amiens, Reims, and Bourger. France seems to be the dominant location for the Gothic era, more than likely due to the brilliance of Philip Augustus who reigned from 1180 to 1223. One interesting aspect of the Gothic style was that every artist—whether he was creating a cathedral or a small manuscript page—was consistently involved with an infinite number of minuscule details, each deliberately and intensively defined. In this sense Gothic art has a predominant linearity.

Another significant aspect of Gothic architecture was that the need for geometric order was absent. In classical art this was an extremely important part of the design. This lack of symmetry or geometry is readily apparent in Chartres cathedral. The two towers are completely different: one is highly decorative, almost like frosting on a birthday cake and the other is angular and conical.

Gothic art is a visually aggressive art. There are many angularities, spires, points, and spear-like projections. Perhaps this was the result of the European background of rivalry and war. Gothic art is extremely involved with forms that were grotesque. This applied not only to the human body but to gargoyles and to whatever form in which distortion appealed to the artist. The Gothic artist is a derivative of the barbarian style.

It is usually thought there are three subdivisions within Gothic architecture:

1. Early Gothic, later half of the twelfth century
2. High Gothic, thirteenth century and
3. Late Gothic, anything after the thirteenth century.

The peak of Gothic art is considered the thirteenth century, particularly in France. There were also many other cathedrals, including the ones at Salisbury, Toledo, St. Francis at Assisi, St. Elizabeth at Marburg, etc. Laon Cathedral is an example of early Gothic. It was started in 1165 and was finished in 1225. Examples of High Gothic include the cathedral of Amiens. This is probably one of the most elegant and architecturally cohesive of all Gothic cathedrals. It was begun in 1220. Many of these cathedrals were built over an extensive period of time by different architects and artisans who proceeded to add their own little nuances and artistries. Most of the cathedrals in France were built on city squares and on this assumption the façade was considered most important in relation to the remainder of the building, for it faced the main center of the city (this was not necessarily so in England or Germany). In most of the cathedrals a statue of Christ is located near the central doorway on a base known as a trumeau. With the linear decorative design of the exterior surfaces of the cathedrals one could also be aware of the great textural feeling from a visual standpoint. The play of light and dark against such an undulating surface is remarkable from a visual standpoint. This is in the very greatest contrast to classical architecture such as the Parthenon with its high emphasis on simplicity and straight geometric configurations. The cathedrals in France are highly suggestive of fortresses.

Construction of the Cathedrals

Another artistic technique which developed during the Gothic period was stained glass. Gothic architects had learned to structure the buildings in a way that small windows were no longer a limitation. As a result, many of these cathedrals could be flooded with colored light, thus a new media was introduced. As an example the cathedral at Chartres is probably one of the finest examples in the use of stained glass as part of the architectural form.

The cathedrals were constructed of cut stone and except on some occasions did not use cement as the Romans had done. It is truly amazing that these gigantic cathedrals could have been made under the conditions of the time. An interesting architectural innovation was the development of the flying buttress, which served as support for the vaulting of the cathedrals. It connected the vaultings with the spires on the outer edges or fringes of the cathedral. The thirteenth century was a period in which many Gothic churches were built and the Gothic style was predominant in each of the churches. This was not the case in the previous two centuries of Romanesque art in which there was great diversity within churches of their respective locales. However, with the centralization of Catholicism in Rome this unification apparently united the populations in various regions under one central governing authority, and it is reflected in the similarity and unification of the cathedral construction. The zenith of cathedral building, in terms of what may be called Gothic perfection was considered to be northern France, particularly the Isle of France or the region surrounding Paris. Certain variations by other countries lent a unique variation to the Gothic style as pioneered by the French. The Germans in particular developed the Gothic cathedral in which one tower was constructed at the main entrance, whereas in the French cathedrals, two towers—one on either side of the main façade—were commonplace. The towers of the German cathedrals at Freiburg and at Ulm stand more than 370 feet and 528 feet respectively. For comparison, the Washington monument is 555 feet. In St. Elizabeth Cathedral at Marburg the Germans eliminated the traditional triforium and clerestory and equalized both sides of the walls of the cathedrals on the interior, forming a long hallway type structure. As such, cathedrals of this sort have been referred to as hall churches. Saint Elizabeth of Marburg is an example. It was started in 1235. England also built many cathedrals, including the Cathedral at Salisbury. Its tower is 404 feet high and was taller than any other structure in England.

The fourteenth century is in contrast to the great church-buildings of the thirteenth century. Wars once again inflicted on Europe a delay in creative activity. The fourteenth century was a time of the Hundred Years War. France in particular was devastated. In 1348, all Europe was swept by a plague known as the Black Death. At this time, probably half the population of Europe died from the plague. However, in the midst of the plague and the wars and the pillaging, great names come to light including Dante, Giotto, Chaucer, Petrarch, and others.

References (Prehistoric to Renaissance)

General Literature

ACKERMAN, JAMES and CARPENTER, RHYS, *Art and Archeology*, New Jersey: Prentice-Hall, Inc., 1965.

ELSEN, ALBERT, *Purposes of Art*, 2nd. ed., New York: Holt, Rinehart & Winston, 1967.

JANSON, H., *History of Art*, New York: Abrams, 1963.

JANSON, H., *Key Monuments of Western Art*, New York: Abrams, n.d.

MILLON, H. A., *Monuments of the History of Architecture*, New York: Abrams, 1964.

PEVSNER, NIKOLAUS, *An Outline of European Architecture*, 6th Jubilee Edition. Penguin Books, 1960.

ROBB, DAVID and GARRISON, J. J., *Art in the Western World*, 4th ed., New York: Harper & Row, 1963.

Prehistoric Art

BATAILLE, GEORGE, *Lascaux*, Geneva: Skira, 1955.

BREUIL, HENRI, *Four Hundred Centuries of Cave Art*, Montignac (France): Centre d'etudes et de Documentation Prehistoriques, 1952.

GRAZIOSI, PAOLO, *Paleolithic Art*, New York: McGraw-Hill, 1960.

Egyptian Art

LANGE, KURT, *Egypt: Architecture, Sculpture, Painting*, London: Phaidon, 1961.

MEKHITARIAN, ARPAG, *Egyptian Painting*, New York: Skira, 1954.

SMITH, STEVENSON W., *The Art and Architecture of Ancient Egypt*, Pelican History of Art, 1958.

WAAGE, FREDERICK O., *Prehistoric Art*, Dubuque, Iowa: Wm. C. Brown Company Publishers, 1969.

The Art of the Ancient Near East

FRANKFORT, HENRI, *Art and Architecture of the Ancient Orient*, Pelican History of Art, 1955.

LLOYD, SETON, *Art of the Ancient Near East*, London: Thames and Hudson, 1961.

PARROT, ANDRE, *Sumer, the Dawn of Art*, New York: Golden Press, 1961.

STROMMENGER, EVA, *5000 Years of the Art of Mesopotamia*, New York: Abrams, 1964.

Aegean and Mycenean Art

DEMARGUE, PIERRE, *Aegean Art*, London: Thames and Hudson, 1964.

MARINATOS, SPYRIDON, *Crete and Mycenae*, London: Thames and Hudson, 1960.

Greek Art

ARIAS, PAOLO, *A History of 1000 Years of Greek Vase Painting*, New York: Abrams, 1961.

BERVE, HELMUT, *Greek Temples, Theatres, and Shrines*, London: Thames and Hudson, 1963.

BIEBER, MARGARETE, *The Sculpture of the Hellenistic Age*, New York: Columbia University Press, 1955.

BOARDMAN, JOHN, *Greek Art*, London: Thames and Hudson, 1964.

BOHR, R. L., *Classical Art*, Dubuque, Iowa: Wm. C. Brown Company Publishers, 1968.

LAWRENCE, A. W., *Greek Architecture*, Pelican History of Art, 1957.

LULLIES, REINHARD, *Greek Sculpture*, New York: Abrams, 1960.

RICHTER, G. M. A., *A Handbook of Greek Art*, London: Phaidon, 1963.

ROBERTSON, MARTIN, *Greek Painting*, Geneva: Skira, 1959.

YALOURIS, NICHOLAS, *The Elgin Marbles of the Parthenon*, New York: New York Graphic Society, 1960.

Etruscan and Roman Art

GOLDSCHEIDER, LUDWIG, *Etruscan Sculpture*, New York: Phaidon, 1941.

HANFMANN, GEORGE, *Roman Art*, Greenwich, Conn.: New York Graphic Society, 1965.

KAHLER, HEINZ, *The Art of Rome and Her Empire*, New York: Crown, 1963.

MACDONALD, W. L., *The Architecture of the Roman Empire*, New Haven: Yale University Press, 1965.

MAIURI, AMEDEO, *Roman Painting*, New York: Skira, n.d.

PALLOTTINO, MASSIMO, *Etruscan Painting*, New York: Skira, n.d.

STRONG, D. E., *Roman Imperial Sculpture*, London: Tiranti, 1961.

WHEELER, ROBERT, *Roman Art and Architecture*, New York: Praeger.

Early Christian Art

BOVINI, GIUSEPPE, *Ravenna Mosaics*, New York: New York Graphic Society, 1956.

KRAUTHEIMER, RICHARD, *Early Christian and Byzantine Architecture*, Pelican History of Art, 1965.

VOLBACH, WOLFGANG, *Early Christian Art*, New York: Abrams, 1963.

Byzantine Art

BECKWITH, JOHN, *The Art of Constantinople*, London: Phaidon, 1961.

GRABER, ANDRE, *Byzantine Painting*, Geneva: Skira, 1953.

RICE, DAVID, *The Art of Byzantium*, London: Thames and Hudson, 1959.

Early Medieval Art

BECKWITH, JOHN, *Early Medieval Art*, New York: Praeger, 1964.

BUSCH, HAROLD, *Romanesque Europe*, London: Batsford, 1959.

GRABER, ANDRE and NORDENFOLK, CARL, *Romanesque Painting*, Geneva: Skira, 1958.

GRABER, ANDRE and NORDENFOLK, CARL, *Early Medieval Painting*, Geneva: Skira, 1957.

SAALMAN, HOWARD, *Medieval Architecture*, New York: Braziller, 1962.

SMITH, NORRIS K., *Medieval Art*, Dubuque, Iowa: Wm. C. Brown Company Publishers, 1968.

SWARZENSKI, HANS, *Monuments of Romanesque Art*, Chicago: University Press, 1954.

Gothic Art

BONY, JEAN, *French Cathedrals*, Boston: The Riverside Press, 1951.

BRANNER, ROBERT, *Gothic Architecture*, New York: Braziller, 1961.

BUSCH, HAROLD, *Gothic Europe*, London: Batsford, 1958.

DUPONT, JACQUES, *Gothic Painting*, Geneva: Skira, 1961.

FOCILLON, HENRI, *The Art of the West*, 2 vols., London: Phaidon, 1963.

"The Virgin With the Monkey"
by Albrecht Durer, ca. 1498-99
Engraving

Chapter 8

Renaissance Art: The Age of Innovation Begins

The beginning of the Renaissance and the subsequent years mark a point in time and history in which man was given value. Prior to this time, man was always subservient to higher powers. The Renaissance marks a point in which the medieval church declined as a dominant power in Western society. Religion became a more reasonable possibility and human values of which men were capable were brought to light. We might consider the Renaissance as the first realization of the potential of human achievement. With the advent of the Renaissance man realized that he could harness the elements of his environment and reshape them into an image that he saw possible. The Renaissance then was an age of exploration and realism. The symbolic representation of humanity as represented in the medieval ages was no longer sufficient to represent man's more realistic approach to the world. As a result Renaissance artists were specifically involved in the nature and substance of many things. We might also think of the Renaissance as an age of draftsmanship, in which skill and vision were united. The Renaissance was a time in which man became a viewer. He fixed his view on all things in his immediate environment and studied them closely and in detail, always from his fixed point of view. As a result of this realistic fixation he developed ways of representing space on a pictorial canvas; he developed the vanishing point in which all lines in a particular view appear to converge in the distance. This contrasts with the medieval period when man was concerned with gathering enough nourishment for his body, when he sought shelter from the elements, and constantly battled plagues, famines, and war. Contrast this with the Renaissance where individual dignity and human right began to assume importance—where man sought pleasures above and beyond the basic needs of the body. The Renaissance was also marked as a time for expressing human values, human needs, and human vanity. It was a time when personal monuments to oneself, particularly those with the power and prestige to accomplish such, were enacted— that is, men of power and prominence paid first-rate artists to make them immortal through canvas, stone, or other artistic means, such as architecture. So ushers in the era in which artists placed their personal signature on their work. Artists were men of prestige in the Renaissance community and were treated much like emperors. That is hardly the case today. Only a few years ago the artist, be he writer, painter, or sculptor, had to make personal sacrifices in order to continue with his work. In one sense the architect has gained a prestige in the world today that the painter has not been able to achieve.

Two key locations which spawned artists of considerable merit were Italy and Flanders. Florence, Italy was *the* city of the Renaissance.

Flemish Art

Realism was a highly significant feature of Flemish style. The tiniest, most minuscule detail such as warts, moles or even hairs on the skin were not excluded from the discerning eye of the Flemish painter. In fact, much of the detail work in Flemish painting was probably completed with the aid of a magnifying lens. Such is the most beautifully precise detail, and though in miniature, many tiny details are beautifully executed as though they were completed on normal scale. Pictorial scale for Flemish artists such as Van Eyck, was completed in three planes, such as foreground, middleground, and background. It is estimated but not provable, that the Van

Courtesy, University Art Collections, Arizona State University Gift of Mr. and Mrs. Orme Lewis

"Christ Before Pilate"
by Rembrandt Van Rijn, Dutch, 1606-1669
Etching

Eyck brothers, Jan and Hubert, were among the first to invent oil painting. At any rate they used it extensively and to its full potential. Their know-how regarding oil painting is still a mystery today. Interesting also is the fact that most Flemish painting was done on wooden panels covered by a gesso ground (fine cement). The gesso provided a smooth working surface. Prior to painting, the Flemish artist would draw his picture completely in ink. When the composition and the drawing was exact to the artist's taste, varnishes and glazes mixed with color were applied. The Flemish style as developed in the beginning by Jan van Eyck set a trend that continued for a century and the only artists who did not come under its spell were the Italians who were also busy developing their own particular approaches to painting.

While Flemish realism had its origins with painters, Italian realism was sculpture-oriented in the beginning and is assumed to have begun with Donatello. We might consider Donatello as the father of the early Renaissance for most of the other painters and sculptors of this time followed in his style, with few exceptions. One of Donatello's monumental commissions was the "Gattamelata" statue which consisted of a horse and rider, reaching a height of nine feet.

The first great painter of the Renaissance was *Masaccio*. He was born in 1401 and died at the age of twenty-seven. There aren't many pictures surviving to attest to such greatness, but apparently there is high significance in the work that was left behind by an artist who painted for such a brief period—five years. The reason for Masaccio's significance as a key figure in the art world is the attribution to him for inspiring the High Renaissance "Grand Style." Masaccio was the first painter of the Renaissance to handle space in a significant way. Had he lived he probably would have been a moving force in bringing the High Renaissance into play at an earlier date.

Another artist of the Early Renaissance was Fra Angelico whose original name was Guido and who was given the name of Fra Giovanni when he entered the Dominican Order. However, he acquired the nickname of Angelico because of the angelic figures that appeared in his early paintings. He is considered to be less of an artist than Masaccio or Donatello. However, his work has considerable merit for his craftsmanship and stylistic presentation.

In every age there have been artists who have appealed to their patrons and for the most part these artists are reasonably successful at their art and many of them have become extremely wealthy because of their ability or intent to please their commissioners. On the other hand we might consider Masaccio and Donatello more of the avant-garde of their time and those patrons willing to take a chance on such artists could not be as sure of their choices. It might be better expressed by stating that Fra Angelico's work was probably reasonably eclectic; that is, he took the best of what went before him and that which surrounded him and interpreted it in an intelligent and masterly style. On the other hand, Masaccio, Donatello, and a few others were not willing to follow the mode of the day, but choose to interpret in what was then their own unique and individual approach to painting and sculpture.

Botticelli and Pollaiuolo

Probably the first painter to be influenced by Neoplatonism was Sandro Botticelli. Botticelli was a man of sensitive tastes and mystery. Even in his time his work was restricted to a small circle of tasteful persons who appreciated his genius. Botticelli received his art training in the shop of Filippo Lippi. He also worked with *Antonio Pollaiuolo* (1429–1498).

Pollaiuolo is noted for his expertise in the representation of anatomy and his ability to portray the figure in exaggerated and action poses. While Pollaiuolo was involved in portraying man in violent action poses, Botticelli was concerned with the delicacy of the human figure and always represented the figure in a softly handled idyllic manner, forceful but silent. Botticelli's involvement with Neoplatonic philosophy is evident in his painting, "The Birth of Venus" for the idealization of the feminine form. Botticelli's work easily reflects his involvement with Greek ideas; that is, with gods and goddesses particularly Venus. For all of Botticelli's concern with interpreting visually the theories of Neoplatonism, Botticelli remains an artist of the very first order. His paintings are uniquely original and serve to illustrate the great talent that he possessed.

Courtesy, The Frick Collection, New York

"Hercules"
by Antonio Del Pollaiuolo

Courtesy, University Art Collections, Arizona State University
Gift of Mr. and Mrs. Read Mullan

"Christ Presented As King of Jews Before Multitude"
by Albrecht Durer
Engraving

"The Massacre of the Innocents"
by Marcantonio Raimondi, Italian, 1480-1530
Engraving

Botticelli was the last of the Early Renaissance artists. The close of his career marks the point at which the High Renaissance began.

The High Renaissance

Leon Battista Alberti, who was born in approximately 1404 and died in 1472, is considered the "Father of the High Renaissance." He was both writer, architect, sculptor, and painter, although few of his artistic works exist. Numerous poems, plays, and essays provide us with the magnitude of this great Renaissance figure. In addition, some of his architectural monuments are among the most innovative in Renaissance architecture. This includes St. Andrea at Mantua. Most of the work was completed after Alberti's death. The significance of Alberti's design for St. Andrea achieves lucidity when we learn that Michelangelo designed St. Peter's cathedral in Rome on the basis of Alberti's design for St. Andrea. St. Peter's thus became the foundation for nearly all churches built in Rome thereafter. One of the differences between the Early Renaissance and the High Renaissance was the fact that the artistic capital changed from Florence to Rome particularly when the Sistine Chapel was constructed at the Vatican and Michelangelo did his heralded ceiling frescoes.

The High Renaissance was a search for a return to antiquity, a return to an expression of idealized form, whereas in the Early Renaissance man had rediscovered nature and was interested in reproducing the real world of his immediate environment.

"St. Helena"
by Marchesi de Cotignola, Italian, 1481-1550

Courtesy, University Art Collections, Arizona State University Lewis and Lenore Collection

Leonardo, Raphael, and Michelangelo

One of the true giants of the Renaissance was Leonardo da Vinci, who was born in 1452 and died in 1519. He left behind him thousands of pages of notes in many different fields. While his genius is apparent in painting and he is probably best known for his "Mona Lisa" and "Last Supper," he was more proficient in science and several other fields. Imagine a man who not only could paint, but also designed plans for helicopters, airplanes, submarines, and all sorts of machines, canals, and water systems. He was a brilliant anatomist long before anatomy became a science. He designed artillery cannon, milling machines, firearms; he dissected eyes, bodies, circulatory systems, and recorded nearly everything he ever examined or ever did in his notebooks, which are located in museums across the breadth of Europe. As a youth Da Vinci was apprenticed to the artist Andrea Verrocchio, 1435–1488. (Verrocchio is best known for his sculpture, "Boy with a Dolphin.") Leonardo was the most influential man of the Renaissance as far as other artists were concerned.

It is recorded that Raphael was a quiet, gentle man and his paintings reflected this. He is noted for an entire series of paintings of Madonnas that have been collectively referred to as the "Florentine Madonnas," each one challenging and fresh in its vitality and approach. Raphael is also considered to be one of the greats of the High Renaissance.

One of the best known giants of the High Renaissance was Michelangelo Buonarotti 1475–1564, who died at the age of eighty-nine years. He was probably one of the greatest sculptors and painters that has ever lived. One of Michelangelo's first works was his relief, "Battle of the Centaurs" and the first work for which he is well noted is his "Pieta" made in 1498, and located in the Vatican. An interesting aspect of Michelangelo's work is the fact that while it retains the vestiges of representation, that is, a figure is a figure, it also contains subtle but powerful exaggerations of the physical being. On looking at Michelangelo's sculptures without observing intently one might remark at the wondrous detail and naturalness. On closer inspection, particularly in the "Pieta" and the "David"

Courtesy, University Art Collections, Arizona State University

"Diogenes"
by Ugo da Carpi, Italian, 1479-1532
Chiaroscuro Woodcut

there is a tremendous exaggeration of the various anatomical parts. The "Pieta" for example is a good deal larger than the Christ and therefore is not a true representation in the realistic sense. But seen as an entity it holds together. What Michelangelo was doing was expressing his own feelings, his uniqueness as an individual. He was probably one of the first artists to regard his work as his own. To put it another way, Michelangelo interpreted and created his sculptures in the way that he desired and not in the way his patrons commissioned him. As a result he had many flare-ups with patrons, colleagues, and with those who worked with him or who came in contact with him. One of Michelangelo's best known and greatest works are the frescoes that he completed for the ceiling of the Sistine Chapel of the Vatican in Rome. The painted surface of the ceiling was roughly 700 square yards and was executed almost entirely by Michelangelo. The frescoes deal with the Biblical Creation, Noah, and various passageways through a life of religious and historical significance. Another great work that was never finished but was done around the time of the Sistine Chapel was the Medici Chapel, a family mausoleum for the Medici. In addition to his great works in painting and in sculpture Michelangelo was also the chief architect for St. Peter's Cathedral at the Vatican in Rome.

A Glossary to Understanding the Signs and Symbols of Renaissance Art

The artist of the Renaissance period, as well as those who preceded him, was deeply involved with his religion. In his art he expressed symbolically his interpretation of God and creation. The medieval period as well as the Renaissance is mainly the story of the Christian church in visual form. The artist interpreted his church in his work. Many of these images were represented in the paintings created during the period from 300 A.D. to 1700 A.D. The following symbols were often used in paintings from these periods and are defined thus:

Symbol	*Meaning*
1. Ape	represents sin, the devil, greed
2. Almond	divinity
3. Apple	evil, salvation
4. Bee	purity, sweetness, unification
5. Birds	the spiritual aspects of the being, the soul
6. Blackbird	temptation
7. Blood	life, soul
8. Breasts	motherhood
9. Bull	strength
10. Butterfly	resurrection of Christ
11. Cherry	blessedness
12. Clover	Trinity
13. Daisy	innocence
14. Dog	faithfulness
15. Dove	peace, the Holy Ghost
16. Dragon	the devil
17. Ear	betrayal of Christ
18. Eye	God
19. Ermine	purity
20. Falcon	courtly
21. Fern	sincerity
22. Fig tree	lust, fertility
23. Fish	Christ, baptism
24. Fly	sin, pestilence
25. Foot	humility
26. Fox	the devil, cunning
27. Frog	sin
28. Fruit	spiritual reward
29. Glass	purity
30. Goat	damned soul
31. Grapes	blood of Christ
32. Hair	penitence
33. Hand	Trinity
34. Heart	love and understanding
35. Hog	gluttony
36. Horse	lust
37. Iris	Virgin Mary
38. Ivy	death and immortality
39. Lamb	Christ, Christianity
40. Leopard	sin, the devil
41. Lily	Virgin Mary
42. Lion	strength, majesty
43. Mirror	Virgin Mary
44. Moon and sun	Christ
45. Olive tree	peace

	Symbol	Meaning
46.	Owl	Satan, Prince of Darkness
47.	Ox	Jewish nation
48.	Palm	triumph over death
49.	Peacock	immortality
50.	Phoenix bird (mythical)	eternal life over death
51.	Pomegranate	Christian church
52.	Rat	evil
53.	Raven	devil
54.	Red rose	martyrdom
55.	Scales	justice
56.	Scorpion	evil
57.	Scythe	death
58.	Ship	church of Christ
59.	Skeleton	death
60.	Skull	transitory nature of earth life
61.	Strawberry	righteousness
62.	Sword	martyrdom
63.	Woodpecker	devil

English Art 1500

The time period of English art coincided with the Renaissance in Italy, however it was a style in contrast to that of Italian art. English artists have always been rather indivdual and quite apart from artists on the Continent. In part, this was due to King Henry VIII who suppressed the Church (one of the main patrons of the arts in Italy). There was no classical tradition or strong interest in mythology to which France, Italy and other countries of the Continent were attracted.

A major artist to influence English art was Anthony van Dyck, 1559–1641. Van Dyck went to London on Rubens' advice. Rubens had visited London in 1629 and was taken with the vast beauty of the country. There were few artists of note in London or in all of England at this time. Van Dyck undoubtedly knew this and proceeded to seek his fortune. Van Dyck was a portrait painter who painted the wealthy aristocracy. His portraits followed a standard initiated by Titian and perpetuated by Rubens. English nobility and English government was not concerned with producing a tutelage of native artists. Many of the artists who worked in the early growth of the country were imports such as Van Dyck and Holbein.

William Hogarth was probably the first artist of native extraction with any considerable talent to arrive on the scene. In succession after Hogarth came Joshua Reynolds, Thomas Gainsborough, George Romney, Henry Rayburn, and Thomas Lawrence—all competent portrait artists who made their living by painting portraits. Gainsborough also did landscapes, primarily for his own gratification as there was not a great market in this field. While each of these men was a competent professional portrait painter, none could be considered of the stature of a Rubens, a Titian, or a Michelangelo. Hogarth is probably one of the few artists in the development of English art who had any great ability. Hogarth had much of the same flavor as Pieter Breughel, whose work has the touch of the Gothic, barbaric element in it. There was nothing aristocratic about his work, yet it is human, warm and artistically fine. Hogarth was extremely satirical. In looking at his paintings and engravings, one is never certain of the intention in many respects although there is a fine cutting edge in all of his work. Many of the other artists such as Reynolds and Gainsborough used inferior paints or did not use the paints properly, while Hogarth's paintings remain in excellent condition. The next artist of note was Joseph Mallard William Turner, 1775–1851. Turner was somewhat of a mystery. Apparently he was a highly seclusive man who traveled extensively, and one who loved the landscape of Europe as well as England. He was a Captain Easy type, an adventurer of sorts who carried a paintbrush instead of a rifle. Mr. Turner was a prolific painter. He was England's contribution to the Romantic movement. (Spain had Goya.) Turner is considered to be among the finest painters England has ever produced. He had an ability with line and organization that is all too rare in the world of painting. Turner existed at a time when the Industrial Revolution was picking up steam, the sailing ship was on its way out, railroads were on their way in. Turner was there to paint sailing vessels, tugboats, and the "Edinburgh Express," and the "Fighting Temeraire," in 1838. Turner was unlike the Impressionists who were concerned with light on the surface and other scientific innovations pertaining to light. Turner was involved with history, with man in his environment and he often included man's inventions within the natural environment; he was concerned with atmosphere, storms, night, mist, and with the effects of natural climate in environment. Whereas the Impressionists created their environment based upon their studies of sunlight in nature.

Another English landscape artist who was a contemporary of J. M. W. Turner was John Constable who painted natural effects of atmosphere as illustrated in "The Cornfield" and "The Haywain." Constable painted at the scene. He would do most of his sketching and his organization on location and finish the painting in his studio. Prior to this time landscape painting was done in the studio away from any scene itself. In fact landscape painting was allegorical and often based on Greek or Roman mythology. Constable was very much like the Dutch—he painted everyday life.

Baroque and Rococo Art

The next epic stage in the growth of art in history since the Renaissance is known as the baroque. When we think of the baroque period we think of the seventeenth century. We think of the rococo as the eighteenth century. Baroque art is a type of art that, descriptively speaking, refers to curvilinear movement. The baroque began with Michelangelo in Rome. The baroque period was significant in terms of the scale which was employed. It was an age in which monumental art, or art on a colossal scale, was created, for example, St. Peter's in Rome and Versailles in France to name a few. One of the first churches in Rome to be considered reflective of the baroque style, which in many instances was an architectural style although it extended over into painting and sculpture, was the Church of Jesu. Construction began four years after Michelangelo's death. This church became an example for many churches to follow across the world including churches in America. The baroque style was the style in which the spectacular was commonplace; the scale of everything was greatly increased. Visually, baroque art is also active. It suggests a feeling of motion or action, whether it be in architecture, painting, or sculpture. A characteristic of baroque art

Courtesy, The Cleveland Museum of Art
Purchase from the J. H. Wade Fund

"Portrait of a Lady in a Ruff"
by Frans Hals, Dutch, ca. 1581/85-1666
Oil on Canvas

which permeated music, painting, sculpture, architecture, and theatre of the period was eclecticism. Technical one-up-man-ship or virtuosity became the aim of the baroque period in which colossal scale was the order of the day, whether it be a painting commission, a sculpture, or an architectural plan. Certain artists did evolve from the baroque age, notably the Flemish artist Peter Paul Rubens, the Spanish artist from Greece, El Greco, and the Italian artists Caravaggio, Caracci and Bernini the sculptor.

The most typical types of buildings of Italian baroque were the churches and the palaces. The churches represented religious power and the palaces indicated the power of newly established monarchies. Baroque art was colossal in scale and it had contributors, but it was mainly an art in which greatness from various periods of the past, including Greece, the Renaissance, and Roman art fragments, were borrowed and included in painting, architecture, sculpture, and everyday life. It was felt that if an artist were to take the best ideas from Raphael, Michelangelo, da Vinci, and other great Renaissance and pre-Renaissance masters, the beauty that was the Renaissance could once again be re-created in seventeenth century Europe. Baroque painting is especially characterized by the strong lighting contrasts of chiaroscuro. (It means light and dark, or contrast of). Sometimes as in Dutch art the light comes from natural sources or appears to come through doorways and windows or out-of-doors, but with the work of some artists such as Caravaggio, Velasquez, Rubens—particularly Caravaggio—the light comes from mysterious sources and in Rembrandt's or Ruben's work, the light is also like stage or theatrical lighting, coming from some ethereal source and in many instances illuminating specific features of a painting rather than everything that would normally be bathed in a natural light. El Greco in Spain is particularly noted for his mystical lighting effects as was Tintoretto in Venice. Rubens, the Flemish artist who studied and painted in Rome for years, is probably one of the "par excellent" masters of baroque expression. He was exposed to and came under the influence of Carracci and Caravaggio and, of course, could not miss being influenced by the High Renaissance masters. Rubens' paintings are a composite of all of these men, and yet because of his own creativity, his own

uniqueness and originality, his work stands on its own. A less talented man using the same ideas and media would have perhaps fallen flat on his face. Rubens' talents with media and varieties of expression ranges extensively. He was able to paint great religious masterpieces as well as serene quiet countrysides, such as his "Landscape with Rainbow."

On the other hand, baroque art was an art that tried to reestablish the power of religion. As such it was an emotional art. Idealization of the times was also characterized by baroque artists. Vestiges of Greece, Rome, and ancient empires are often depicted.

Baroque art in the Netherlands was interpreted differently from the highly academic, rigid art of France, Italy and the rest of Europe. For the art of the Netherlands was a Protestant art, and had more to do with the middle class than with the aristocracy. Dutch art was not a church art as such. The commonplace scene became the content of painting. The Dutch artists relied less on the patronage of the church or the aristocracy. Financially, the Dutch artist was more independent and as such was able to choose more of what he wanted to paint. As a result landscape, still life, private residences, and other more commonplace subject matter was predominant, although some classical or literary themes were still painted. The Dutch baroque artist was extremely interested in portraying realism or naturalistic effect (particularly Vermeer and Rembrandt). A new element was introduced into the painting scene—the gallery director or third man, the one who sold paintings. As such, public demand influenced the type of pictures desired.

The baroque art of Dutch artists reflected or mirrored the aims and aspirations of the rising middle class. In the absence of a religious art as such, the artist of this era in the Netherlands portrayed the everyday life of the merchant class. In another sense these artists carried on the meticulous tradition of the Van Eyck style in which detailed precision is portrayed with exactitude. We might say that the baroque style picked up where the final phases of the Renaissance leave off.

Baroque art began in Rome about 1600. It began in the Vatican with several commissions by the Pope which had as its aim, the remaking of Rome into a beautiful religious city. The baroque style however did not confine itself to Rome or to Italy. It spread through-out the world in fact, and one of its main contributors was the Flem-ish artist, Peter Paul Rubens. In France the influence of baroque art was also a signal that France had become the dominant capital of the visual arts. Nicholas Poussin who spent most of his life in Italy is regarded as one of the greatest of the French artists and one of the first to achieve success as a Frenchman in painting.

Rococo: the Curvy Art of Movement

The rococo was a world-wide style and it was the last world style before the contemporary age. Most all of Western civilization was brought under its spell. The rococo was an eclectic compilation of many things that had been discovered in painting, sculpture, ar-chitecture down through the ages wrapped up in a grandiose style known as the rococo. The rococo style sprang directly from the baroque and was indeed a variation of it. One of the best known artists was Antoine Watteau, 1684–1721. Rococo painting might be described as a painting that was subtler, gentler, and more refined than the baroque. It was a more delicate approach to the visual arts. Lighting effects were softer. The textures were handled modestly. The overall feeling tended to be more lyrical. Rococo was a gentle art-style suggesting early summer, soft evenings, gentle breezes, ro-mantic moods and highly sentimentalized feelings. The rococo painter often worked in terms of an entire decorative scheme; that is, his paintings were intended to fit within a broader rococo drama of decorative appeal. Rococo in description is an art of curving, gentle, graceful movements. The rococo style emerged in France about the beginning of the eighteenth century and par-alleled the reign of Louis XV. It held Europe in its sway until the later stages of the eighteenth century. The rococo is manifested in painting, sculpture, and both interior and exterior architecture. We might refer to rococo as a decorative manifestation. It was a com-plete visual and textural ornamentation of surface. We still feel its impact today in tableware, furniture, guns, iron fences, anything that man has had an opportunity to decorate. The rococo as a world style had some powerful influences on Western civilization. The influence of the rococo style was evident in turn of the century art

Courtesy, University Art Collections, Arizona State University
Gift of Oliver B. James

"Le Ventre Legislatif" (Legislators)
by Honore Daumier, French, 1808-1879
Lithograph

in both Europe and America and was known as art nouveau (where the same decorative theme is replayed).

The Art World Turns to France

Nineteenth century art in France, known as the neoclassic style, was notably influenced by painting. The neoclassical style was a result of the French Academy of Art. It was an art derived from the influences of classical Greek and Roman and reinterpreted for the period. Any art that is based on previous art forms is not the same as the original; it comes on much stronger. The neoclassical style was the result of the aftermath of the French Revolution which occurred in the later stages of the eighteenth century (1789). Neoclassicism or the neoclassic art of France became the most suitable propaganda subject for the new government of France.

One of the first artists to be part of this neoclassic ideal was Jacques-Louis David, 1748–1825, a painter who had appeal both for the educated and the lower class. Many of his paintings, although completed during the rococo period, had a certain simplicity and quiet noble style that apparently wore well with the ruling government. He ultimately became the spokesman for the Academy. He painted several paintings in a neoclassical style using as subject matter Greek stories and epics such as the "Oath of Horatii," "Andromache Mourning the Death of Hector," "The Lictors Bringing Back to Brutus the Bodies of his Sons," and "Paris and Helen." A more or less vicarious approach—someone painting Greek mythology without having a Greek background. It might be compared to someone of our contemporary era painting subjects in a Renaissance vein. David's work was in complete contrast to Boucher or Fragonard who were strictly rococo; his style was more suitable to the greatness of the new regime with its nobility, power, and circumstances. It also should be noted that the classical revival was spurred by excavations of ancient ruins, which had gotten underway. Certain events revived the interest in classical art; modern excavations had begun at ancient city sites such as Pompeii and Herculaneum. Also some books had been printed; one in particular, contained much information about Athens and Greece that for Western Europeans had been little known up to this time. The publication of this book as well as Winckelmann's *History of the Art of Ancient Times* resulted in Lord Elgin of England shipping what remained of the sculpture on the Parthenon and sailing it back aboard ship to the British Museum. These were the events that helped to shape and form the Academy of France and which also influenced David in his painting style.

In Spain, Francisco Goya was a contemporary of David. Goya was a study in contrast to David who was always correct in technique, subject matter and precise detail, bloodless, with cold emotion, while Goya painted compassionately the horrors and tragedies of war. His etching series titled "The Disasters of War" illustrate this point well. Also his famous painting "Execution of the 3rd of May, 1808" reveal the carnage that is part of war. The painting depicts the sacking of a Spanish town by the French conquering army led by Napoleon. Goya's work is rather barbaric and has strong echoes of Gothic undertones. In contrast, David borrowed greatly from the Chiaroscuro discoveries made by Caravaggio.

The Empire of Napoleon lasted a short ten years after which the French Academy was re-established by David's star pupil, Jean-Auguste Dominique Ingres. Ingres was also a politician and a highly sagacious individual who always seemed to be in the right place at the right time, saying the right thing. Ingres was a better drawer than David, although most artists would probably decline to be in a contest with either of these two artists as their opponents. The neo-classical period extended from approximately 1775 to 1830 while romanticism, a more romantic interpretation, developed about mid-nineteenth century.

The Romantic Movement

The main aspects of the romantic movement began about 1830 in Paris. In 1827, Delacroix had exhibited his "Death of Sardanapolus," which now hangs in the Louvre, Paris. In viewing romantic art, especially that presented to us by Delacroix, we see an art of idealization combined with deep emotions. Color helps to establish the mood in romantic art. Delacroix painted most of his works from literary sources, including Shakespeare, Byron and Goethe. He was intrigued by Goethe's "Faust" and did many lithographs and paintings on various aspects of the "Faust" theme. Rubens was his hero as well as Rembrandt, for he was also concerned with dramatic lighting in order to heighten the effects he sought to achieve on canvas. Another one of his famous paintings was "Dante and Vergil in Hell," 1822; it is also in the Louvre, Paris. These are the paintings that inspire young students for they are handsomely painted, brilliantly executed and their story is readily identifiable today.

The romantic style pervaded all of French life. It might be described as a coming of age for man in which contemporary events needed contemporary expression and thinking. The romantic period was also a period in which exotic subject matter was interpreted—Turkish baths, Arabian knights, Oriental influences—all contributed to the fanciful, imaginary world of the romantic.

The beauty of the art of the past is that each era produced a number of artists who have been able to make a mark on the history of their time and we who study this work can bring it back to life through our own vicarious experience with it.

The Movement toward Impressionism

Parallel to romanticism, the realistic and impressionistic style of art began about 1850 in Paris, the world's new art capital. A number of artists who were no longer interested in classical beauty, romantic phantasy, or allegorical heroes were emerging into the limelight. They pursued their subject as they found it, much in the manner of the artists of the Low Countries, Brueghel, in particular. Such artists as Daumier, Courbet, and Manet, to mention a few, no longer portrayed historical or exotic subject matter. These artists were concerned with social commentary in a sense. Daumier tried to show ugliness and the depressing qualities of the poor. Another artist involved in social commentaries was Theodore Gericault whose famous picture "The Raft of the Medusa" created extreme controversy when exhibited for the first time in the Salon of 1819. His subject matter was an actual disaster of a shipwreck at sea in

Courtesy of The Art Institute of Chicago
Potter Palmer Collection

"Little Circus Girls"
by Auguste Renoir, 1879

which some sailors did survive to tell of their horrifying experience with starvation, cannibalism, injury and insanity. The trend in the work of these artists was away from middle class life, aristocratic life or classical life; it was gradually moving toward nature, without any message involved. Claude Monet exhibited a picture titled "Impression: Sunrise." The term was picked up and coined as such. Events in science at this time also would lead us to believe that artists were aware of recent discoveries such as the daguerrotype, an early photographic process. The physicist, Helmholtz, discovered the prismatic effects of light, while several scientists pursued the effects of colors in the spectrum. It seems only natural that the artist would become involved in this type of experience and more than likely pursued visual effects of color and light in their paintings. They reasoned that harsh lines do not exist in nature and that shadows are soft and based on colors from the objects from which they were derived. Impressionism then, is concerned with impressions, not concrete hardedge effects, but more in the nature of what we observe in nature. Many impressionist artists such as Manet, Monet, Renoir, and Seurat were particularly involved with the effects of placing one hue next to another hue with the eye doing the mixing. Up to this time the artist mixed his hue and applied it to the canvas, but artists such as Seurat and others such as Monet would put a color next to another color with their brush and these colors would fuse at a distance much in the same way that the colors would if mixed on a palette previous to their application on the canvas. This system developed by Seurat for applying color is referred to as pointillism.

Impressionism was also a style of painting where the artist moved his canvas to the out-of-doors. Prior to this time he worked in his studio for the most part or indoors and derived his subject matter from interior scenes. Impressionism was an easy kind of art. It was an art without pomp and circumstance. It was probably an art in which the artist was concerned with pictorial space and the effect of such space in regard to the manipulation of pigment. Impressionistic painters selected the city and the country as their subject: cabarets, street scenes, lily ponds, train stations. No subject was too ordinary for their purpose. If one considers that the im-

Courtesy of The Art Institute of Chicago
The Kate L. Brewster Bequest

"May Milton"
by Henri de Toulouse-Lautrec
Oil on Cardboard

pressionists were involved with the effects of light on surfaces, then any subject, any surface, becomes interesting, because they were not painting epics, or monumental creations depicting the greatness of Greece or Italy. They were involved with the problems of *painting* per se. They were involved in *how* one can look at a subject rather than simply what the subject was. It was not so much water or a lake but the visual atmosphere of water when sunlight plays across its surface. Impressionism as such lasted probably 15 to 20 years, although its effects are still felt today and American artists of the recent past have been willing pupils of such French masters, particularly Childe Hassam.

An artist who was able to take the best of impressionism and extend it to new frontiers was Paul Cezanne. He began his career in the 1870's but soon discovered that impressionism had certain limitations. He became interested in artistic considerations other than application of light on a surface. He is often referred to as the father of modern art. Cezanne tells us that painting is not only a visual phenomenon, but also an intellectual adventure and that color could be a means not only of describing light, but of describ-

ing masses and forms. He was a mixer of colors; he did not apply the color merely to the surface, but mixed it first on his palette and then applied it, sometimes as a hue alone, sometimes as a form to suggest a mass. Cezanne composed his pictures and synthesized them to form a new whole. He often worked from the actual subject, most of which were from his own daily experiences. He painted figures, the landscape, still life. One has a feeling that it is not so important what he painted but how he painted it and what he suggested through his interpretation of what he saw. He was probably one of the first to see that a line or a color could be an esthetic entity in itself even though he still retained some essence of its pictorial content. Contemporary innovators of painting such as Hans Hoffmann would take this philosophy the entire distance and make the line an esthetic entity in itself devoid of content.

The following chronological check sheet lists most of the great masters of art of all time, beginning with the early Renaissance. The artist, his life span, and one or more examples of his significant works is included. This list is intended as a beginning spur to further investigation.

A Checksheet of the Great Masters (Old and Modern)

Who They Are and Some of Their Masterpieces

Artists of the Early Renaissance in Italy		*Great Art Works*
Giovanni Cimabue	1240–1302	Madonna Enthroned
Duccio di Buoninsegna	1255–1319	Pieta
Giotto di Bondone	1266–1336	Joachim Returning to the Sheepfold
		Pieta
		Portrait of Dante
		Madonna Enthroned
		Death of St. Francis
		Last Judgment
Niccolo Pisano	1205–1278	Marble Pulpit at Baptistry, Pisa
North of the Alps in Flanders		
Jan Van Eyck	1380–1441	Ghent Altarpiece
		Madonna with Chancellor Rolin
		Giovanni Arnolfini and His Wife
Hans Memling	1433–1494	The Annunciation
Hieronymus Bosch	1462–1516	The Garden of Delights

Artists of the High Renaissance in Italy

Masaccio	1401–1428	Expulsion from the Garden
		Tribute Money
Filippo Lippi	1406–1469	Nativity
Piero della Francesca	1416–1492	Resurrection
Antonio Pollaiuolo	1429–1498	Battle of Ten Nude Men
		Hercules Strangling Antaeus
Sandro Botticelli	1444–1510	Adoration of the Magi
		Birth of Venus
		Venus and Mars
Domenico Ghirlandaio	1449–1510	Adoration of the Shepherds
Leonardo da Vinci	1452–1519	Last Supper
		Mona Lisa
		Madonna of the Rocks
Lorenzo Ghiberti	1378–1455	Gates of Paradise (church doors, Florence, Italy)
Donatello	1386–1466	Monument of Gattamelatta
		David
		Prophet

Early Renaissance in Italy, Fifteenth Century   *Great Art Works*

Donatello	1386–1466	The Annunciation
		Feast of Herod
		Gattamelatta
		David
Masaccio	1401–1428	Expulsion of Adam and Eve from the Garden of Eden
		Tribute Money
		Madonna Enthroned
		Expulsion from Paradise
Fra Angelico	1387–1455	Annunciation
		Deposition from the Cross
Botticelli	1444–1510	Birth of Venus
		Allegory of Spring
		Mystical Nativity
		Crucifixion
Filippo Lippi	1406–1469	
Antonio Pollaiuolo	1429–1498	Hercules and the Hydra
		Battle of Ten Naked Men

High Renaissance

Leon Battista Alberti	1404–1472	Designed Sant'Andrea, Mantua
Leonardo da Vinci	1452–1519	Madonna of the Rocks
		Last Supper
		Mona Lisa

Raphael	1483–1520	Dream of a Knight
		Marriage of the Virgin
		Colonna altarpiece
		School of Athens
		Disputa
Michelangelo Buonarrotti	1475–1564	Battle of the Centaurs
		Pieta sculptures
		David
		Holy Family
		Sistine chapel ceiling
		Last Judgment

Artists of the High Renaissance in Italy

Luca della Robbia	1400–1482	Madonna and Angels
Michelangelo Buonarroti	1475–1564	Sistine Chapel
		David
		Moses
		Pieta
Andrea del Verrocchio	1435–1488	Colleoni Equestrian Statue
Benvenuto Cellini	1500–1571	The Saltcellar of Francis I
Raphael Sanzio	1483–1520	School of Athens
		Julius II

High Renaissance in Venice

Rubens	1577–1640	Garden of Love
		Crucifixion
		Lion Hunt
		Descent from the Cross
		Landscape with Rainbow
Titian	1477–1576	Rape of Europa
		Sacred and Profane Love
		Bacchus and Ariadne
Tintoretto	1518–1594	Presentation of the Virgin
		Miracle of Saint Mark
		The Last Supper
Veronese	1528–1588	Marriage at Cana
Giovanni Bellini	1430–1516	Madonna and Child
Giorgione	1475–1510	The Sleeping Venus

Northern Artists of the High Renaissance

Hieronymus Bosch	1450–1516	Temptation of Saint Anthony
		Christ before Pilate
		Garden of Delights
		Prodigal Son

Albrecht Durer	1471–1528	Four Horsemen of the Apocalypse
Pieter Brueghel	1528–1569	Peasant Dance
		Peasant Wedding
		Parable of the Birds' Nest
		Wedding Dance
		Hunters in the Snow
		The Corn Harvest
Mathias Grunewald	1485–1528	Isenheim altarpiece

Baroque Artists

Giovanni Bellini	1430–1516	St. Francis in Ecstasy
Titian	1490–1576	Sacred and Profane Love
		Bacchus and Ariadne
		Assumption of the Virgin
		Venus and the Organ Player
Giorgione	1478–1510	Tempest
		Sleeping Venus
Jacopo Tinoretto	1518–1594	Last Supper
Paolo Veronese	1528–1588	Marriage at Cana
El Greco	1541–1614	Burial of Count Orgaz
		Expulsion from the Temple
		View of Toledo
Michelangelo da Caravaggio	1573–1610	Conversion of St. Paul
		Calling of St. Matthew
		Death of the Virgin

Highlights of the Baroque in Italy

Annibale Carracci	1560–1609	Virgin Mourning over the Dead Christ
		Ceiling of Farnese Palace
Caravaggio	1573–1610	The Bacchus
		The Calling of St. Matthew
		The Death of the Virgin

Highlights of the Baroque in Flanders

Peter Paul Rubens	1577–1640	Garden of Love
		Crucifixion
		Lion Hunt
		Descent from the Cross
		Landscape with Rainbow

Highlights of the Baroque in Holland

| Frans Hals | 1580–1666 | Laughing Cavalier |
| | | Malle Babbe |

Rembrandt van Rijn	1606–1669	Man with the Golden Helmet
		Nightwatch
		Dr. Tulp's Anatomy Lesson
Jakob van Ruisdael	1628–1682	The Jewish Graveyard
Jan Steen	1629–1679	
Pieter de Hooch	1629–1683	Mother and Child
Jan Vermeer	1632–1675	View of Delft
		Artist in his Studio
		The Letter
		Young Woman with Water Jug
		Officer and Laughing Girl

Highlights of the Baroque in France

Nicolas Poussin	1593–1665	Cephalus and Aurora
		Rape of the Sabine Women

Artists of the Rococo Period

Antoine Watteau	1684–1721	Les Plaisirs du Bal
Francois Boucher	1703–1770	The Toilet of Venus
J.B.S. Chardin	1699–1779	Bowl of Plums
		Boy Spinning Top
		Back from the Market
Jean Honore Fragonard	1732–1806	The Swing
		Bathers
		The Meeting

Artists of the Neoclassic Period in France

Jacques Louis David	1748–1825	Oath of the Horatii
		Andromache Mourning the Death of Hector
		Death of Marat
		Battle of the Romans and the Sabines
Jean A.D. Inges	1780–1867	The Turkish Bath
		Apotheosis of Homer
		Louis Bertin
		Odalisque

Artists of the Romantic Period

Francisco Goya	1746–1828	Executions of the Third of May
		Family of Charles IV
Theodore Gericault	1791–1824	Raft of the Medusa
		The Madman
Eugene Delacroix	1798–1863	Liberty Leading the People
		Dante and Vergil in Hell
		Death of Sardanapalus

| Honore Daumier | 1808–1879 | Third Class Carriage |
| Francois Millet | 1814–1875 | The Sower |

English Artists Worth Knowing

William Hogarth	1697–1764	The Rake's Progress
		The Harlot's Progress
		The Four Stages of Cruelty
J.M.W. Turner	1775–1851	The Slave Ship
		Fighting Temeraire
John Constable	1776–1837	The Haywain
		Corn Field
William Blake	1757–1827	The Simoniac Pope
Joshua Reynolds°	1723–1792	
Thomas Gainsborough°	1727–1788	
George Romney°	1734–1802	
Henry Raeburn°	1756–1823	
Thomas Laurence°	1769–1830	

Imports to London

| Hans Holbein° | 1497–1543 | Henry VIII |
| Anthony van Dyck° | 1599–1641 | |

Nineteenth Century Artists of France

Gustave Courbet	1819–1877	The Artist's Studio
		The Stone Breakers
Edouard Manet	1832–1883	The Fifer
Edgar Degas	1834–1917	Prima Ballerina
Camille Corot	1796–1875	The Bridge at Mantes
Paul Cezanne	1839–1906	The Card Players
Claude Monet	1840–1926	Water Lilies
		The River
Pierre Auguste Renoir	1841–1919	Luncheon of the Boating Party
Paul Gauguin	1848–1903	Yellow Christ
Vincent Van Gogh	1853–1890	Starry Night
Georges Seurat	1859–1891	Sunday Afternoon on the Island of the Grande Jatte
		Side Show
Henri de Toulouse-Lautrec	1864–1901	At the Moulin Rouge

European Painters Worth Knowing

| Georges Braque | 1882–1963 | Cubistic Still Lifes |
| Pablo Picasso | 1881– | **Girl Before a Mirror** |

° Painters of nobility and class

Juan Gris	1887–1927	Cubism
Fernand Leger	1881–1955	The City, Three Women
Marcel Duchamp	1887–	Nude Descending a Staircase
Henri Matisse	1869–1954	Roumanian Blouse
		Blue Window
Andre Derain		Head of a Girl
Maurice de Vlaminck		Houses and Trees
Raoul Dufy		The Studio
Georges Roualt	1871–1958	The Judges
Amadeo Modigliani	1884–1920	Reclining Nude

Non-Objective Painting

Wassily Kandinsky	1886–1944	Improvisation No. 30
Kasimer Malevich	1878–1935	White on White
Piet Mondrian	1872–1944	Broadway Boogie-Woogie
Ben Nicholson	1894–	Painted Relief

Neo-Expressionism

Fritz Scholder	1937-
Earl Linderman	1931-

Pop Art

Wayne Thiebaud	Pies
Jasper Johns	Flags
Robert Rauschenberg	Canyon
Andy Warhol	Campbell Soup
Roy Lichtenstein	Comic Strip Art

Expressionism

Georges Roualt	1871–1958	The Judges
Vincent Van Gogh	1839–1890	Starry Night
Edvard Munch	1863–1944	The Scream
James Ensor	1860–1949	Intrigue
Oskar Kokoschka	1886–	Self-Portrait, 1917
Lyonel Feininger	1871–1956	Church
Max Beckman	1884–1950	Self-Portrait, 1927
Amadeo Modigliani	1884–1920	Reclining Nude

Surrealism

Henri Rousseau	1840–1910	The Dream
Odilon Redon	1840–1916	The Kiss
Giorgio de Chirico	1888–	Infinite Languor
Marc Chagall	1887–	I and the Village

Salvador Dali	1904–	Persistence of Memory
Max Ernst	1891–	The Red Cow
Marcel Duchamp	1887–	Nude Descending a Staircase
Kurt Schwitters	1887–1948	Collage
Jean Hans Arp	1888–	Mountain, Table, Anchors, Navel
Paul Klee	1879–1940	Senecio
Joan Miro	1893–	Flight of the Bird over the Plain III
Rene Magritte		Mental Calculus

Painters of Young America

John Singleton Copley	1738–1815	Watson and the Shark
Charles W. Peale	1741–1827	Exhuming the Mastodon
Benjamin West	1738–1820	Death of General Wolfe
Gilbert Stuart	1755–1828	George Washington
Edward Hicks	1780–1849	The Peaceable Kingdom
Washington Allston	1779–1843	Elijah in the Desert
Thomas Cole	1801–1848	Expulsion from the Garden of Eden
Albert Bierstadt	1830–1902	Merced River, Yosemite Valley
Samuel F. B. Morse	1791–1872	The Dying Hercules
Albert Pinkham Ryder	1847–1917	The Race Track
John James Audubon	1785–1851	Birds
George Bingham	1811–1879	Fur Traders on the Missouri
John Singer Sargent	1856–1925	The Daughters of Edward D. Boit
Winslow Homer	1836–1910	Gulf Stream
		Eight Bells
Frederick Remington	1861–1909	
Thomas Eakins	1844–1916	Max Schmidt in a Single Scull
		The Gross Clinic
James McNeill Whistler	1834–1903	Arrangement in Black and Gray

Sculptors Worth Learning About

Constantin Brancusi	1876–1957	Bird in Space
Ernst Barlach	1870–1938	Expressionist Sculpture
Jean Arp	1887–	Two Heads
Henry Moore	1898–	Reclining Figure
Alberto Giacometti	1901–1966	The Palace at 4 A. M.
Wilhelm Lehmbruck	1881–1919	Kneeling Youth
Jacob Epstein	1880–1959	
Alexander Archipenko	1887–1964	
Richard Lippold	1915–	Variation Number 7: Full Moon
Aristide Maillol	1861–1944	The Mediterrean
Alexander Calder	1898–1977	Mobiles
Jacques Lipchitz	1891–	Girl With a Braid
John Battenburg		Bronze Sculptures

Ivan Mestrovich		Atlantide
Auguste Rodin	1840–1917	The Kiss
John Chamberlain		Sculpted Car Parts
Frank Gallo		Bikini Girl
Mark Di Suvero		Chains and Beams
Marisol		Painted Wood
Ed Keinholz		Barney's Beanery

References

Renaissance to Neoclassic

CARLI, ENZO, *Duccio*, Milano: Martello, n.d.

DE WALD, ERNEST, *Italian Painting, 1200–1600*, London: Phaidon, 1957.

DUBY, GEORGES, *Foundations of a New Humanism, 1280–1440*, Geneva: Skira, 1966.

GNUDI, CESARE, *Giotto*, Milano: Martello, 1955.

PECCAGNINI, GIOVANNI, *Simone Martini*, Milano: Martello, 1957.

POPE-HENNESSY, JOHN, *Italian Gothic Sculpture*, New York: Phaidon, 1955.

WHITE, JOHN, *Art and Architecture in Italy, 1250–1400*, Pelican History of Art, 1966.

The Early Renaissance in Italy (1400–1500)

BERENSON, BERNARD, *The Italian Painters of the Renaissance*, New York: Phaidon, 1952.

BERENSON, BERNARD, *Italian Painters of the Renaissance*, Venetian School II, New York: Phaidon, 1957.

BERTI, LUCIANO, *Masaccio*, Pennsylvania State University Press, 1967.

CASTELFRANCO, GIORGIO, *Donatello*, New York: Reynal and Co., 1967.

CHASTEL, ANDRE, *Botticelli*, New York: New York Graphic Society, 1958.

CLARK, KENNETH, *Piero della Francesca*, London: Phaidon, 1951.

GOULD, CECIL, *An Introduction to Italian Renaissance Painting*, London: Phaidon, 1957.

JANSEN, H. W., *The Sculpture of Donatello*, 2 vols., Princeton: Princeton University Press, 1957.

KRAUTHEIMER, RICHARD, *Lorenzo Ghiberti*, Princeton: Princeton University Press, 1956.

ORTOLANI, SERGIO, *Il Pollaiuolo*, Milano: Ulrico Hoepli, n.d.

PALLUCCHINI, RODOLFO, *Giovanni Bellini*, Milano: Martello, 1959.

POPE-HENNESSY, JOHN, *Italian Renaissance Sculpture*, New York: Phaidon, 1957.

SALMI, MARIO, *Luca Signorelli*, Novaro: Istituto Geografico Agostino, 1956.

SEYMOUR, CHARLES, JR., *Sculpture in Italy, 1400–1500*, Pelican History of Art, 1966.

TIETZE-CONRAT, E., *Mantegna*, London: Phaidon, 1955.

The High Renaissance in Italy (1500–1520)

POPE-HENNESSY, JOHN, *Italian High Renaissance and Baroque Sculpture*, New York: Phaidon, 1963.

SALMI, MARIO (Forward), *The Complete Work of Michelangelo*, New York: Reynal and Co., 1965.

WEINBERGER, MARTIN, *Michelangelo, the Sculptor*, 2 vols., New York: Columbia University Press, 1967.

CLARK, KENNETH, *Leonardo da Vinci*, Cambridge: Harvard University Press, 1961.

FISCHEL, OSKAR, *Raphael*, 2 vols., London: Kegan Paul, 1948.

FREEDBERG, SYDNEY, *Andrea del Sarto*, 2 vols., Cambridge: Harvard University Press, 1963.

FREEDBERG, SYDNEY, *Painting of the High Renaissance in Rome and Florence*, 2 vols., Cambridge: Harvard University Press, 1961.

GOLDSCHEIDER, LUDWIG, *Leonardo da Vinci*, London: Phaidon, 1954.

MARIANI, VALERIO, *Michelangelo, the Painter*, Milano: Arti Grafiche Ricordi, 1964.

VENTURI, LIONELLO, *The Sixteenth Century, from Leonardo to El Greco*, New York: Skira, 1956.

WOLFFLIN, HEINRICH, *Classic Art: the Great Masters of the Italian Renaissance*, New York: Phaidon, 1959.

Mannerism and Venetian School of Sixteenth Century

BRIGANTI, GIULIANO, *Italian Mannerism*, London: Thames and Hudson, 1962.

BOUSQUET, JACQUES, *Mannerism, the Painting and Style of the Late Renaissance*, New York: Braziller, 1964.

FREEDBERG, SYDNEY, *Parmigianino*, Cambridge: Harvard University Press, 1960.

MORASSI, ANTONIO, *Titian*, New York: New York Graphic Society, 1964.

ORLIAC, ANTIONE, *Veronese*, New York: Hyperion Press, 1940.

POPHAM, A. E., *Correggio's Drawings*, London: Oxford University Press, 1957.

QUINTAVELLE, AUGUSTE, *Correggio: the Frescoes in San Giovanni Evangelista in Parma*, New York: Abrams, n.d.

RICCI, CORRADO, *Correggio*, New York and London: Frederick Warne, 1930.

TIETZE, HANS, *Tintoretto: the Paintings and Drawings*, London: Phaidon, 1948.

TIETZE, HANS, *Titian: Paintings and Drawings*, Vienna: Phaidon, 1937.

WURTENBERGER, FRANZSEPP, *Mannerism*, New York: Holt, Rinehart & Winston, 1963.

Early Netherlandish Painting (1400–1500)

BALDASS, LUDWIG, *Jan van Eyck*, New York: Phaidon, 1952.

BALDASS, LUDWIG, *Hieronymus Bosch*, New York: Abrams, 1960.

BENESCH, OTTO, *The Art of the Renaissance in Northern Europe*, Cambridge: Harvard University Press, 1945.

DE TOLNAY, CHARLES, *Hieronymus Bosch*, New York: Reynal and Co., 1966.

FRIEDLANDER, MAX, *From Van Eyck to Bruegel*, London: Phaidon, 1956.

LASSAIGNE, JACQUES, *Flemish Painting, the Century of Van Eyck*, Geneva: Skira, 1957.

LASSAIGNE, JACQUES and ARGAN, GIULIO, *The Fifteenth Century from Van Eyck to Botticelli*, Geneva: Skira, 1955.

PANOFSKY, ERWIN, *Early Netherlandish Painting*, 2 vols., Cambridge: Harvard University Press, 1958.

TOVELL, RUTH, *Rogier van der Weyden*, Toronto: Burns and MacEachern, 1955.

The Renaissance in the North

GANZ, PAUL, *The Paintings of Hans Holbein*, New York: Phaidon, 1950.

GROSSMAN, F., *Bruegel, the Paintings*, London: Phaidon, 1966.

MUNZ, LUDWIG, *Bruegel, the Drawings*, London: Phaidon, 1961.

PANOFSKY, ERWIN, *Life and Work of Albrecht Durer*, Princeton: Princeton University Press, 1955.

PEVSNER, NIKOLAUS and MEIER, MICHAEL, *Grunewald*, New York: Abrams, 1958.

Baroque Art (1600–1700)

BAZIN, G., *Baroque and Rococo*, London: Thames and Hudson, 1964.

GOMBRICH, E., *Meditations on a Hobby Horse*, London: Phaidon, 1963.

KITSON, MICHAEL, *The Age of Baroque*, New York: McGraw-Hill, 1966.

LEES-MILNE, J., *Baroque Europe*, London: Batsford, 1962.

STECH, VACLAV, *Baroque Sculpture*, London: Spring Books, 1959.

Baroque in Italy

BALDINUCCI, FILIPPO, *The Life of Bernini*, Pennsylvania State University Press, 1966.

BLUNT, ANTHONY and COOKE, HEREWARD, *The Roman Drawings of the XVII and XVIII Centuries at Windsor Castle*, London: Phaidon, 1960.

DE LOGU, GIUSEPPE, *Caravaggio*, New York: Abrams, 1965.

FRIEDLANDER, WALTER, *Caravaggio Studies*, Princeton: Princeton University Press, 1955.

HIBBARD, HOWARD, *Bernini*, Baltimore: Penguin Books, 1966.

LEES-MILNE, *Baroque in Italy*, London: Batsford, 1949.

POPE-HENNESSY, JOHN, *Italy High Renaissance and Baroque Sculpture*, London: Phaidon, 1963.

TAPIE, VICTOR L., *The Age of Grandeur*, New York: Praeger, 1960.

WATERHOUSE, E. K., *Italian Baroque Painting*, London: Phaidon, 1962.

WITTKOWER, RUDOLF, *Art and Architecture in Italy, 1600–1750*, 2nd rev. ed., Pelican History of Art, 1966.

WITTKOWER, RUDOLF, *Drawings of the Carracci at Windsor Castle*, London: Phaidon, 1952.

WITTKOWER, RUDOLF, *Gian Lorenzo Bernini*, 2nd ed., London: Phaidon, 1966.

Baroque in Holland

BERGSTROM, INGVAR, *Dutch Still Life Painting*, New York: P. Yoseloff, 1956.

BREDIUS, A., ed., *The Paintings of Rembrandt*, London: Phaidon, n.d.

GOLDSCHEIDER, L., *Vermeer*, London: Phaidon, 1958.

HECKSCHER, WILLIAM, *Rembrandt's Anatomy Lesson of Dr. Tulp*, New York: New York University Press, 1958.

ROSENBERG, J. and SLIVE, SEYMOUR, *Dutch Art and Architecture 1600–1800*, Pelican History of Art, 1966.

SLIVE, SEYMOUR (introd.), *Frans Hals Exhibition*, Haarlem: Frans Hals Museum, 1962.

TRIVAS, NUMA S., *The Paintings of Frans Hals*, New York: Oxford University Press, 1942.

VRIES, A. B. DE, *Jan Vermeer van Delft*, London: B. T. Batsford, 1948.

Baroque in Belgium

RUBENS, PETER PAUL, *The Letters of Peter Paul Rubens*, Cambridge: Harvard University Press, 1955.

Baroque in France

BLUNT, ANTHONY, *Art and Architecture in France, 1500–1700*, 2nd ed., Pelican History of Art, 1958.

BLUNT, ANTHONY, *Nicolas Poussin*, London: Phaidon, 1966.

CRELLY, W., *Simon Vouet*, New Haven: Yale University Press, 1963.

FRIEDLANDER, WALTER, *Nicolas Poussin*, New York: Abrams, 1965.

Baroque in Spain

KUBLER, GEORGE and SORIA, MARTIN, *Baroque Art and Architecture in Spain and Latin America*, Pelican History of Art, 1959.

LEES-MILNE, J., *Baroque in Spain and Portugal*, London: Batsford, 1960.

TAPIER, ELIZABETH, *Velasquez*, New York: Hispanic Society of America, 1948.

Baroque in England

WATERHOUSE, E. K., *Painting in Britain, 1530–1830*, London: Pelican History of Art, 1953.

WHINNEY, M. D., *English Sculpture, 1530–1830*, Pelican History of Art, 1958.

WHINNEY, M. D. and MILLAR, O., *English Art, 1623–1714*, Oxford, 1957.

The Eighteenth Century (Rococo to Neoclassic 1700–1760)

ANTAL, FREDERICK, *Classicism and Romanticism*, New York: Basic Books, Inc., 1966.

BOURKE, JOHN, *Baroque Churches of Central Europe*, London, 1958.

FOSCA, FRANCOIS, *The Eighteenth Century from Watteau to Tiepolo*, Skira, 1952.

HAWLEY, HENRY, *Neo-Classicism, Style and Motif*, Cleveland: Cleveland Museum of Art, 1964.

KIMBALL, FISKE, *The Creation of the Rococo*, Norton, 1963.

LEVEY, MICHAEL, *Painting in the 18th Century*, London: Phaidon, 1959.

LEVEY, MICHAEL, *Rococo to Revolution, Major Trends in Eighteenth Century Painting*, New York: Praeger, 1966.

MORASSI, ANTONIO, *The Paintings of Giambattista Tiepolo*, London: Phaidon, 1955.

SCHONBERGER, ARNO, *The Rococo Age*, New York: McGraw-Hill, 1960.

WATERHOUSE, ELLIS, *Gainsborough*, London: Edward Hulton, 1958.

WATERHOUSE, ELLIS, *Reynolds*, London: Kegan Paul, 1941.

WILDENSTEIN, GEORGES, *Chardin*, Zurich: Manesse, 1963.

WILDENSTEIN, GEORGES, *The Paintings of Fragonard*, London: Phaidon, 1960.

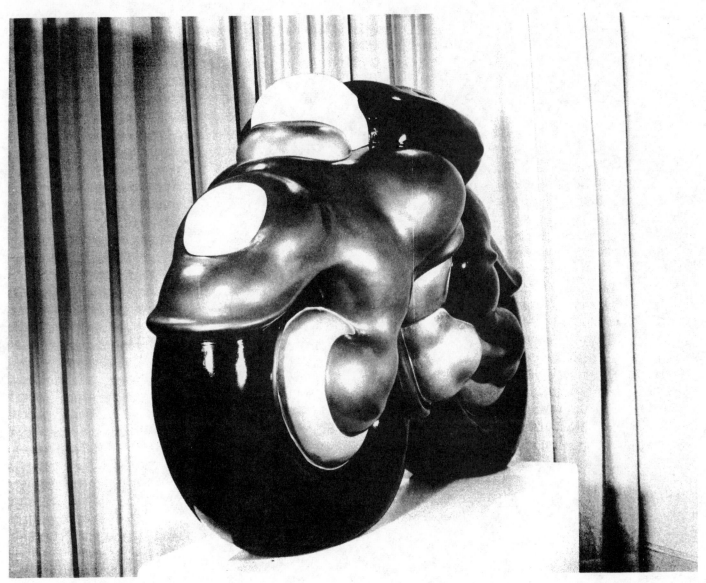

Courtesy, Graham Gallery, New York

"Cyclist"
by Luis Jimines, 1969
Fiberglass and Epoxy

Chapter 9

Art should be an intimate part of our communal life, as it was in Ancient Greece, as it was in the Middle Ages; and it should enter our lives at their formative stage, as a natural function of human relationships, as the language of form and color, as universal and as innocent as the language of words.

HERBERT READ,
The Grass Roots of Art,
New York: Meridian, 1961, Chapter V

Pursuing Art Skills through Search and Practice

Teaching Studio Art and Skills

Today's art emphasizes ideas and skills. Artists, while mindful of values derived from past traditions are willing and eager to try new things. They are pushing boundaries in directions that have never before been tapped. The entire theme of the creation of an art work today stresses emphasis upon the uniqueness of an idea as well as the technical carry-through to complete the work. The artist breaks with traditional ways of working although he acknowledges tradition. As in the outer world in general, innovation has become an important aspect of the aspiring life. In science and technology change is often extremely super-rapid, so rapid in fact that most of us barely digest the changes. Traditional attitudes, assumptions, and styles of working have been challenged so that the artist is in a searching period of change and continual flux. Even the materials are of the space age—plastics, resins, steel, aluminum—and the exciting thing about it all is that the secondary art teacher can be right smack in the middle of the action!

The important thing for the art teacher to keep in mind is that at the foundational base of artistic growth is the feeling for art itself in terms of what it can do for the student as individual. Art teachers need to encourage in their students the growth of artistic vision. Artistic vision means learning to see beyond the ordinary ways of seeing. It means seeing the world with a new eye, a way of seeing that may never have happened to an individual before, but an adventure once embarked upon that can never be forgotten. The greater the degree of visual sensitivity the greater the degree of opportunities for detecting aesthetic possibilities. Man is unique among the animals for he can reason, invent, imagine, explore and reshape the world and *recreate entirely new worlds never seen before.* The artist primarily is an experimenter, a person who is not afraid of changes, in fact seeks new possibilities through his vision and thinking. In teaching students to be visually sensitive, we can change their entire attitude toward art, and to the manner in which they comprehend the visual world. We can open doorways that could never be opened without the experience of art.

"Good Time Charley"
by Jasper Johns, 1961
Encaustic, Canvas with Objects

Courtesy, Leo Castelli Gallery, New York

Developing Art Skills Is Part of Learning about Art

Even though most students in art may never choose some phase of art as a career, it is essential to the process of understanding and enjoying art that students engage in the making of it. Art works will never be sensitively understood by remaining a mere spectator. Deep involvement, and this necessitates making, is necessary to opening up one's range of comprehension to what art can be. Art skills reveal the high degree of perfection necessary to construct an art work. It is not a simple process of easily administering pigment to a canvas, or manipulating a few lines to achieve a high quality product. Indeed, as in all experiences of value, there will be frustration, heartache, despair, as well as the joy experienced in seeing improvement in one's own efforts.

In art, it should be remembered there can be no compromise. The art product must represent the complete and total effort of the student in his involvement, his persistence and dedication to the task that he has elected to forge, in order to take his art work in process toward a hopefully successful conclusion. It would be erroneous to think that all art works produced will turn out successfully. Even the best known artists of the world do not achieve success each time. In fact, many artists feel that if they achieve one good work out of ten completed, a measure of success has been possible. Success, of course, is relative to one's own goals. Being able to sense accomplishment from one work to the next can become the substance of artistic growth. Most of us will agree that every person varies in his inherited capacity to create art works. Some of us may have greater artistic talents, but this is no different than any other field. What is important is that we engage in the processes of art practice, regardless of innate talent or gifts.

Teaching Art Media

In teaching art media to students in a studio-type experience it might be of value to open up thinking in the beginning by giving them a broad base of various types of art experiences, such as procedures in discovering different tools for drawing. The teacher

Courtesy of The Art Institute of Chicago
Gift of Mrs. Leigh B. Block

"Portrait of Mary Block"
by Ivan Le Loraine Albright
Oil on Canvas

"Walnut Table"
by Tom Eckert
56" L x 14" W x 16" H
Hollow, Weight 40 pounds

might employ rapid units in charcoal, pencil, ink, pastel, crayon, etc. As the students become familiar with the materials, it might become more beneficial to go into depth in which the students can be encouraged to concentrate at length with a particular tool on a particular subject. An aesthetic understanding of the subject is not found through one pencil rendition of a vase. Discovery might not occur until the twentieth or for some the fiftieth time. For the fortunate few discovery may happen on the second try, but a concentration in depth with a particular media through constant practice and constant observation can open up pathways of discovery that would never occur if the student is kept hopping from media to media and subject to subject. Indeed, the artist may work for months or even years and not exhaust the possibilities that exist in a particular subject. Georges Braque, the famous French artist, worked the major part of his entire life with cubism, finding in each new interpretation ideas and possibilities, threads based upon the previous product of his endeavor.

Where Does Art Begin?

Art exists most of all in our imaginative vision. Imaginative vision is man's way of skillfully and systematically bringing order from chaos. He is able to flavor his life by arranging and constructing his personal ideas into visual statements of beauty with art media. The artist may select any type of materials as his means of expression. They may be of a conventional nature such as oil paint and canvas, marble and chisel, or printers' ink and lithograph stone; or they may be unorthodox in nature, such as newspaper and paste, or acetylene torch and metal. Ultimately, the processes of creating are as personal as they are complex. It involves searching, exploring, experimenting, building, destroying, taking apart, adding, changing, modifying, forming, and repetitions of such stages again and again until an art work reaches a point at which the artist feels he can proceed no further.

The process of creating an art work demands complete involvement and dedication to the pursuance of the idea. During such a process, the artist attempts to unify basic components into an aesthetically pleasing organization. Understanding organization presupposes that one has developed a dexterity and awareness of the structural properties necessary to compose an art form. These structural properties or raw materials are often referred to as the *art elements*, and include such components as *line, shape, texture, color,* and *space.* The art student can gain an understanding of such traits during an intensified program of search and experimentation with art media.

All of the ways of art cannot be explained by the use of concrete rules and verbal dictums. There are many intangible factors in experiencing art which must be intuitively *felt* by each individual in his own way. He must become sensitive to the tiny but significant nuances of his experiences. His aesthetic receptors must be finely tuned if he is to fully savor the richness of art. The experiences of living are reflected in the individual's attempt to express life through the media of art. The student of art can be led to the proper door, but *he* must open it in order to see the wonders beyond. The direction indicated is not always a roller coaster ride. There will be disappointments and frustrations, as well as occasional rewards for the effort one must give to the processes of art. The pace may consist of two steps forward, and one back; or it may come in great leaps only to become snarled again in a tangled maze.

The art student sometimes assumes that he must be a highly trained technician before he can say anything expressive in his art work. This is not so, for both the ability to express ideas and the talent necessary to state such ideas in art form must grow hand in hand. It must be realized that personal uniqueness in *seeing* forms with originality of vision is a very necessary quality which the art student must develop.

Developing Artistic Attitudes

Building an inner sensitivity or "artistic sense" is largely dependent on attitudes and assumptions which we hold regarding the individuals, objects, and events in our experiences. If we remain rigid and *fixed* in our ideas concerning the environment, or in terms of how we feel about art, our thinking may remain within narrow boundaries. One does not consciously plan to shut out parts of the world, but when we close our minds to new possibilities and sources for expression, we may also restrict opportunities to broaden our viewpoints toward art.

Learning to discover and grow with art media first necessitates a decision to be *open from within* to fresh ideas, feelings, and viewpoints even though they may seem totally foreign to one's present attitudes and beliefs about art. In order to create with artistic vision one must learn to think in the manner of an artist. This means strengthening *new* habits of inquiry by discarding our old and worn art jackets and beginning a *new* period of boundary pushing. With the drag of mediocrity discarded, the barriers will slip away, and we shall be ready to take in fresh information about our world so that we have something to start with. We cannot adequately express ideas in artistic ways if we have no knowledgeable backlog from which to build our ideas.

To the inexperienced eye, it may appear that all of a certain artist's pictures are identical because of his consistency of theme. Therefore, it may appear that the artist is repeating himself unnecessarily. However, the minutest variations of an image or even a shape may serve to completely restructure his thinking on the subject. For an artist, a single art product is seldom more than the *barest trace of an idea.* Until that idea has been expanded several times, with many variations, it usually remains as a temporary statement.

Through the development of imagination, strongly personal statements or "truths" can emerge in art media. Without imagination, art remains mere technical training in which skill alone replaces personal imagery in the production of art works. Great art works as well as qualitative lesser works are created by a combination of imagination and skill exerted in just the right consistency. Great art can move, inspire, and even startle us. Most of all it expresses human experiences, either factually or abstractly. Finally, when skill and expressive intent have been accomplished within the art work, the rest is up to the observer.

"Horn and Hardart"
by Richard Estes, 1967
Oil

The Instruction of Art

It is often difficult to know when to provide instructions to students and when to encourage them to go it on their own in order to push for discoveries. It is assumed that a specific degree of rudimentary skill within any given medium is fundamental to learning further in art. Skills might include:

1. Shading
2. The drawing of an ellipse
3. An understanding of perspective.

On the other hand, there may be a point at which the student can work quite freely and inventively while having only a limited instruction in standard art technique. All art lessons need to be planned with care and thoughtfulness.

It might be challenging for teachers to include materials which have never been considered as art media. Some possibilities for explorations include light, reflections, movement, a new way of handling space, or sound. Art may result from electronic gear.

Considerations in Drawing and Painting

When drawing or painting a picture, while using any type of tool, and while creating any subject matter keep in mind some of the following suggestions:

1. Always try to make each line aesthetic and visually sensitive to behold. Avoid permitting your hand to control your mind by merely making lines which communicate *only*. (A pencil line drawn without feeling is merely a line on a surface.)
2. Try to achieve as many variations in your lines as possible.
3. Work for a range of values, running from light to dark and vice versa.
4. Overlap lines and intertwine. Build a visual surface of lines which can describe a form. The manner of interpretation or solution is your own. It is perfectly all right to be influenced by a known master or your teacher (who may be a modern master!).

5. Always try to be inventive and imaginative in your approaches and solutions. Make your realism exciting, as well as your abstraction!
6. When drawing, keep this approach in mind: observe the details, remember, and draw. Observe the details, remember, and draw. Observe the details, remember, and draw. (Get the idea?)
7. Vary the hand and finger pressure when drawing. This creates variations in the value of the line as well as the thickness of the line. Press down, let up, press down, let up, then let the line tail into silence! Develop varying approaches to how you make lines and marks for your drawings.
8. Make your lines flicker, dart, come on strong, swirl, hesitate, go very straight, be sharp, fuzzy, dim, stark. Work for an infinity of variations, while keeping in mind the mastery of each.
9. Make your lines count. Try to avoid making any lines which do not have meaning. Here again, make your mind the boss, not your hand.
10. Try to make your lines describe your intentions in the subject or idea.
11. Aim for organization, balance, harmony. Try to feel visual order intuitively.

In the beginning art program, the student should have an opportunity to explore with a variety of materials. He will discover that different materials will suggest different approaches and vice versa. For instance, there are a variety of pencils to work with. Different weight pencils will produce different lines. For example, a 4-B pencil produces a soft, dark line while a 4-H produces a thin, light line. Get the students to seek visual answers in working with tools. For example, can your students answer the following questions:

1. What happens when you draw with a 4-B pencil and you press hard and let up?
2. What happens when you turn a pencil on its side?
3. Have you ever rolled a pencil between your fingers as you draw?
4. What happens when you go back into a drawing with an eraser?

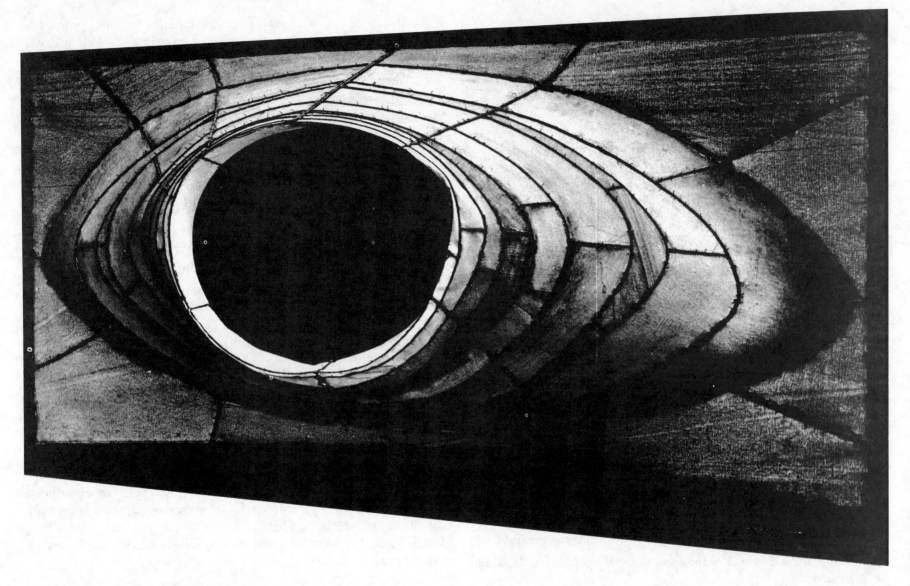

"Untitled"
by Lee Bontecou, 1960
Welded Steel and Canvas

Courtesy, Leo Castelli Gallery, New York

5. Have you ever made a loud line? A quiet one? A violent one?
6. What happens when you draw with pen and ink? How about stick and ink?
7. Have you ever drawn on wet paper?
8. Have you ever drawn with white pastel pencil over oil crayons?
9. Can you make a line skip or hop?
10. How do you indicate form or tone with a pen line?
11. What is the difference between a pattern and a texture?
12. What else can you discover?

Getting Started on a Subject

Where does one begin to draw? What subject? You could start anywhere. A scarf tacked to the wall, a kitchen sink, a watch, a group of paint jars, or even a shoe. Anything is subject for drawing. (See Chapter 10.)

Some Possibilities for Drawing

1. Can you complete a drawing with a variety of textures to indicate space?
2. Can you draw with oil crayons over paint?
3. Can you draw with pastels over watercolor?
4. Can you draw with oil crayons and turpentine?
5. Have you ever drawn with oil crayons on wood?

Some Possibilities for Painting

1. What is intensity and value?
2. What happens when you mix colors?
3. What happens when you overlay colors?
4. What happens when you glaze colors?

Points to Consider When Painting

Drawing ability is significant to all types of painting. One is seriously handicapped without some practice in drawing. Here are some pointers to think about when preparing a picture for painting.

1. Balance your vertical strokes or lines with horizontals. Make large movements on the paper first. Let one stroke be counterbalanced by an opposing stroke, such as vertical-horizontal.
2. Repeat your strokes by distributing them around the painting surface.
3. Repeat the lines and shapes, but vary the direction of the lines and shapes.
4. Avoid making any two shapes the exact same size.
5. Have some dominating shapes.
6. Let the different parts of your picture breathe.
7. Let some forms extend off the page.
8. Try to keep the entire picture going simultaneously. Don't over-complete one part of the painting without considering each of the other parts.
9. Balance your picture by using strong colors opposed by larger shapes. Keep all of the parts working in relation to each other.
10. Don't become overly formalized. Keep the possibilities open during the entire creation of a picture.

Keep in mind that it is best for the beginning student to learn some rules. Then he has a basis for action. Rules can always be broken later when one achieves some facility with the media. Most beginners do much better if they learn to walk first before running. Skills and idea-understanding must come first. This is only possible through hard and persistent effort, and *an unbeatable desire to learn.* With this type of spirit, any media can be mastered. The student must be willing to suffer through all of the disappointments which are part and parcel of the artistic process. The teacher should encourage the student not to give up after a flop of a painting. It will often take several paintings before some glimmer of success is attained. Growth is not always evident in the work. It first appears in one's thinking and new attitudes about art. As the eye perceives more acutely, growth will begin to take place on the painting surface.

In the high school program, students need an opportunity to work with materials that challenge and in themselves are rugged

"In Sober Ecstasy"
by Hans Hofmann, 1965
Oil on Canvas

Courtesy, Andre Emmerich Gallery, Inc., New York

and rough. They need opportunities to put massive pieces of lumber together, to chisel on logs, and to chip and hack away. They need also to work with tools and media that require finesse in handling, such as the brush or pencil. Each student is different, and media will vary with the individual. It might be better that a student learns one media well rather than a skimpy knowledge with several media.

There are so many possibilities for secondary students. Jewelry, because of its very richness, can be challenging. Working on canvas or a surface with paint provides a different response. Students need a variety of options available to them so that decisions are possible. We want things to really happen in the classroom, and the materials as well as the ideas have to speak to youth.

Using Carbon Paper Drawing Techniques as a Freeing Device

Take carbon paper, place over surface and draw subject with fingers and other drawing instruments, such as pencils, pens, knives, brushes, blunt instruments and any other instrument that will not tear the paper. Tones can be achieved by using the side of the tool or the hand. The carbon paper, if small in size, can be shifted around the drawing surface. If the drawing paper is larger, the drawing will be approached slightly differently because it can be completed without moving the carbon. IBM computer paper is an excellent source for obtaining larger carbon sheets as well as a ready-made package for a drawing surface. It might be interesting to approach this technique with carbon paper covering a complete large-size surface such as a three by four foot sheet where nothing can be seen in drawing the subject until it is finished so that the tactile effects of drawing are emphasized. This loosens up the student. This type of approach to drawing is valuable because it is inventive, odd-ball in nature, unorthodox, and does not permit stereotypes to enter into one's thinking, especially for beginning students. The carbon paper drawing technique, using a combination of drawing paper and regular drawing technique, might be a useful approach on one surface where you have a reproduced line on one surface and a directly drawn line in another area.

"Bather and Small Seated Nude"
by Frank Gallo, 1964
Polyester Resin

Courtesy, Graham Gallery, New York

Utilizing Multiple Drawing Tools Together

Another technique for loosening up the beginning student is to combine two or more pens or pencils together by taping, and then proceeding to draw a subject. In this type of approach multiple lines are created instantly. Overlapping occurs immediately as the lines merge into each other. The building up of form develops rapidly. The ordinary approach in drawing is to make one mark with one tool at a time. Making that one mark at a time may be quite a hurdle for beginning students who are loaded with fears of their own inabilities. Taping several tools together (such as pencils or pens) creates multiple lines simultaneously! The teacher can take it from here. Techniques or approaches such as this are not intended to become crutches or replacements for basic foundational approaches in using drawing tools. The following is one approach in planning objectives for helping students develop art sense.

Some Basic Rules for Drawing Flowers with Pastels

1. Use the side of the chalk as well as the point.
2. Use colors that are close in value to each other.
3. Overlap one color over another to achieve a new color, plus transparent effects.
4. Use colors that show contrast. Can you make a color that makes your eye quiver?
5. Use stick, twig, or feather to obtain a linear effect aside from chalk line.
6. You can select from what you see to compose your picture. Don't feel that it is necessary to draw everything exactly as it appears. Select the most interesting flowers and arrange them as you feel they should go.
7. Make some flowers lighter than others. This gives a feeling of depth.
8. Make some flowers detailed, while leaving others more vague. Background flowers can be more vague or fuzzy.
9. Make flowers at the bottom of the paper larger.
10. Make some flowers larger than the others.

Courtesy, University Art Collections, Arizona State University
Gift of Oliver B. James

"I Am Glad I Came Back"
by George Grosz, American, 1943
Oil on Masonite

11. Don't place your dominant flower exactly in the middle. This creates a propeller effect.

12. Don't make lines that only fill up the page. Make all of your lines count. Don't overwork the picture.

13. Don't be content with colors as they come from the tube. Mix your colors on the paper to obtain richer effects.

14. Work directly with the chalk. (Crayon can be handled the same way.)

15. Try to utilize the whole paper.

16. Let some flowers drift off the page (as in life)

17. Rub with your finger, or use a cloth, to get soft effects.

18. Wet the paper in spots and draw over those spots with ink and pastel. Don't over-wet; the paper should be just damp.

19. Plan your composition for the whole paper. Don't work one flower in detail while leaving the rest waiting. You must feel the whole work; you should have your plan for the whole work.

20. Keep one hand free from chalk at all times. Keep extra paper towels handy for keeping hands clean.

21. Flip paper to get rid of chalk dust. Don't blow it.

22. Spray your picture at the close.

23. Try not to have objects running from corner to corner.

24. Make the mind control the hand.

25. Remember, you can break the rules *after* you learn them.

The Line and Other Art Elements as a Basis for Drawing, Design and Art

There are countless ways in which linear techniques can be employed to build an art product. Line can be used to organize and structure a composition, as well as indicate a sense of compositional direction within the work. It can also become simply *line* which is beautiful to behold in itself. Linear properties are part of all natural and man-made objects, although their character is not always readily apparent. Line as a visual phenomenon is most observable in such objects as *spider webs, vines, railroad tracks, telephone lines, fabric, wood grains, fences, television aerials, wheel spokes, supporting beams* and *posts, billboard lettering, grain fields, grasses, radio towers, seed puffs, bridges, street markings, decorative wall units, wet tire marks, flower stems, petals, tree trunks* and *branches, pins* and *needles,* and *strings, ropes,* and *wires.*

Many other elements exist in our visual field which are not immediately apparent in terms of their linear properties. This is clear if we realize that *all objects* are first observed in outline or contour form. Such a phenomenon is a result of the human eye's tendency to see the *edge* of a form as most dominant within the visual path. An extension of this process takes place when two colors having contrasting value ratios are joined at one edge. Their meeting point or joined edge produces a distinct linear response.

Line in nature is an integral part of the forms therein. In a composition, line *can* exist by itself. It need not rely on the emotional impact of color or the decorative aspects of texture and pattern. In other words, the line *can* be the total artistic product, devoid of any other structural support. Drawings are fine examples of how the skillful use of lines creates an artistic statement.

How the individual perceives or reacts to linear elements in a composition is often related to past experience. For example, if an artist draws a straight, horizontal line across the width of his paper, it is possible to respond to such a line as a horizon. A drawn circle may suggest a sun or moon if positioned above such a horizontal line. This is because we tend to relate linear elements in a composition to images which are consistent with our previous experiences. In this instance, we relate to past experiences with horizontal and circular images which appear in combination; i.e., skyline with sun or moon. Lines which are drawn vertically and repeated consecutively across the paper become suggestive of objects which are vertical. Depending upon the length of such lines, they may imply a fence, or strings on a musical instrument.

The drawn line is an element of communication between observer and line. It contains visual signals intended for the observer. If that observer is able to "read" the signals, transmission is complete. The art work is like the printed word inasmuch as both

"American Gothic"
by Grand Wood, 1930
Oil on Beaver Board

Courtesy of The Art Institute of Chicago
Friends of American Art Collection

transmit information to a receiving source. In art forms, it is possible for lines to become *more* than standard communication signals. Through the skills of the artist, lines may also possess *aesthetic* properties which extend the original message by giving it a more exquisite form. We call this form beauty.

The beginning art student may draw lines which communicate the idea intended, but remain completely lacking in any aesthetic sensitivity. It should be realized however, that sensitivity to aesthetic qualities grows with practice. The student must train the hand as well as the imagination. To paraphrase a familiar adage, *artists are made, not born.*

The Visual Characteristics of Lines

Line as an art element serves three major functions in the creation of an art product. These include:

> *line as contour or structure in delineating form*
> *line as expressiveness in communication of ideas*
> *line as pure aesthetic quality*

1. **Line as contour or structure.**   Line in its pure form is an artistic device originated by man to help provide him with a method of giving meaning to his world of shape, form and design. Whenever we observe an object, we mentally scan the surface in search of an understandable image. What we perceive first is a total outline of the object which serves as a visual shorthand in comprehending the form. This outline image gives us clues relating to structure by condensing the total form into a communicable order. When an artist draws a picture in outline, he is essentially putting forms into a comprehensible order. The linear skeleton of a building under construction is a composite of structural lines bonded in unison to support the overlaying material.

Lines which are structural serve many purposes in terms of artistic production. They enclose shapes to form outlines, as when making an initial sketch or composition for a painting. Lines can suggest the surface modulation of a form when combined in a planned order or sequence. Lines can also be incorporated to create textural effects within a composition. The drawn line enables the artist to relate three dimensional characteristics of environment to the two dimensional structures in picture making.

2. **Line as expressiveness.** If the aesthetic quality of a line were reduced to its barest common denominator, we would perceive such a line without sensitivity. It would tend to be uniform in thickness and length, and would function as a vehicle for transmitting messages or ideas, devoid of personal emotion. Lines of this nature are often suited to technical drawings, blueprints, and the printed page which functions largely as communication. These lines are clean, crisp, and precise, for their purpose is to relay specific

The Cleveland Museum of Art, Mr. and Mrs. Charles G. Prasse Collection

"Le Jockey" 67.234
Henry de Toulouse-Lautrec, French, 1864-1901
Medium Lithograph   Measurements 516 x 363 mm.

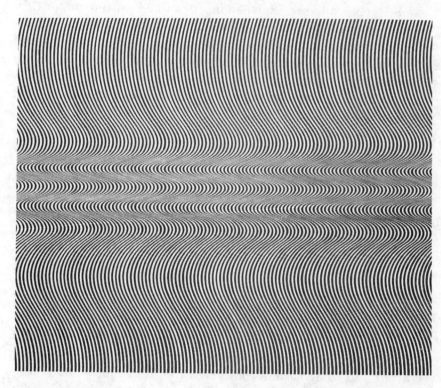

"Current"
by Bridget Riley, 1964
Emulsion on Board

Courtesy, Richard Feigen Gallery, New York and Chicago
Collection, The Museum of Modern Art, New York

content. By contrast, the lines of artistic arrangement are deliberately created to help convey the mood or feeling of the images they represent. When such lines become more than vehicles of communication, they assume characteristics which can provoke an emotional response within us. For example, certain lines can suggest softness and grace, as seen in dancers, or other lines can be vigorous and forceful to suggest a violent thunderstorm. The daily experiences of living appear to influence our emotional reactions to linear arrangements. For example, whenever we see curved lines we relate to things which are graceful, delicate, feminine. If we think of *curved lines* from our immediate experiences, we might think of ballet dancers, children and babies, women, the edges of white clouds, billowy pillows, furry kittens, marshmallows, or powder puffs. In drawing a curved line on a surface, we may find ourselves identifying with the curved lines of our environment.

Horizontal lines generally suggest things which are restful, slow moving, drifting, spacious, and quiet. Whenever we draw horizontal lines on a surface, we are reminded of our bodies when we sleep, the distant horizon, a table top, a flowing river, a still lake, a highway stretching across the plain, or a landing strip.

Vertical lines suggest strength, stability, and poise. The images which come to mind when viewing vertical lines include our bodies when standing erect, trees, supporting members and posts of buildings, telephone poles, church steeples and spires.

Diagonal lines suggest motion, rapid flight, action, and speed. Diagonal lines remind us of our bodies when we run, jump, dive. They also suggest hills and mountains, leaning structures, explosions, lightning, and rockets.

Combining different linear directions in one arrangement usually produces a multiple response. The effect becomes one which is determined by the lines which dominate in the composition. If the total linear structure is largely curvilinear, the viewer's response will be related to the graceful, soft qualities of curved lines.

3. **Line as pure aesthetic quality.** Wedded throughout any linear design is a characteristic trait known as *aesthetic quality*. This refers to the inherent beauty of the line itself regardless of representation. If a line were removed from its context within a composition, it should still retain a visual sensitivity in terms of its aesthetic attributes, i.e., it should be pleasing to behold with or without content. At one extreme, we may create a line which is uniform in width throughout its distance on a surface, and lacking in any spatial variation whatever. This type of line could become tedious to look at simply because of its monotony. A line must come alive as a quivering, bold, pulsing, dynamic throb of energy! It can be timid, aggressive, retiring, extravagant, explosive, subtle, striking, or delicate. A line projects its aesthetic qualities through the skillful strokes of its master. Lines may vary widely in the manner in which they expand, contract, curve, or otherwise change their appearance. The line can be swiftly flowing and smooth, or scratchy and lumpy. It can be shredded, sticky, hairy, or fibrous. It can possess features of transparency, translucency, or opaqueness. Lines can be technically precise when made with an instrument, or they can be very willowy when made with a tool such as a feather. Often, the tool used will determine the type of lines which can be created. A brush line will be quite different from lines which are made with a pencil or pen. Each tool used has a potential number of possibilities for linear construction depending on the skill of the individual artist.

Line as it is used in painting or drawing can be thought of as the backbone of a picture. It helps us to describe form, as well as provide us with a point of view. It establishes moods, and it is pleasing to examine as a quality in itself. At times it may serve the function of decoration.

Tools and Materials for Exploring Lines

It is important in designing a composition that careful consideration be given to the selection of the tools and materials to be used in the construction of the art work. In the beginning it is of value to consider many possible materials before selecting those which will be most appropriate to the problem. Commercially prepared tools such as pen, pencil, brush, or pastel will serve the beginning as well as advanced artist very well. These tools, along with crayons and charcoals are considered *traditional tools* for creating art works. Needless to say, all of the above materials should be fully explored to understand their properties and potential. Of course, we would limit our *discovery potential* if we only experimented with traditional media. There are many tools which are not ordinarily thought of as art media, but which serve to stimulate fresh thinking through their unusualness. Listed below, are some tools that are not ordinarily thought of as art tools. The art student should certainly consider all such tools as possibilities for making interesting and variable linear structures.

Unorthodox Tools

bamboo pen	soap
dried twigs	pointed instruments
feathers	rags
rubber gloves	sponges
erasers	dipped string
corks	edges of cardboard
felt-tip pens	cement and glue

In experimenting with traditional as well as unorthodox tools, the working surface for the art work should also be considered as a means to create interesting variations of linear structure. Each surface will produce a different effect that is dependent on the particular tool utilized. Surface materials upon which to draw or paint vary considerably.

It should be remembered that tools and materials alone do not make an artist. It is more the individual's awareness and sensitivity to the uniqueness of such materials that enables him to discover their potential. Each material or tool has an individual uniqueness, and as such is capable of providing the art student with the means to create the specific effect he may be seeking. The student must search, experiment, and continue to search for those possibilities which he can discover. He must give each material and tool the proper chance to reveal its best qualities. This can only be done through the process of *consistent practice*. In art, it is essential that we build up a sufficient backlog of information, data, and practiced skill in knowing what each tool and material can do.

Courtesy of the Artist

"Head Dress #2"
by Fritz Scholder, 1978
Monotype

Building an Art Notebook

Search out and write in your notebook the objects in your environment which contain aesthetic potential. In addition, magazines, illustrations, and literary sources provide an excellent means for developing your awareness to forms. The notebook should become an invaluable source of ideas and information, containing a sufficient body of related material which can be drawn from when the need arises.

The reason for such a notebook is that it is impossible to retain or recall huge amounts of data which comprise one's experiences. When you do discover something of value, it can be captured on the spot by means of a note or sketch. In this fashion, it will not slip away into the stream of life. The notebook will also help one to think more clearly by keeping many ideas closer to the conscious level of thinking. The need to retrace our steps is lessened and we can move to extended viewpoints with greater sensitivity and clarity of mind. Putting down information serves to clarify what we think, and it strengthens the original image. It helps us to *listen to ourselves.*

More Art Problems to Explore

Since the beginning of the history of man, sensitivity to art has been exhibited in two distinct types of artistic behavior: (1) the making of art and (2) looking at works of art.

The two categories of art are often interfaced and a program of art instruction can be designed to relate the concepts and skills developed in the skill area to the aesthetic objectives involved in learning to critically appreciate works of art.

Idea-Pushing Possibilities with Art History as a Base

The following list suggests possible lessons where art theory and art practice would be inter-related:

I. *Studio Experience Relevant to the Teaching of Art History-Art Appreciation and for Aesthetics.* Theme for these units: do as the artists do.

A. Explore the *materials* of the artists as you study them.

1. Make an oil painting on canvas or masonite in the manner of artists such as Van Gogh, Cezanne, Hals, Picasso, Delacroix, El Greco or Rubens.

2. Do a series of pastels when studying Edgar Degas and Toulouse-Lautrec.

3. Try a series of watercolors when studying John Marin or Paul Cezanne.

4. Do a woodcut when studying Japanese prints.

5. Make a sculpture (both additive and subtractive methods) to help you understand the art of Michelangelo, Henry Moore or Auguste Rodin.

6. Make a found-art sculpture, a pop art sculpture or an assemblage when studying Jasper Johns, Claes Oldenburg, Marisol, and Louise Nevelson.

7. Experiment with drawing materials such as charcoal, pen and ink, Conte crayon and litho crayon when trying to understand the drawings of Daumier, Da Vinci, Picasso, Matisse, Rembrandt, Durer.

8. Make a relief sculpture (low, medium or high) when studying Egyptian art, Greek, Medieval or Renaissance art.

9. Try a *small* fresco to understand the process as used by Giotto, Masaccio, and Michelangelo.

10. Do a mosaic when studying Byzantine art.

11. Do a collage when studying Braque, Picasso, Rauschenburg, Wesselman, Ernst and Schwitters and the Dada movement.

B. Explore the *subject matter* (content) of the artist and methods of handling subject matter.

1. Make a series of landscapes when studying Constable, Turner, Ruisdael, Van Gogh, Cezanne, Winslow Homer, Monet, Pissarro, El Greco.

2. Do a still life when studying Matisse, Cezanne, Peale, Chardin, Harnett, Van Gogh, Max Weber.

3. Paint or draw a scene of everyday life when studying the Ash Can school, Courbet, Van Gogh, Ben Shahn, Chagall, Vuillard, Vermeer, De Hooch.

4. Try to interpret a religious theme in paint, to understand the work of Van Eyck, Fra Angelico, Giotto, Rembrandt, Roualt, Dali, El Greco.

5. Make a portrait bust in clay or papier mache when studying classical Roman art.

6. Interpret a personality through a figure study when studying Kokoschka, Picasso, Rembrandt, Holbein, Titian, Modigliani, David, Van Dyck, Velasquez, Gauguin, Munch.

7. Do a group figure composition putting in as many figures as you can when studying such works as:

Title	Artist

The Last Judgment—Michelangelo
Guernica—Picasso
Liberty Leading the People—Delacroix
Raft of the Medusa—Gericault
The Great Bathers—Cezanne
Nude Descending a Staircase—Duchamp
The Last Supper—Da Vinci
The Night Watch—Rembrandt

8. For abstract art, make a series of geometric and free form compositions when studying Mondrian, Kandinsky, Klee, Malevich, Kline, Hoffmann, Pollock, Rothko, Delaunay, Albers, Motherwell or Arp.

C. Explore the *styles* of art forms of various periods.
   Paint a subject as:

   a pop artist would
   a cubist artist would
   a classical artist would (idealized)
   an Egyptian artist would
   an impressionist would
   a surrealist would
   a pointillist would
   a little Dutch master or Flemish painter would.

Courtesy of The Art Institute of Chicago
Joseph Winterbotham Collection

"Still Life, Geranium Plants,
Fruit on Table"
by Henri Matisse, 1906
Oil on Canvas

Understanding Space in Art Practice

In composing an arrangement or picture, the space involved in the actual arrangement is a special type of space. It requires a special kind of seeing. In order to understand the space of the artist; that is, the space created on a picture surface, it is important to understand it as a shorthand version of the space around us. In our own experiences, we are part of the greater atmosphere around us. We walk, talk, breathe, and move through space with our own bodies. We are objects, just as tables, chairs, autos, planes, are objects ad infinitum, which occupy this greater space. Space is the air around us. It is the position which is occupied by all unfilled air. It fills all surfaces not occupied by a mass of some sort or another. When an area is determined to be the painting or drawing, or design surface, it becomes this space around us on a smaller scale. The minute we prescribe a boundary on a surface, and intend to work within this limit, we have set up a kind of space which is similar to the space we experience around us. The prescribed space becomes the representation on a two dimensional surface for three dimensional reality. What we do to the space will affect its arrangement to us. The painting or drawing surface is like the heavens in the sky. It can go on and on forever into infinity within the limitations of the space itself. It is primarily an aesthetic space. Our intention in creating an art work is to arrange and construct pleasing forms within a prescribed space.

The moment we place a line or shape of any sort into the prescribed space, we have introduced a form into the void. An object in itself is limited by its aloneness. When another object is placed within the space, a relationship exists between the two objects. We can relate the objects' shape to each other, or we can relate them to the edge of the paper, or the boundary. Each shape thereafter introduced will relate to each and every shape already within the confines of our boundaries. It can relate in terms of identity, or similarity of form or shape, such as two squares. Lines which are of various lengths and directions will relate to each other, because they are lines. *Straight lines*, for instance, can relate to the *straight edges* of a *shape*, such as a square. Shapes, lines, and what have you within the arrangement which is growing can relate in terms of *position* to

each other. *Shapes which are in close proximity* to each other will indicate a relationship. Shapes will relate according to placement. Shapes and lines which are horizontal in position or placement will relate their horizontalness, and so on. Vertical elements will express their verticality. Elements can relate according to similarity in color and value. Anything which reflects a similarity will establish a relationship. When we compose a picture, we try to relate all objects in a composition to all other objects in the composition. We must do this with delicate balance and decision. The more elements that we work with, the greater is the challenge to put the arrangement together.

The thing to consider here first of all, is that the space created by the boundaries of the paper or surface is not a flat space. At all times the illusion is one of visual depth. We must maintain the depth illusion of our picture space. We must see the space as infinite to our vision, just as in actual vision of the world nothing is flat—objects appear farther and farther away. On the picture surface, objects appear farther and farther into space for several reasons. A change in value between objects will change their relative position on the working surface. A change in size will affect their relationship. A change in position on the surface will create the effect of depth or distance. Size, value, and position appear to be the main factors affecting depth of space on the two dimensional surface. Objects placed lower on the page, for example, will create an illusion of being closer than objects farther up on the working surface. Even though we know all objects are in fact on the same surface and on the same plane.

Some space in an arrangement can be referred to as captured space. It is the space within an object which has been trapped by a linear or color boundary all around it. For instance, a shape with an opening within it is a captured space. The space around objects is known as the background space. It is often referred to as negative space, not used space, secondary space, and so forth. All space is used in an arrangement. The space will relate to the objects and shapes which are placed on the spatial surface. It is also referred to as quiet space, or busy space. The positive areas, or the areas which contain shapes are the busy areas, and the untouched spaces are the quiet spaces. It is possible to have quiet space within a large shape, within the space already occupied by a shape or form. This could be thought of as a transformed space or an occupied space. Captured space may also be used here. Objects which are placed on a painting, drawing or design surface are surrounded and permeated by the space within the boundaries of the composition. What we do to the initial space will affect the manner in which we see objects in such a space. We can achieve realistic impressions of depth in space by using rules which pertain to reality, such as perspective. This gives an impression of depth by relating the space to the space of our known environment.

Space within a composition does not have to be occupied to be used. It is at once in relationship to the objects. Space is that invisible entity which forms the picture surface. Within this space will go all the attempts by an artist to say something visually pleasing. Artists who create successful art works have solved the problems of how to handle space. The space around objects is often as important as the objects represented. In a realistic picture much of the space can become atmospheric in nature; that is, we tend to relate the picture surface and its areas to the world around us which is similar to the image. In this instance, the space is much easier to comprehend.

Change of size pushes objects back and forth in space. Change in light and dark also pushes the objects. Color pushes the objects. The angle and direction of the shapes and lines also indicate movement backwards or forwards. Space can be uniform in sequence, as when a shape is repeated several times in a row. This sets up a rhythm or pattern through repetition. The repetition of the shapes becomes much like the musical notes in a sequence. A rhythm is established. One may repeat a square shape six times and then change the position of the next square to provide variation. Where this is multiplied several times, we achieve a rhythm. If it is organized, it will work for us. Space can be thought of in terms of direction. Space which is bounded by vertically positioned objects is known as vertical space. When we relate the space around objects to horizontal positions, it is horizontal space. We also have curvilinear space, and diagonal space. The space tends to relate to the objects within the surface. The space takes the shape of the outer edges of the objects which border it. It also takes the shape of any cut-out portions of the shapes and forms themselves.

Balance

There are several means to achieve balance in the picture arrangement. Balance is a feeling that the picture is organized and the parts relate. There is a sense of equilibrium on the parts of the objects. Balance can be achieved by equal weighting of the parts in respect to each other; by change in value and size of some of the parts; by combining several smaller parts to equal the visual weight of a larger part; by relating lighter valued objects to darker valued objects in the proper portion; by spacing the parts in positions which modify the other. Colors can be balanced. Shapes can be balanced. Space can be balanced. Lines can be balanced. Textures can be balanced. All objects in the picture surface can be balanced. Objects or parts can be balanced by color, spacing, size, value. Balance can be formal or informal.

Rhythm

Rhythm is a regulated movement of parts which relate to each other in unison. Shapes which are repeated in a sequence can be rhythmical. Rhythm can have many variations yet still relate to the whole picture. Rhythm brings life to the composition. It is the music of art. Rhythm provides the unity. Rhythm can be achieved in many ways. Repetition of shapes, colors, lines, textures can set up rhythms in the composition. Rhythms can be very noticeable or very subtle. Rhythms can have dominant rhythms and secondary rhythms which echo the dominant rhythms. Rhythm is a regulated flow of the elements which make up the composition. The position of elements can establish a rhythm. Spacing contributes to the compositional rhythm.

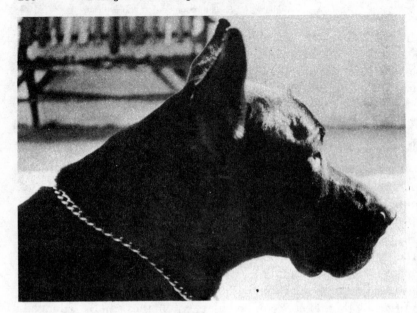

Courtesy of the Artist

A great dane served as the model for a
charcoal drawing done by Heather, a
sophomore in high school.

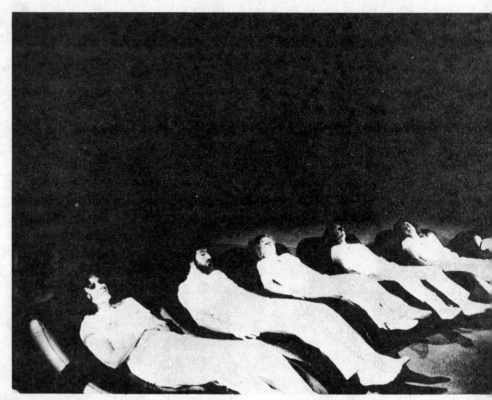

"House and Field" C. 1923-28
by Edward Hopper
Conte Crayon

Single frame from
"Enervate: The Artist's Lounge"
by Muriel Magenta and Karen Stone
16 mm Black and White Silent Film

Courtesy of Muriel Magenta

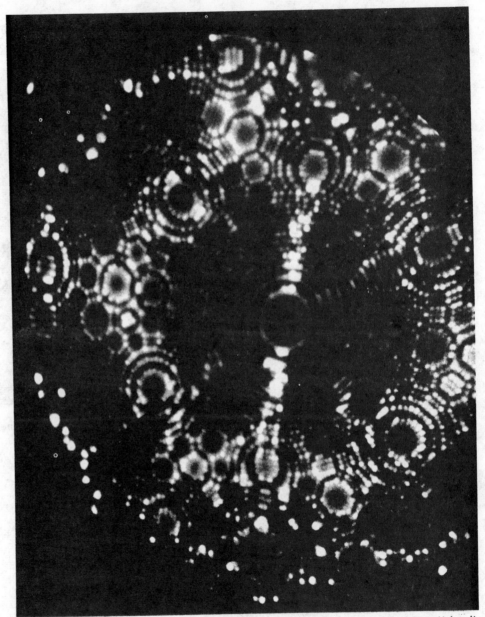

Electron Micrograph photo of
an atom, smallest unit of life
of any object. Magnification at
1,000,000 times normal scale.

Chapter 10

Discovering Idea Sources

Where does one find ideas for art which go beyond the ordinary and stimulate us to create exciting aesthetic arrangements?

The *initial* phase in working out a problem in art form concerns the actual *search for ideas*. In this search to increase one's idea-index, it is necessary to put into operation an intake framework that is equipped to receive the raw idea data. Our eyes, hands, ears, and body form this sensory network which can enable us to detect and bring in signals which are suitable for manufacture in terms of artistic potential.

In the first stages of searching, we should cultivate our *awareness* so that large amounts of information or idea potential can be taken in. At this point it is not necessary or desirable to select or focus our thinking in a specific direction. If the search for ideas which relate to a particular problem is narrowed too soon, we may restrict the number of possibilities to a confined margin. Instead, we should encourage many ideas to flow forth initially in order to provide a larger base from which to select. Once we feel that our collected information on a given subject is sufficient to generate many ideas, we can begin to relate this information to our problems.

The next step involves actual experimentation and manipulation of the art media. The objective of this point is to create several working studies of the problem by rendering as many variations as possible. In this manner, the rough ideas are brought into focus and insight can be gained prior to a final selection and ultimate completion of the art work.

Finding Idea Sources in Nature

There are no limitations of sources for developing ideas from nature. One can begin almost anywhere! Our natural curiosity about things could serve as a starting point. It is important to develop the habit of searching for the most minute details of an object. This means that we must use the eyes for *observing;* the hands, knees, cheeks, and body for *feeling;* the ears for *listening;* and the nose for *smelling.* Of course, ideas for artistry do not "flow" from everywhere to touch us with inspiration. The artist must develop his *own* mental wellspring from which ideas can pour forth when needed. This is done by becoming aware and responsive to the possibilities which each experience, event, or material offers. We are limited only by our own capacity to develop insights which will extend our vision.

Discovering and investigating sources from which artistic ideas can develop is unlimited. The following categories are offered as reference and stimulation. In addition, they may also suggest other possible sources for inquiry.

1. **Forms from the Sea.** The diversity of forms from the waters of the world offer a wealth of visual material to stimulate artistic thinking. The most likely forms to consider can be found in the many different varieties of fish. Each style of fish offers a unique type of visual treat. Fish possess a remarkable variety of exterior styles in terms of shapes, surface patterns, and color diversification. Some fish are extremely narrow and elongated, while others appear short and pudgy. Some are transparent, while others dazzle us with their brilliance. In addition to fish, the beauty of coral, sponge, and other marine animals can also be studied. This type of sea life has magnificent textural qualities which appeal both to eye and touch. Films, slides, illustrations, and collections in biological and marine laboratories provide an immediate source for close analysis of both exterior and interior surfaces.

2. **Animal and Bird Forms.** The animal and bird world is an excellent idea source. In the case of domestic animals, first-hand experiences are always best if the subjects are available. Each specific type of animal has special identifying characteristics which can be studied in terms of visual imagery. In general, cattle have long, stocky profiles with short stubby legs and a large head. They give one a lumbering, plodding appearance. By comparison, cats are small in scale, furry and soft; have long narrow bodies, and a graceful but furtive appearance. In the case of a wild animal, the deer is characterized by a sleek, horizontal body, thin tapering legs, a long curving neck, and a convergent head. They are graceful of movement and project a delicate but alert stance. Characteristics such as these are immediately apparent at first glance. A closer examination should seek to answer questions such as the following:

In what direction does the body hair grow?
What shapes are the facial features?
What color are the eyes?
Where are the ears located?
What is the shape of the foot?
Where does the tail begin?
Are the body muscles pronounced?
Do all animals have whiskers?
How does the jaw operate?
Does the animal stand flat on all feet?

In asking questions about nature, the artist or student goes beyond mere surface impressions in order to form a richer concept of the object. All animals have unique body structures which offer the art student various sources for the study of form. While each animal has characteristic traits, the artist must select those aspects which best provide aesthetic potential for him. A horse to one person may suggest a sleek, proud form for racing. For another, a horse may suggest a powerful machine denoting astonishing strength.

Birds also suggest aesthetic forms. Some birds reflect flight or motion, while others such as the golden eagle, indicate strength and stateliness. The swan or flamingo reminds us of graceful qualities, while the birds of tropical jungles may suggest decorative appeal.

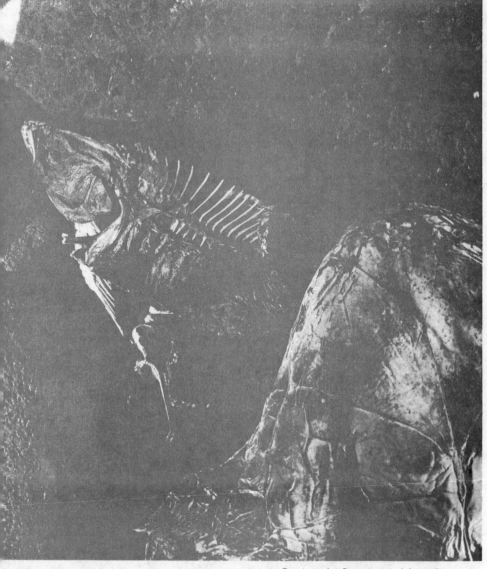

Courtesy, Art Department, Arizona State
Photo by Cavalliere Ketchum, 1963

"Engulfment"

Courtesy, Dr. James Pearcey, Oregon State University

"Eel Larva of an Unknown Species Captured off Oregon Coast"

All birds have certain characteristics in common, including claws, feathers, wings, and beaks. These are general traits which must not be overlooked by the designer. He must also search further for the wealth of material which lies beyond the first glance. Some questions to ask oneself in investigating the characteristics of birds might include:

Are all feathers the same size?
Are they soft or stiff?
How does the beak attach to the head?
What is the shape of the eye?
Is there an eyelid?
Where is the comb located?
How does a bird turn his head?
How does he cling to a branch?
How many claws does he have?
Where do the wings attach?
How does the bird use his wings in flight?
How does a bird bend his neck for food?
What is the texture of his legs?
Do birds have good eyesight?
Why does a bird have a tail?
Do birds have teeth?
Are all feathers water repellant?
Do all birds fly?
Where does the egg come out?

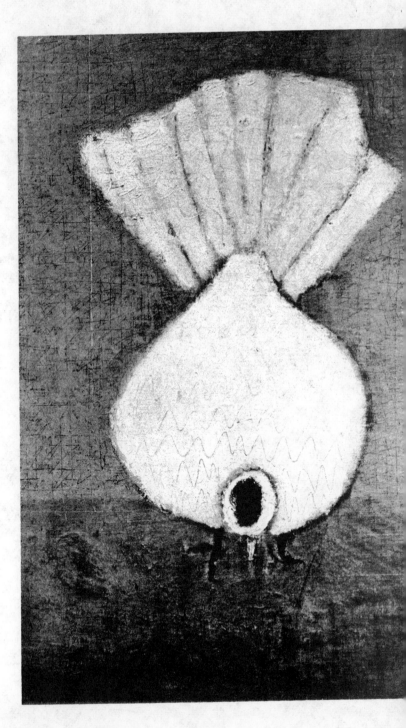

"Fantail Pigeon" 1953
by Milton Avery
Oil on Canvas Board

"Reconstructed"
photo by Jack Stuler

Courtesy of the Artist

The artist used a reflective screen to
recapture the human form and
compose it into a new assembly
with his camera.

3. **Trees, Flowers and Growing Things.**   The curving shape of a leaf, the twist of a tree limb, the gentle grace of a blossom in bloom —all reflect an unharnessed beauty within natural forms which offers the student a continual source of aesthetic stimulation. The aspiring artist must become aware of such details within the larger, more haphazard landscape. This demands observation, search, and persistence to see relationships of form which must be sought out in order to be discovered. More intense searching can reveal the underlying structure of petal growth, the textural quality of a stem, the pocket which holds the nectar, or the subtle changes in light values from petal to petal as sunlight skips across surfaces. By extending our awareness, we are able to discover how a tree anchors itself to the soil, how shadows glide across grassy fields, how a daisy grows in clusters, or how a mass of granite pushes upward in a silent crescendo. These observations and impressions coupled with many others of a similar nature become the fuel which *quickens* one's aesthetic sensitivities.

In the natural world, along with the usual aspects of discovery such as terrain, sky, and water, plus trees, there are some more unusual items that can be challenging to the artist. One subject includes insectivorous plants. These are plants which consume insects and other forms of animal matter in order to maintain nutrients for growth. Plants of this nature capture insects alive, and absorb their juices after they have become immobilized. While this subject is admittedly more imaginative in theme, some plants to study along this order include the Venus flytrap, the Pitcher plant and the Sun dew. Aside from the extreme beauty of color and form of these plants, the motion of the parts in catching the prey is fascinating.

Other idea possibilities in constructing composition might deal with white flowers on a white background; it might be challenging to study plant cross-sections which reveal minute interior details. The size of flowers might be an artistic consideration. In some portions of the world such as Sumatra, flowers attain petal lengths in excess of one foot per petal. Other plants have gigantic flowers with weights exceeding 100 pounds. Some flowers reach a diameter of five to six feet. In this respect, what compositional possibilities exist if we were to paint a flower six feet in diameter? Here again, changing the point of view.

5. **Insects, Bugs and Spider Forms.**   The tiny kingdom beneath man's feet shelters a multitude of fascinating creatures. Many of them exist at our doorstep, but are frequently overlooked as compositional material because of their minuteness. While investigation of an insect in its natural scale is difficult and tedious, one need only consult various entomological journals to discover excellent sources of diagrammed close-ups of specific insects and spiders.

Insects offer the artist surfaces of repetitive patterns in which all parts are harmoniously related. Some parts, such as wings, are transparent and permit visibility through the form. Other parts, such as legs are delicate in appearance, yet are jointed and suggest grace of movement. Butterflies are among some of the more obviously beautiful insect forms. While spiders have interesting structures, they do not enjoy the same popularity as the butterfly. The significant role these insects can play in arousing our awareness relates to the fact that they are not part of the usual world we experience. In fact, they represent a visual stimulus quite different from what we are accustomed to viewing and experiencing. In this respect, they offer us an opportunity to see with fresh insights. Experiences such as these are invigorating to our senses in the same manner that anything new or unusual is exciting to discover! When we are not familiar with a form, we should approach it with curiosity and enthusiasm. At first the mere thought of studying the characteristics of a spider may seem repulsive to us. Once the initial hesitancy has passed, creatures which previously appeared foreign to our thinking will not seem so strange after all. Growing in artistic awareness means to expand one's cathedral through many intense experiences.

6. **Forms from Magnification and Films.**   The more recent electron microscope provides for magnification that can reach one million times normal scale. This means that for the artist, forms never before dreamed of can come into view as artistic potential. Much of the preliminary groundwork has been accomplished by the scientist. Photomicrographs of various substances can offer new insights into design sources and structures. Through magnification,

inside and outside structure can be revealed simultaneously (we call this transparency of form). An opaque substance such as a tree trunk or a nautilus shell can be internally viewed.

Breathtaking worlds can unfold before the artist's observation through the use of magnification. Under the revealing lens, daring new idea sources can be brought into focus. There are several methods of enlarging the diminutive landscape around us. One simple means is to obtain an inexpensive magnifying glass of a type ordinarily used for reading. Objects take on a different appearance when enlarged, and details can be detected that would otherwise go unnoticed. When using a magnifying lens, one is better equipped to observe the inside of a flower, the body of an insect, the textural property of a seed pod, the porousness of skin, or the external structure of the eye.

Another means for examining tiny forms is through films which reveal details of plant life, insect forms, and microorganisms in nature. Motion picture film allows the eye to witness astounding sequences that would otherwise be lost in normal vision. For example, through time-sequence photography the camera can capture the complete unfolding of a flower, the mechanics of birds in flight, or the flow of blood through an artery.

Slides offer a stimulating view of cellular life. The microscope enables one to examine living cells, structural qualities of various subjects, and to discover forms which are invisible to the eye.

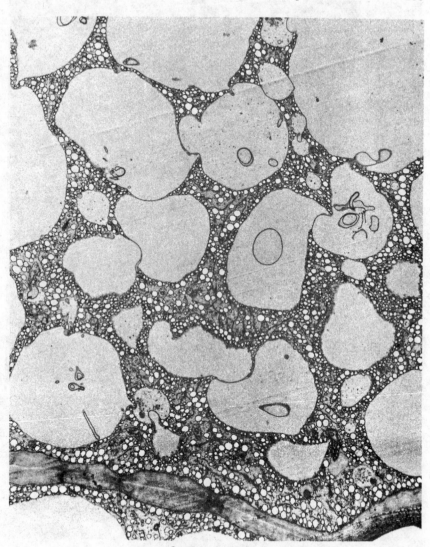

Courtesy, Cell Research Institute, The University of Texas
Photo by F. R. Turner

"A Stage in Spermatogenesis of Zamia, A Cycad"

Courtesy of the Artist

"Cave Formation, Tonto Natural Bridge
near Payson, Arizona"
photo by Jack Stuler

Natural forms can often suggest many ideas.
Note the textural surface, which the artist
has highlighted through his skill with the
camera.

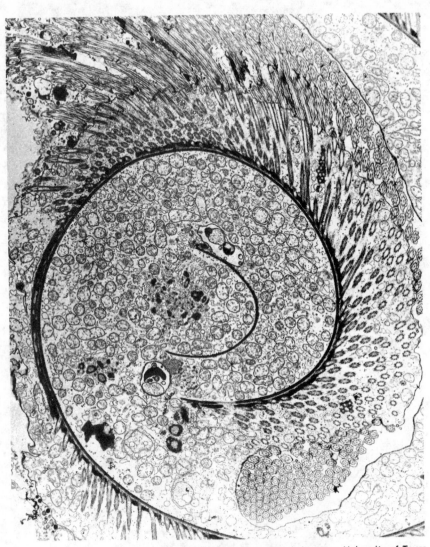

*Courtesy, Electron Microscope Laboratory, University of Texas
Photo by Hilton H. Mollenhauer*

"Cells from a Soybean Cotyledon"

All of these means are usually available through college and high school libraries, science laboratories, and audio-visual departments. These sources can serve as another reference point for stimulating imagination and opening new doors for developing our artistic sense.

7. **Skeletal Structures.**   The skeletal structure of vertebrate creatures offers an interesting opportunity to view internal organization. Bone formations can be pleasing to look at visually from the standpoint of multiple shapes seen in a unified relationship. The shapes of bones are both subtle and graceful in appearance. They suggest a certain fascination which may be attributed in part to their vital function of supporting the human frame.

Through observation of a skeletal structure, the designer is able to relate internal format with the surface variations it supports. Museum collections, college science and art departments are excellent sources of actual skeletal models, as well as detailed visual reproductions.

8. **Discovering the Human Form.**   One might in addition to the conventional aspects consider only a fragment of the figure at extremely close range. Drawing the head in greatly enlarged scale could suggest new directions. Consider the challenge in painting a figure on canvas that is ten times or more life size. Billboards are a fascinating consideration here. At close observation, the scale is so extensive that original intent becomes lost. This forces us to seek new details which come into focus. We may instead pick out a painted watch worn by the figure on the billboard, or a view of an eye that is two feet across. When scale is so extensive, our manner of interpretation of subject is forced to change. Positioning a slide reproduction out of focus changes the point of view also.

Disguising the figure, such as putting a stocking over the face, or an exaggerated application of theatrical makeup, or the placement of colored lights on the subject can stimulate aesthetic directions. The subject viewed under blue light, or purple light, causes our visual field to be spontaneously altered. In a recent film that I saw, one of the actors painted a room completely white—furniture, walls, accessories. The visual effect was startling. Our past perception of what a room looks like changes under such conditions. See-

ing a subject in a new way *under unique visual conditions* can help us to interpret form with a fresh awareness.

Studying the figure through binoculars offers the artist an interesting point of view. Details can be observed that would otherwise go undetected. Viewing the subject through the opposite end of binoculars gives an immediate change of position to the subject. The subject can also be turned out of focus for the study of shapes and related abstract form.

Recent experiments by Bell Telephone Laboratories reveal that voice sound patterns can be transferred into visual images. This might be a direction to pursue.

9. **Shops and Stores** can offer exciting visual material to the eye. Some that are particularly worth mentioning include antique shops. Here, echoes of life gone before reverberate endlessly. Antique dealers are masters at collecting and sorting out the residue of past generations. Without going on at length here, one might find hand-carved pieces of furniture, dishware unlimited, horse-driven hearses, grandfather clocks, rusted implements, old posters, stuffed birds, gilded frames, lost keys, and all the items of childhood experience, and much more to tempt the visual appetite.

10. **Wrecking Yards** are full of the remnants of old vehicles. In a yard of this sort, cars have been stripped, shorn, mangled, and otherwise eviscerated. Front sections are intertwined with frames and fragments of tail gates. Some autos have been burned and charred, and present an alarming scene. In many ways, these auto graveyards tell us something of life and death, beginnings and endings for all things.

11. **Coin Shops.**   Investigating a coin shop might suggest directions for exploration. While coins are extremely interesting to view, their size often causes us to bypass visual gems. Foreign currency is especially interesting. Civil war greenbacks are a visual delight. Other sources of visual possibility in this direction include lamp shops, grocery stores, bakery shops, candy counters, music stores, and amusement centers.

12. **Precision Instruments** are an important source of visual discovery. An aspect for consideration here is motion. Recent experiments in kinetic sculpture relate very closely to this subject. In

Photo by Jack Stuler

this type of world, clocks, relay systems, computers, and signal systems of infinite variety offer visual possibilities that do not exist in the traditional studio set-up. There are a vast network of tubes, wires, signal systems, patterned circuits, and colored units. Of especial interest to the artist here are the light patterns created by the operational sequences of the machine in motion, and the memory banks, which store particles of information. Much of what is aesthetically intriguing in precision instruments is contained under the surface, or relates to the internal components. Watch and clock parts are infinitely more interesting on the inside than on their chromy or wooden exteriors.

In all of the examples thus far mentioned, there are artists whose work can be related. Consulting these works by artists who have explored within a specific area can open insights. Consider precision and automation. Artists such as Sheeler, Leger, Davis, and Pereira come to mind. You may have your own choices.

13. **Camouflage** is a characteristic that has seldom been explored by the artist. In nature, it is of prime importance for survival. The artist could very well utilize these principles in the articulation of an art work. Let's think in terms of colors, tones, and textures that might change ever so subtly on canvas or paper, without being immediately apparent to the eye. Those artists working with optical effects of color have encountered such possibilities. Like the moth who blends into the tree trunk, or the caterpillar who assumes the posture and color of the stem, forms in art can also experiment with such principles. The surrealists incorporated some of this feeling into their work, especially Dali.

14. **Fossils**, or impressions that have been left in ancient rocks, offer much in the way of aesthetic challenge. Fossils can reveal evidence of insects, fish, birds, lizards, and organic matter in nature. An interesting aspect of fossils is that a once three dimensional form has now been flattened into an impression which appears in low relief, and in many cases is merely an abstraction of its former self. This type of visual information would seem pertinent to any-

one working in a pliable material, such as on the surface of a ceramic bowl.

15. **Ideas from Old Photographs.** Old photographs are windows to the past. They are also fantastic sources for generating art ideas. In old photos, every object appears different from today. This includes architecture, clothes, store products, lighting, whatever can be viewed. In addition, the photos themselves have a nice patina or glow, which only comes with age. I often utilize old photographs (as well as contemporary ones) to obtain ideas and forms that can extend my thinking about art. Old photographs can be obtained from historical books in libraries, from magazines that discuss periods in history, and the actual old photographs can often be found in thrift shops or other places which sell "used" items. The actual old photo is much more exciting to view than a printed version in a book.

Photo by Jack Stuler   "Pool, Natural Bridge, Near Payson, Arizona"

Additional Sources for Awareness and Idea-Exploration

ADAM, MARCELLE, *Album of Cats*, New York: Arco Publishing Company, Inc., 1964.

ADAMS, ANSEL, *These We Inherit: The Parklands of America*, San Francisco, California: Sierra Club, 1963.

ALBERT, C., and SECKLER, D., *Figure Drawing Comes to Life*, New York: Reinhold, 1957.

ANDERSON, DONALD M., *Elements of Design*, New York: Holt, Rinehart & Winston, 1961.

ARGIRO, LARRY, *Mosaic Art Today*, Scranton: International Textbook Company, 1961.

AUBERT, DE LaRUE, BOURLIÈRE, FRANCOIS, and HARROY, JEAN-PAUL, *The Tropics*, New York: Alfred A. Knopf, Inc., 1957.

BAKER, RICHARD ST. BARBE, *The Redwoods*, London: George Ronald, 1960.

BAKER, STEPHEN, *Visual Persuasion*, New York: McGraw-Hill Book Company, 1961.

BANDSMA, A. T. and BRANDT, R. T., *The Amazing World of Insects*, New York: Macmillan, 1963.

BARRY, SIR GERALD, et. al., *The Arts: Man's Creative Imagination*, Doubleday Pictorial Library of the Arts, Garden City, New York: Doubleday and Co., Inc., 1965.

BUCHSBAUM, RALPH and others. *The Lower Animals: Living Invertebrates of the World*, Garden City, New York: Doubleday and Co., Inc., 1960.

BUDDENBROCK, WOLFGANG VON, *The Senses*, Ann Arbor: University of Michigan Press, 1958.

BURTON, MAURICE, *Life Under the Sea*, London: Spring Books, 1961.

BUTLER, JOSEPH T., *American Antiques*, 1800–1900, New York: Odyssey Press, 1965.

CAEN, HERB, et. al., *Our San Francisco: America's Favorite City*, Garden City, New York: Doubleday and Co., Inc., 1964.

CAIDIN, MARTIN, and YARNELL, JAMES, *This Is My Land*, New York: Random House, 1962.

CARRINGTON, RICHARD, *Elephants*, New York: Basic Books, Inc., 1959.

CLYMER, JOSEPH FLOYD, *Treasury of Early American Automobiles*, 1877–1925, New York: McGraw-Hill Book Company, 1950.

COCHRAN, DORIS M., *Living Amphibians of the World*, Garden City, New York: Doubleday and Co., Inc., 1961.

COLLINGWOOD, G. H. and BRUSH, WARREN D., *Knowing Your Trees*, Washington, D.C., The American Forestry Association, 1955.

CRUICKSHANK, ALLAN D. and HELEN G., *1001 Questions Answered About Birds*, New York: Dodd, Mead, & Co., 1958.

EDMONDSON, CHARLES H., *Seashore Treasures*, Palo Alto, California: Pacific Books, 1949.

FEININGER, ANDREAS, and LYMAN, SUSAN E., *The Face of New York*, New York: Crown Publishers, 1964.

————, *The Anatomy of Nature*, New York: Crown Publishing, 1956.

FELLIG, ARTHUR, *Weegee's Creative Camera*. Garden City: Hanover House, 1959.

GERTSCH, WILLIS J., *American Spiders*, New York: D. Van Nostrand Co., Inc., 1949.

GREULACH, VICTOR A., and ADAMS, J. EDISON, *Plants: An Introduction to Modern Botany*, New York: John Wiley & Sons, Inc., 1962.

HALSTEAD, BRUCE W., *Dangerous Marine Animals*, Cambridge, Maryland: Cornell Maritime Press, 1959.

HAUSMAN, LEON A., *Birds of Prey of Northwestern North America*, New Brunswick, N.J.: Rutgers University Press, 1948.

HEINROTH, OSKAR and KATHARINA, *The Birds*, Ann Arbor: University of Michigan Press, 1958.

HELLER, JULES, *Printmaking Today*, New York: Holt, Rinehart & Winston, 1958.

HERALD, EARL S., *Living Fishes of the World*, New York: Doubleday and Co., 1961.

HUTCHINS, ROSS E., *This is a Leaf*, New York: Dodd, Mead & Co., 1962.

————, *Wild Ways: A Book of Animal Habits*, Chicago: Rand McNally & Co., 1961.

HUXLEY, ANTHONY J., *Exotic Plants of the World*, Garden City, New York: Hanover House, 1957.

HYLANDER, CLARENCE J., *The Macmillan Wildflower Book*, New York: The Macmillan Company, 1954.

JACK, ANTHONY, *Feathered Wings: A Study of the Flight of Birds*, London: Methuen & Co., Ltd., 1953.

JAEGER, PAUL, *The Wonderful Life of Flowers*, New York: E. P. Dutton & Co., 1961.

JIROVIE, O. BOUCEK, B. and FIALA, J., *Life Under the Microscope*, London: Spring Books.

KEPES, GYÖRGY (ed.), *Education of Vision*, New York: George Braziller, 1965.

KEPES, GYÖRGY (ed.), *Structure In Art and Science*, New York: George Braziller, 1965.

KEPES, GYÖRGY (ed.), *Language of Vision*, Chicago: Paul Theobald, 1944.

KLEIJN, H., *Mushrooms and Other Fungi: Their Form and Colour*, Garden City, New York: Doubleday and Co., 1962.

KLOTS, ALEXANDER B. and KLOTS, ELSIE B., *Living Insects of the World*, New York: Doubleday and Co., 1959.

————, *The World of Butterflies and Moths*, New York: McGraw-Hill Book Company, 1953.

KŌJIRO, YŪICHIRŌ, *Forms in Japan*, Honolulu: East-West Center Press, 1965.

KUH, KATHERINE, *The Artist's Voice*, New York: Harper & Row, 1962.

LINDERMAN, EARL W. and HERBERHOLZ, DONALD W., *Developing Artistic and Perceptual Awareness*, Dubuque, Iowa: Wm. C. Brown Company Publishers, 1964.

LORD, FRANCIS ALFRED, *Civil War Collector's Encyclopedia*, Harrisburg, Pennsylvania: Stackpole Company, 1963.

MANNING, HARVEY, *The Wild Cascades*, San Francisco, California: The Sierra Club, 1964.

MATTIL, EDWARD L., *Meaning In Crafts*, Englewood Cliffs, New Jersey: Prentice-Hall, 1965, 2nd ed.

MAYER, RALPH, *The Painter's Craft*, New York: D. Van Nostrand Co., Inc., 1948.

————, *The Artist's Handbook of Materials and Techniques*, New York: Viking Press, 1957.

McCURRACH, JAMES C., *Palms of the World*, New York: Harper & Row, 1960.

McDARRAH, FRED, *The Artist's World in Pictures*, New York: E. P. Dutton & Co., Inc., 1961.

MERTENS, ROBERT, *The World of Amphibians and Reptiles*, New York: McGraw-Hill Book Company, 1960.

MOHOLY-NAGY, LASZLO, *Vision in Motion*, Chicago: Paul Theobald & Company, 1947.

MOSES, MORRIS, *Printed Circuits*, New York: Gernsback Library, Inc., 1959.

MUYBRIDGE, EADWEARD, *Animals in Motion*. New York: Dover Publications, 1957.

NELSSON, LEINART, *Life in the Sea*, New York: Basic Books, Inc., 1964.

NEUTRA, RICHARD, *Survival Through Design*, New York: Oxford University Press, 1954.

NEWHALL, BEAUMONT, *The History of Photography, 1839 to the Present Day*, Garden City, New York: Museum of Modern Art, 1964.

NICOLAIDES, KIMON, *The Natural Way to Draw*, Boston: Houghton Mifflin Company, 1941.

PESSON, PAUL, *The World of Insects*. New York: McGraw-Hill Book Company, 1959.

PLATT, RUTHERFORD, *The Great American Forest*, Engelwood Cliffs, N.J.: Prentice-Hall, Inc., 1965.

POPE, CLIFFORD HILLHOUSE, *The Giant Snakes*, New York: Alfred A. Knopf, Inc.,1961.

————, *The Reptile World*, New York: Alfred A. Knopf, Inc., 1955.

RICH, JACK C., *The Materials and Methods of Sculpture*, New York: Oxford University Press, 1947.

RICKETT, H. W., *The Odyssey Book of American Wildflowers*, New York: Odyssey Press, 1964.

ROSS, EDWARD S., *Insects Close Up*, Berkeley: University of California Press, 1953.

SACHS, PAUL J., *Modern Prints and Drawings*, New York: Alfred A. Knopf, Inc.,1954.

SCHINNELLER, JAMES A., *Art: Search and Self-Discovery*, Scranton: International Textbook Co., 1961.

SCHMIDT, KARL P. and INGER, ROBERT F., *Living Reptiles of the World*, New York: Hanover House, 1957.

SHAHN, BEN, *The Shape of Content*, New York: Harvard Press Books, 1957.

SMITH, ALEXANDER H., *The Mushroom Hunter's Field Guide*, Ann Arbor: University of Michigan Press, 1958.

SMITH, MAXWELL, *World Wide Sea Shells*, Ann Arbor: Edward Brothers, Inc., 1940.

SMYTHE, R. H., *Animal Visions: What Animals See*, Springfield, Illinois: Charles C. Thomas, 1961.

STANEK, V. J., *Pictorial Encyclopedia of the Animal Kingdom*, New York: Crown Publishers, 1962.

STEICHEN, EDWARD, *The Family of Man*, New York: Maco Magazine, Museum of Modern Art Publication, 1955.

STRACHE, WOLF, *Forms and Patterns in Nature*, New York: Pantheon Books, Inc., 1956.

TAYLOR, NORMAN, *The Ageless Relicts: The Story of Sequoia*, New York: St. Martin's Press, 1963.

TEALE, EDWIN WAY, *The Strange Lives of Familiar Insects*, New York: Dodd, Mead & Company, 1962.

———, *A Book About Bees*, Bloomington, Indiana: Indiana University Press, 1959.

TYLINEK, ERICH and STEPANEK, OTAKAR, *The Animal World*, London: Spring Books, 1964.

VESEY, NORMAN, *Arms and Armor*, New York: G. P. Putnam's Sons, 1964.

VOGEL, ZDENAK, *Reptiles and Amphibians*, New York, Viking Press, 1964.

WINEBRENNER, D. KENNETH, *Jewelry Making As An Art Expression*, Scranton: International Textbook Co., 1963.

"Mouth Number 14 (Marilyn)"
by Tom Wesselman, 1967
Oil on Canvas

Chapter 11

How and where the arts are learned may be of greater significance than how successfully they are taught. The arts are learned in university lecture halls and in small hallways, at concerts and through the hi-fi in the gallery and on the street, in crowds and in isolation, and the learning may be carefully structured and formal or casual and accidental. The arts are taught by teachers who enjoy students and who find teaching a rewarding, creative delight, and by teachers who find teaching a dull, interfering bore and think of students as the enemy.

EDWARD L. MATTEL,
"Teaching the Arts," from *The Arts in Higher Education*,
San Francisco: Jossey-Bass Inc., Publishers, 1968, p. 60

Art Teachers and Artists Provide Learning Clues on Art

A Letter from Tom Wesselman, East Coast Painter

Dear Earl,

There are just about three things that I feel are important enough to stress about essentials for becoming an artist:

1. Challenge *every* aspect of your life—every value you had taught to you or accepted—every idea you ever considered valid. Throw out all you can't accept or justify and keep all that are justifiable. (Under whatever standards you bring to bear, and challenge more standards.) However, realizing human fallibility, be open to re-evaluations.

2. Study and learn about other things than art, for the most part. Art should get the least attention.

The above two seem to me indispensable to being mature enough and your own person enough to have a personal point of view and deep enough conviction to compel you to work.

3. Look at as many paintings, especially, but not only, rather contemporary works. (And other art forms too—theater, dance, books, etc.)

That's it. The manual ability comes easily enough when the necessity to paint is strong enough.

A Statement by Larry Foster, West Coast Artist

Most physics students know more about physics than Galileo or Newton, but most art students don't know more about art than Leonardo or Michelangelo. It's true because knowledge in science is cumulative and knowledge in art is not. Contemporary art is not better or poorer than Egyptian art, but contemporary medicine is a whole lot better than Egyptian medicine.

If you want to study art you could start at any point in history. For in terms of which is easy to understand, there is no beginning or end in art. However there are beginning art students and they can start by looking at the greatest pieces of painting and sculpture in the world. If they give the student pleasure then there is understanding just as one understands a fine steak, a rose garden or a new Porsche. If he rejects them, or they simply aren't enjoyed, then I believe he is the product of conditioning which has to some extent excluded art.

Developing understanding and abilities in art is actually an uncomplicated matter. It simply takes incentive to look and exposure to see. I've encouraged my students to make quick poster paint copies of artists they are curious about, either for or against. The value in this exercise isn't in having a copy of a painting around the house, but what happens in the process of producing the copy itself. In order to copy, one must be exposed and the exposure nearly always extends the student's approval of the artist, for in order to copy one must look carefully. The exercise is also good for the students because it helps them get over the "I want to be different." We all want to be different. That's all well and good, but the difference must be a result of study and not a substitute for study. After all, Rembrandt didn't start off by being Rembrandt. First, he was that serious kid over in the corner that was always drawing.

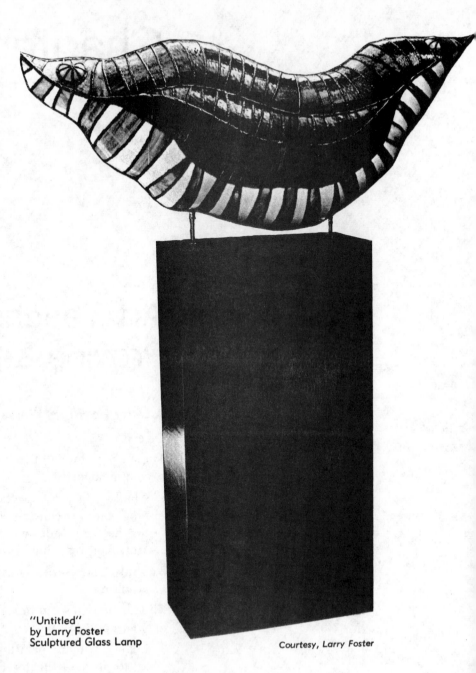

"Untitled"
by Larry Foster
Sculptured Glass Lamp

Courtesy, Larry Foster

A Conversation with Mel Ramos, West Coast Painter

Q. The first question that I would like to ask you is how did you get started painting comic heroes such as bat man?

Like most college students you have hero types that you are interested in, and at that time De Koonings woman series really caused me a lot of trouble. I couldn't get over them for a long period of time, so consequently the paintings from '58 to the end of the year were very much in that vein. At the same time I was interested in figures. My work looked a lot like Diebenkorn for a couple of months. Then, since I couldn't handle color very well I became very muted in terms of tonality. I was painting in greys. I began to develop a series of paintings of straight ordinary figures with a lot of grey. But, I remember about 1960 there seemed to be something in the air. I started thinking very seriously about some things that I wanted to paint, and I remember thinking about some things that I was very interested in as a young kid, and that was comic books. As a kid in courses I used to draw Captain Marvel in English and arithmetic, in high school and grade school because it bored me. So, these grey figures that I was doing, one day I just put a costume on it and it was funny, it was really a funny painting. I never thought of taking it seriously. I need coaxing, I need praise. I was hoping someone would say, "Wow, what a great painting." But of course, no one did. And, then I went over to a friend of mine and saw a painting that he did about the same time of a piece of pie. He had the same feeling about his piece. He was always involved with counters and food displays, but he always did them in a very romantic abstract expressionist style. One day he stripped all the romance out and painted it just straight out. When I saw this and I knew that someone else was doing the same type of thing, I went home and did a whole series of them. Then I saw in *Time* magazine that Leo Castelli had come out and proclaimed Roy Lichtenstein one of the geniuses of this whole epic, because of his comic book painting that he made. When he did this of course, I was sold on it. It convinced me that I was really doing the right thing. I started collecting early pre code comic books and did a whole series of cul-

Courtesy, Mel Ramos

"Chic"
by Mel Ramos, 1965
Oil on Canvas

Courtesy, Mel Ramos
Collection of William Zierler, New York

"Mysta of the Moon"
by Mel Ramos, 1962
Oil on Canvas

ture heroes, which I was very much interested in. Out of this came maybe thirty or forty paintings of people like Bat Man, Robin, Superman. But, the very funny thing, one hero that I never did, one that I always remember in my mind and who probably impressed me the most was Captain Marvel. I had a whole collection of his comic books. I had never done a painting of Captain Marvel. And, I finally realized about two years later why I had never done him. It was because I look just like him. He's kind of fat, curly hair; he's got a dimple on his chin, a round face, like I do, and it's like a sacred cow sort of thing.

Q. How did you evolve to a change from your comic book series?

Actually there never was a change. The work from that period was a very slow subtle transition, a process. The paint was very thick at the beginning, right now it's very thin. When I ran out of male heroes, I just started doing the female heroes. Shena, Queen of the Jungle, Phantom Lady, Wonder Woman, Fau, White Goddess, Roma, empress of the ancient world, and people like that—Cat Girl, Leopard Girl. I began to notice the sort of erotic drawing in these books. In order to make the erotic thing come through more, I stopped using the comic connotations and started using photographs from girly magazines. So, I could draw and paint the anatomy of a real figure and make it more believable. So, I got rid of the comic like drawing and used a kind of academic drawing. This suggested a level of reality which was much different than the comic book. The costumes began to get slinkier and more suggestive. Like we see at the circus with the girls on the elephants, it was a very suggestive sort of thing. This is the way it was in the comic books, until about 1950 when the code came out and banned all that sort of thing. Then I ran that to the logical conclusion, and finally with a painting called Navel Orange I removed the costume and used the girl in an environment which was sort of humorous. I did the first nude picture of a sex queen buried in a pile of oranges. Then the progression gradually moved up until what I'm doing now. What I'm doing now, again is just an extension of these figures. But, my preoccupation has always been with the figure.

Courtesy, Mel Ramos

"Lolita"
by Mel Ramos, 1966
Oil and Rayon Flock on Canvas and Panel

Q. Who do you feel are the outstanding young artists of today?

I try to be objective about making judgments about other peoples work. But, I have certain sympathies, and these sympathies lie in my own idiom. The people that I have the most regard for as strong intellectual painters even visual type of painters are people like Roy Lichtenstein, who because of his direction in what he has done to alter the course of modern art. And, also Claus Oldenberg who I think is probably one of the strongest sculptors around. When I was in college I had a great admiration for Corot, and of the real young, the New York painters. I think that Tom Wesselman is developing a very strong direction in terms of ideas and image. I think artists have to change, even if it's very slightly. They have to keep working. Keep doing things which are going to alter your visual threshold.

Q. What do you mix with your pigment?

In order to make the kind of image that I paint as believable as possible, I really try to use a classical painting media—oil paint. I use a very classical mixer which is ⅓ turpentine, ⅓ linseed oil, and ⅓ varnish. However, recently I'm taking out the varnish because it turns the paint a little brittle. Because of the very sort of cristene surface that I have, any sort of blemish or mark just destroys the whole thing. I've been having trouble with people poking the paint, poking the canvasses or treating them a little roughly. The paint is cracking, that is they put little cracks in the surface. The varnish does this. So I'm getting rid of the varnish and using more turpentine and linseed oil with very little varnish. It makes a nice satin finish.

Q. Do you use any special brushes or canvas?

Canvas I don't. I just use a portrait linen which has a very fine tooth. But, I came across Degas filbert brushes, which have long tapered bristles. This seems to work best for me. I use these almost exclusively when I render things. When I work with large areas I use big flat brushes.

Q. Do you prepare a preliminary sketch or study?

Yes. Usually I spend a lot of time going through photographs, because I paint from photographs. I can't afford models. I go through photographs, collect magazines, and collect photographs from magazines. I collect a lot of photographs that I think that I could use, and then I sit down every three or four days and just pick out component parts of various figures that might suggest an idea for a painting. Then I make a small drawing combining these component parts or two or three of them. If it seems to work out then I blow it up with an opaque projector onto a large canvas. The rest is just working out the paint.

Q. How long a period do you spend on painting, generally?

It varies. If I'm lucky I can get a five-by-six-foot painting done in two days. If I'm unlucky I can get a twenty-by-thirty-inch painting done in two weeks. It really varies depending upon how difficult the problem is, the mood I'm in, and if my bills are paid. If all these things are bothering you then it takes you longer. One of the best paintings I ever did, one of the best known is a painting called Chiquita Banana, which is a very large painting, five-by-six-feet. I started it about four o'clock in the afternoon. I painted the banana, and part of the figure, and I went out the next morning at eight o'clock and finished the figure and put in the background by ten that night. Then I just sat back. I was so delighted with the result. But it happened like within thirty-six hours. The painting was done. But that's rare. I was just lucky.

Q. When do you consider a painting finished?

Never, really. There have been paintings that I have thought were finished, that would just sit around the studio and then later I might have made a correction or changed it, or altered a color or taken out something or another. I guess when they're finished is when I frame them and give them to the gallery, or when they sell them, if they sell them. Even at that I have had some paintings come back from the gallery that didn't sell and I've worked on.

Q. Do you find painting a rigorous discipline?

Painting to me is hard work. I don't know how else to describe it. You can't make good paintings if you paint just when you feel like painting. I'm a fatalist in that regard. I feel that you have so many bad paintings in you and you just have to paint to get them all out of your system before you can get a good one. So, I try to set myself a time limit each week and try to work at least thirty or forty hours whether I want to or not. I force myself to do it. It's nothing else but a discipline to me. It's my work.

Q. Do you feel that each painting you do is successful?

No, not successful in that sense. I think when I finish a painting, if I really like it I consider it successful. If I don't like it, I just keep working and working and working on it and I might never like it, but I finally reach a point where I'm so sick of the painting that I just resolve it to the best possible way that I can at that time, and hope that maybe tomorrow I'll feel differently, but that usually never happens. You can usually tell when the painting is successful. Of course, these are hard decisions to make. Once in awhile I know.

Q. Do you feel that painters should be teachers of their art?

No, I don't think about that much. I teach because I have to. If my work supported me I'd quit teaching, but of course not many of us can do that. The market for painting is very fickle. You might do very well one year and lousy the next. And then again some painters can't teach. They just can't relate to people. But, I personally enjoy teaching. I like to open up people, but I don't impose my image on them. I don't believe in that.

Q. Does your own teaching help you in your painting?

Not my own teaching. I have found a few students who were very excited students and of course you get excited by their work. Their enthusiasm, kind of reminds you of when you were twenty-five and had a lot of enthusiasm. When you get up past thirty you start to get lazy. I think a good students enthusiasm will help regenerate the enthusiasm in me. I like that. I enjoy that part of it.

Q. Do you feel that any one can learn to paint well?

Absolutely. I think anyone can paint well providing that you're not retarded or something like that. But, even then there are retarded people who paint some fantastic pictures. They're very naive and they might not know what they're about but they're great paintings. I think with discipline and the willingness to work at it any one can learn to paint.

Q. Are you speaking of artistically inclined individuals or just anyone in particular?

I don't really know what artistic inclination is other than some people work harder than other people. Some people are born lazy. And, some people like to work. If they direct that enthusiasm towards painting or art, I think they're going to be good at it.

Q. Are there some individuals who are born with a gift to become an artist?

Again, I think it's the same thing. The gift that they have is the ability for lots of work. That is, they are energetic and enthusiastic and this is their gift. I'm saying that these people could do well at anything. If they chose to be a baseball player they could.

Q. What do you feel that should be done in terms of public school art? To improve programs in public schools?

I think they should make art a requirement, like any other discipline. They regard it as an elective course and it gets all the treat-

ment of most elective courses. They get very little money, very little encouragement from administration. Everybody is trying to get their share of the government money and of course it all goes to the sciences and English and languages. There seems to be such a strong kind of emphasis to get people into the universities, and they don't regard art as a prerequisite to get into the universities. I think this is a terrible mistake. Either they make art a requirement or get rid of it. Because you see what's coming out of the schools. They're all eyesores. The very best art that comes out of the public shools is coming out of places where there are professional artists teaching, and not so called school teacher types who took one course in college and are qualified to teach art. If they're going to teach art then they should be specialists at it. Otherwise you see what's happening. It's just like anything else. You have to be a specialist at it. I think they should make it a requirement or else just get rid of it completely, because it's not doing anyone any good, otherwise.

Some Notes on the Disadvantaged Student

Where does the so-called disadvantaged child fit into the picture in relation to the teaching of art programs at the secondary level? The answer, while not in complete focus, is provided in some directions by researchers in the field. Fundamentally, it appears that art experiences can be tremendously significant to the increased perceptual and intellectual performance of students from economically depressed areas. Art experiences open the door for students of all types, and provide options by which they can take a new look at their environment, and perhaps move in the direction of restructuring personal aesthetic vision.

The following interview was by the author and Dr. Eugene Grigsby, professor of art and art education at Arizona State University. Dr. Grigsby is well-known for his work with the economically disadvantaged.

Q. Does economics play a part in the art curriculum?

Yes, it plays something of a factor, but I think the curriculum should be built around the kids. I don't think kids themselves are so different from one part of the city to the other, the Inner City or the suburb. I really don't think kids are that different. You take European or American students—they're kids from any part of the world. Every school should build a curriculum around the kind of kids and the kind of experiences these kids have had. They should capitalize on what the kids can do or what the kids cannot do. I believe in each instance you will find a rich background if you probe deep enough. What we call the Inner City kid, the kid from the lower economic level, may have some advantages that the suburbia kid from the affluent society may not have. For example, he may have been free to roam, get in the mud, get dirty. Tactile experiences may have been his from early childhood. He may bring in tin cans and the sort of thing that we treasure for collages. A kid from the more affluent home, where he has had to keep everything clean; when he walks in, he can't get dirty; if he gets any paint on his clothes, he gets a spanking, so he goes into a shell and becomes disadvantaged in terms of this kind of experience. I suspect, in general, if you could do a study of kids who have not had the freedom to explore a variety of mediums, you might have a different kind of expression from them than those who have been free to do almost anything. Where kids in the Inner City are disadvantaged is largely in verbal communication, in conversational skills, in ability to read. Again, many of the reasons he is able to draw, many of the reasons he's able to roam, to do whatever he wants to, has impeded his progress in the other kind of activities.

I think the curriculum that we need to consider has to also consider the kind of background experiences and the level of development of the individual. I think that at no other time, and in no other place in the curriculum do we have the opportunity to develop certain characteristics or qualities within the individual as in high school. I don't think it's been touched upon because we've been so concerned with bringing in the kind of thing you can get in college —or, bringing in the kind of art techniques and forgetting to let the individual grow almost at will without any direction. In other words it's been a product end in curriculum, where I think that the individual should be the ultimate end.

Q. What could you get from art at the high school level that could be different from art at the college level?

You can develop a sense of integrity because you have the student every day. You have the opportunity to develop understandings of self. You have an opportunity to help people live together, work together, to cooperate with one another and to teach one another. You have this in the curriculum that you don't have at any other time in the secondary school.

Q. Why wouldn't you have this in another class in the high school?

Because they're academically oriented. They have a book that they have to go through. You *can* have; it's possible. Art is a good jumping-off place. I feel that it is important, because this is the last place where many people will ever have a chance to explore art, the visual exploration, the tactile exploration. Even in education, English teachers, history teachers, math teachers don't have time to search visually. But they become teachers in schools, they become business men and sit on boards of directors and dictate what kind of art there shall be; the kind of art experiences they've had is usually very limited because most high schools will guide a kid through an "I.Q." program. If it's high and if he is "capable," this will move him into the academic world. He is deprived of any visual experience at all.

Q. Are kids from the Inner City as visually enriched as kids from the Outer City?

It depends on many factors. They are limited in terms of some experiences. They don't have any books in their home. They don't have anything to read. Verbal command is lower. It's not necessarily low in terms of visual experience. Now I haven't made any studies, but I've had my own experience.

Q. You have a long rich background of teaching at the high school level. Were the students in your classes visually prolific?

I think so. We had kids from some of the poorest areas of Phoenix and then some of the kids were quite well-to-do. I think the confusion of all of this comes about because of lack of experience in people who have done much theorizing, and it seems to me that most of these people have had a lot of experience in the academic areas, but then again very little experience in the visual art areas. It takes a couple of high school generations and when I talk of a generation I'm talking of four years. It takes a couple of generations to grasp the kinds of kids, the variations, the differences, and how they are changing constantly. I think that you need to get someone who has worked very closely with kids over a period of time to see where they can stretch and how far, and what can be done with them. I have a report on Picasso, which I showed to my class last week, done by a high school freshman, second semester, who came from a poor family, which rivals any comparable report from any college student I've seen. I think when we begin to limit what we can say, generalizing as to what you can expect from a student, then we immediately put a limitation on it.

On the other hand there have been some with limited verbal experiences. The first student I ever had create an etching was one whose verbal skills were so limited he wasn't even enrolled in any of the academic classes. He did it beautifully. But this was only through understanding and working with the student, knowing what he might be able to do under certain circumstances.

But I think that it is in this area where we have an opportunity to develop the skills that will help a person to first make a living, and second to enjoy it. We talk about teenagers not being responsible. We talk about them not having ambition, initiative, and not being concerned with the way things around them look. I think this is what we ought to teach. And it's through the arts that we can teach these things. Especially through the visual arts. If a person learns how to work and wants to know how to work, he becomes responsible for himself. He can carry this out on his own. He can go beyond what has been given to create new things. He can learn to use materials and techniques. Then you're teaching something more than just the art. I find that practically every other area teaches something about how to live, how to make a living. This is one thing that I have a quarrel with regarding many of the poverty programs. They teach a person how to make a living; they take him off of welfare and put some money in his pocket, but he changes very little. He may go from a hovel to a $100,000 house, but he's got the same

Courtesy, Phoenix Union High School, Phoenix, Arizona
Photo by Chuck Friedenmaker

problems. He doesn't learn to enjoy being around these things any more than he did before. Just because a person is on welfare doesn't mean that he cannot experience visual things. These kids learn to silk-screen wrapping paper, wall paper, fix up better rooms, and fix up other rooms around them. These things they know how to enjoy and they know how to make things enjoyable and if they have no money, they can still do it. They can still enjoy it. If you don't have the sensitivity—I don't care how much money you have—that's something that no one can give you. You can't buy it. It's like love.

Q. A kid who comes from the Inner City—are his chances of having this sensitivity just as great?

Yes, just as great.

Q. Then could the art curriculum be used as a springboard to enable the student to get started on visual skills? Could this be used as a social force of value?

Yes, this is possible. To learn to respect one another through the arts produced by people of a similar background. For example, we have a misconception that only in the Inner City do we have different groups. America has not been the melting pot it has claimed. I don't care where you go, you have kids that are just as different in their ethnic background in every suburb. All you have to do is fly around the world and you see the Semitic people—Egypt and Israel —are at each other. People that look alike but maybe are far more different than people who don't look alike. Look at Nigeria and Biafra. Almost every place you look—the Irish, the Catholics, and the Protestants—these people are at each other's throats. I feel that through the arts every group has produced important works of art which are highly prized. If individuals can discover for themselves something about these things through the respect of these, they can also learn to respect individuals.

Q. Would the Inner City kid be able to handle art history as part of his curriculum?

The kids would. The problem is the teacher, teaching the idea. If the teacher can communicate with the kids, they can handle it. So it's a question of communication.

Q. Is it possible that the teacher will not be able to use traditional approaches to communication, or are there some kind of barriers there? Earlier we mentioned that the kids were lower verbally.

This doesn't mean they can't verbalize. They are lower in their ability to read certain kinds of things. They have the potential, but it hasn't been developed academically by handing a kid something that has been written some other place or any place. But if you handle this in the sense of Sylvia Ashton Warner handled the children that she worked with, and using their terminology, and taking words that they understand and working with them; they can grasp it—just like any other kid. The kids at that level in all of the areas should be writing materials themselves, should be developing materials, should be working; not out of some esoteric historian's book, but out of their own experiences.

Q. What are some specific ways you would use to reach kids in the Inner City that you would employ, if you couldn't use verbal means?

You can use verbal means. I think we need to use verbal means. I don't think that there is that great a difference between the kids of the Inner City and the kids of the Outer City. The means of reaching them would depend on those particular kids in the class and the particular creativity of the teacher. Suburbs can be deprived just as visually as the ghettos. There is the same problem. Like the ticky-tacky boxes, everybody repeating the same thing. When we talk of driving through, this is the visual impact that we are getting.

Q. In a sense, you mentioned that the Inner City kids might have greater freedoms in a certain area; that is, they are free to explore and to express. The kids in the suburbs might be limited to mothers doting on them.

When we say this, we are talking about generalities, which again you are assuming things which appear to be. But there does seem to be a lot of money from governmental sources going into projects aimed at providing research and discovery aimed at dealing with the disadvantaged, deprived. They talk about disadvantaged kids and things like that. I say this is where much of my quarrel is. I am participating in several of these groups, sitting on boards. Each one of them has difficulty getting over the point that there must be something besides economic improvement. There needs to be just as much concern about a certain aesthetic understanding. Understanding how to enjoy this economic advancement in terms of the visual impact around them.

We in the schools need to understand that there are various areas in which the art program can be most effective. Those kids who are going on to college to take art—they can do it whether they have a terrific program in art in high school or not, for the most part. Those who don't go to college but who drop out of high school, they're the ones who need help and they don't need the kind of orientation that you prepare in the college curriculum.

This little thing of bead-making that we started last summer has gone around like wild fire. Kids get the biggest bang out of this —making things out of nothing. If we can encourage and spread the word that you can take things that are ordinarily thrown away and make something beautiful out of it. We are so affluent that half of our society is just throw-away. Part of the problem with people is that they are treated the same way as things and they feel that they have no value, no worth for themselves. They say, "I'm of no value, there's nothing here for me, so forget it." If they in turn see some self-value for themselves, that they are valuable people and that they have a particular place and something to contribute; then we begin the building-up process. If a person is making things for his own enjoyment, if he is making things for his own room, if he is designing his tiles or walls, then I think art is doing him some good. But if he closes his book at the end of class and never picks up a brush, never does anything else, never concerns himself with his own arrangement, never tries to do any puttering on the lawn, arrange flowers, make shapes or uses textures of rocks or of bamboo, to make his own little environment enjoyable where he wants to come home, where he wants to look around and just sit back and enjoy what's around him; then I think art is doing the job it should be in high school. If instead he's taking it for a grade in order to go to college, I think we are wasting time and money. The purpose of art is to give some meaning to his life.

Q. If you could make some recommendations for Inner City students, what would you recommend?

Good teachers. Teachers who are willing to give time to kids. Teachers who are not on a time schedule activated by bells and paychecks only. Good teachers are willing to work with kids and to help them over some hurdles. They are creative and are willing to relate to kids without giving them their own hang-ups, without forcing their ideas on the kids. Teachers who draw out of the kids ideas that they have that can relate to the community. Teachers who participate in community activities, who go to a home in order to get to know the kids and who develop programs based on the kids that they are working with instead of being based on something that someone told them was the way it has to be.

"Ceramic Cactus"
by Randy Schmidt

Chapter 12

It is a mistake for a sculptor or a painter to speak or write very often about his job. It releases tension needed for his work. By trying to express his aims with rounded-off logical exactness, he can easily become a theorist whose actual work is only a caged-in exposition of conceptions evolved in terms of logic and words.

But though the non-logical, instinctive, subconscious part of the mind must play its part in his work, he also has a conscious mind which is not inactive. The artist works with a concentration of his whole personality, and the conscious part of it resolves conflicts, organizes memories, and prevents him from trying to walk in two directions at the same time.

HENRY MOORE,
from "On Sculpture and Primitive Art,"
New Jersey: Prentice-Hall, Inc., p. 141

Studio Notes for the Studio: Ideas for Art Teachers

Adventures in Ceramics

Here are some suggestions for getting started in ceramics:

1. Demonstrate wedging and emphasize the plastic qualities of clay. Distribute clay to each student, and encourage him to discover its characteristics by pressing, shaping, and twisting it into various shapes. Illustrate the nature of clay in its various forms such as moist, leather-firm, dry, bisque, and glazed.
2. Discuss the aesthetic beauty of hand-formed pieces. Illustrate with slides a survey of ceramic art, from ancient times to the present day.
3. Show examples of slides of contemporary ceramics emphasizing its flexibility and limitations. Have class discussions afterward concerning how the students respond to ceramic art.
4. Form a cup from a clay ball using the hands as tools. Avoid extremely thin edges.
5. From a solid mass of clay, construct an abstract form.
6. Carve a free-shape form from a leather-hard ball of clay.
7. Encourage the students to make an art notebook which shows examples of pottery and sculptured ceramics.

8. Keep idea material handy: ask the students to contribute. Change the displays often.
9. Emphasize care of equipment and respect for property.
10. Experiment with joining clay parts at the leather-hard stage by using slip, and scoring methods.
11. Study clay bodies and the potentialities of specific clays for various methods of pottery and ceramic construction.
12. Discuss the surface embellishment of a piece in relation to its aesthetic form.
13. Make a series of small slabs for textural and glaze experiments.
14. Create unusual surface qualities by the inclusion of unorthodox materials, such as grog, sawdust, cinders, rust, or other substances.
15. Demonstrate the use of engobes as a color source. Develop a sgraffito design on a ceramic piece. Apply oxides to enrich clay bodies and glazes.
16. Emphasize the relationship between function and form in functional ceramics. Construct a pitcher or cup that has a pouring spout and handle.
17. Show how green-ware and bisque-ware differ. Explain how a bisque fire is necessary to the glazing of the piece.
18. Idea-search with various tools on clay surfaces.
19. Demonstrate coil method of building. Coils should be of uniform thickness and length.
20. Show slides of contemporary ceramics which are done in a free or abstract manner. Discuss the transition of ceramics from a functional art form to an expressive statement in art media.
21. Demonstrate the proper method of flattening a slab of clay.
22. Have the students compile good examples of clay products.
23. Experiment with different ways of shaping clay through such methods as pinching, coiling, slabs, modeling, and sculpting.
24. Visit a local ceramics shop. Prepare a report on types of supplies used, glaze, methods and clay preparation.
25. Visit galleries to observe ceramics of both past and contemporary artists. Have students critically prepare a written or oral report.

26. Be alert to university art exhibits. Visit them often to keep abreast of new ideas and examples of the work of teacher-potters.
27. Practice stacking the kiln under supervision. Experiment with the best use of space by fitting pots into the space.
28. Discuss the value of using kiln wash to prolong the life of shelves. Kiln wash is prepared from equal parts silica kaolin, and ball clay.
29. Illustrate various types of glazes and discuss their characteristics, such as transparent, glossy, semi-glossy, matt, etc.
30. Experiment with glaze applications, such as dipping, pouring, brushing, spraying.
31. Discuss firing processes such as oxidation, reduction, and vitrification of clay.
32. Mix different oxides and chemicals to produce various glaze effects. Utilize transparent, white satin or white matt glazes.
33. Experiment with glaze colorants, such as iron oxide, cobalt, copper carbonate, glaze stains and nitrates.
34. Create unusual forms by shaping clay around stones, sand bags, or other forms.
35. Have students exhibit their art work.
36. Have students select a contemporary ceramist whose work the student admires and have him compile a body of information that he can report to the class.

Equipment and Supplies

Kiln—minimum 3-5 cubic feet, gas or electric

Kiln furniture—shelves, supports, stilts, spurs

Work benches—solid, wooden top

Wedging table

Clay storage bin with cover

Damp storage cupboards

Student storage lockers

Storage cabinets for tools and supplies

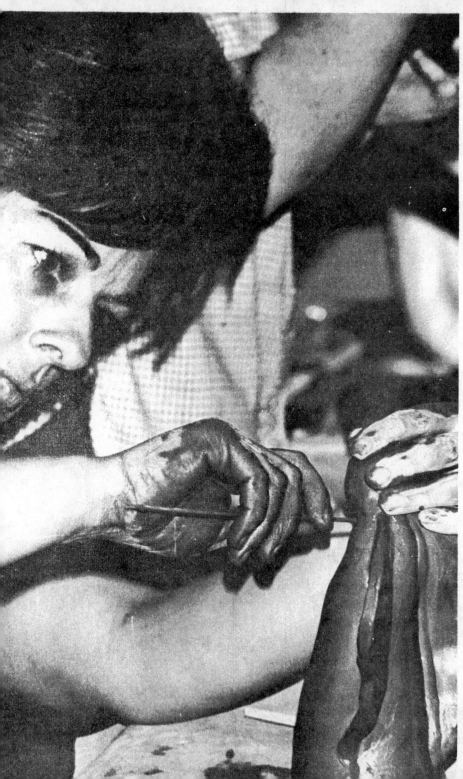

Courtesy, Don Schaumberg

"Ceramic Pot"
by Don Schaumburg

Courtesy, Mesa Public Schools, Mesa, Arizona

Ware racks

Potter's wheels

Spray booth with fan, compressor, spray gun

Pug mill

Sinks

Banding wheels

Plastic sheeting and bags

Plaster of Paris bats

Porcelain mortars and pestles, 16 and 32 ounce

Brass glaze sieves: 60, 80, and 120 mesh

Ball-mill jars: ½ gallon and quart sizes

Balance scale

Containers, plastic: bowls, basins, buckets, cannisters with lids, jugs

Brushes, artists: soft and hard, large and small

Slip trailers and nozzles

Burlap, at least 24 inches wide

Sponges, household cellulose: heavy duty. Small elephant ear or complexion sponges: close texture, natural

Rolling pins

Wood strips or dowels, matching pairs: 24 inches by ⅜ or ½ inch

Pieces of wood to beat or shape clay

Knives: any thin, short, narrow blade. Artist's palette knife: small, 6 inches

Cutting wires: nylon line, or thin copper wire

Scrapers: hacksaw blades, adhesive spreaders or bits of rasp-plane blades. Flexible metal scrapers, kidney-shaped as well as straight-sided, 3–4 inches long. Housepainter's scraper

Pressers or ribs: kidney-shaped, rubber with tapered off edges

Modeling tools: any kind, particularly simple wooden ones and large simple wire loops which have been given teeth by filing

Needle tools

Funnels

Measuring spoons

Clay—gray and red or brown; high-fire pugged

Plaster of Paris—regular pottery plaster

Seger cones

Kiln wash

Wax resist—liquid

Glazes—high-fire, dry-blended:

Semi-clear matt	Eggshell white
Opaque white	Opaque white gloss
Mottled beige	Transparent

(Glaze materials for mixing from scratch are not listed due to the lack of storage space in most high school classrooms.)

Glaze and engobe stains—variety of colors such as:

orange	turquoise
yellow	green
brown	black
red	purple
blue	

Engobe bases

Grog—#20 and #30 mesh

Oxides—variety for colorants:

tin oxide	iron chromate
iron oxide	rutile
cobalt carbonate	vanadium, tin
copper carbonate	zinc oxide
manganese oxide	chrome oxide

Casting slip—high-fire

Clay—high-fire powdered, gray and red-brown for engobes

Photography

Materials for Photography

1. Film—endless varieties. Two basic ones are:
    Plus X
    Tri X—higher speed than Plus X. Good for night shots.

2. Developer:
   Microdol X
   Fixit
   Replenisher
3. Camera—any camera with manual shutter speeds and lens opening.
4. Enlarger
5. Paper holder
6. Dryer
7. Print presser
8. Developing tank
9. Developing apron
10. Funnel
11. Thermometer
12. Light meter

Printing Procedures

The negative to be enlarged must be clean, free of dust and placed emulsion side down in the enlarger.

The next step is to focus and compress the image on the enlarging easel. This is done with the diaphragm of the lens wide open. For the exposure, the lens should be closed to approximately f11 (approximately three clicks on the enlarger lens).

A test exposure strip is then made across the important portion of the image to ascertain the correct printing time. The test strip should then be *developed* for two minutes, *rinsed* for ten seconds, and *fixed* for two minutes.

It should then be taken into the white light and compared with the contact print for evaluation and placement of tones.

Upon choosing the proper exposure time, the print is ready to be exposed.

Print according to your text exposure evaluation.

Step-by-Step Procedure for Film Development

1. Remove film from paper backing (in dark).
2. Wind film carefully in clean plastic apron. Be certain the film does not overlap the serrated edges of the apron.
4. Place apron and film in empty tank.
4. Place metal disk in tank on top of film.
5. Place cover on tank tightly.
6. Light may be turned on at this time as tank is light-tight.
7. Check temperature of chemicals. (Chemicals should not vary in temperature more than 3–5 degrees.)
8. Find corresponding time for your particular chemical temperature.
9. Carefully noting the exact time when you begin, pour developer into the tank.
10. Agitate constantly for the first ten seconds of development, thereafter five seconds every half minute.
11. After prescribed development time, pour developer back into bottle and fill tank with water, agitating for approximately ten seconds.
12. Pour water into sink and fill tank with fixing solution (hypo).
13. Fix for ten seconds.
14. Pour fix back into bottle.
15. Tank may be opened at this time.
16. Wash film in running water for thirty minutes.
17. Film should be hung carefully in drying room; handle film only by edges, being careful not to touch image with anything but air.

Contrast Control

1. Through filters: red filter filters out complementary colors.
2. Inherent contrast: light things against light, dark against dark.
3. Lighting
4. Film: slow speed fine grain
   medium speed Pan Am X
   fast film Kodak Tri-X

5. Film developer: Microdol X with Plus X works well
6. Paper grades: 2, 3

Check List of Terms to Investigate in Photography
(See What You Can Discover!)

1. Aperture
2. Burning in
3. Contact print
4. Depth of field
5. Development time
6. Dodging
7. Emulsion
8. Focus
9. f-stop
10. Gray scale
11. Lens
12. Speed—ASA
13. Spotting
14. Test strip
15. Add to the list here!

Contemporary Explorations for Painting

In this unit the student would develop an awareness of what is being done today, continuity between the artists and styles studied in preceding units and contemporary art would be stressed.

Pop Art

Short for popular art, it has been one of the major trends since the early 1960's. This art uses images from mass advertising, comic strips, and ordinary objects such as pop bottles, soup cans, etc., presented in distortions or exaggerations of size but always recognizable.

Claes Oldenburg—Stove and painted plaster food; sculptor who also uses plastic and ceramics.

Jasper Johns—The American flag painting; also does targets.

Andy Warhol—takes photos and produces multiple portraits using the silk screen process.

James Rosenquist—16 foot long painting "Silver Skies."

George Segal—life-size plaster sculpture.

Roy Lichenstein—comic strip characters.

Tom Wesselman—Great American Nudes, a series in which he uses collage materials paints, glues, and photographs.

Marisol—wood sculpture.

Robert Rauschenberg

Wayne Thiebaud—Cut Meringues.

Mel Ramos—takes slides, puts them together, blows them up; does girls from magazines.

Robert Indiana—uses advertising images.

Nicholas Krushenick—successful; uses bright bold colors and black outlines.

Optical Art

Op artists experiment with precise shapes, wiggly lines, concentric lines, and moire patterns in their concern with unusual visual effects. The optical illusion is defined as a visual experience in which a discrepancy exists between what we see and what is there.

Victor Vasarely—Helion 1960, oil on canvas, ambiguous figure-ground relationships.

Josef Albers—Interiors 1942, lithograph, figures alter their position in space.

Waterworks:

Iain Baxter—plunges chrome poles into the Columbia Glacier (Canada); poles work their way down to river.

Pulsa—a Yale University group of six men are involved with art to "make meaningful use of current phenomena of the technological environment." They placed 55 xenon strobe lights under water in the Boston Gardens' four-acre pond and rigged up 52 speakers programmed by analog and digital computers; effect was light flashes and sound.

Skyworks:

James Lee Byaus—did a "pretend" plane out of satin for 100 passengers.

Forrest Myers—did a skywork of four carbon arcs over New York City.

Thinkworks:

Joseph Kosuth—a series of definitions of words on canvases.

Edward Kienholz—did "The Cement Store" with detailed specifications for construction listed on a separate plaque.

Minimal Art

Ascetic restraint or undetailed. The minimal artists work with light radiation, chromatic temperature changes, elusive spatiality, and illusive tactility. David Diao, Allan Hacklan and Donald Kaufman are minimal artists whose work is a reaction to the major trends of the 60's.

Impossible Art

Defined as art that is impossible to collect, to show; impossible for dealers to handle; but nevertheless a reaching toward a new art form.

Earthworks:

Dennis Oppenheim—covered a New York City asphalt parking lot with salt, called it "Salt Flat."

Robert Smithson—placed rocks in metal bins, a framed earthwork.

Robert Morris—a combination of steel rods, tar, felt, and soil heaped into a mound.

Archiworks:

Christo—erected a 29-story polyethylene "bratwurst" in Kassel, Germany, at an exhibition.

Claes Oldenburg—designed enormous toilet ball-floats for the Thames in London.

Super Realism:

Paintings that look like photographs, sometimes they are copies of photographs.

Malcolm Morley—works from photographs shot by someone else, turning small photos into very large paintings.

Richard Estes—takes his own photos, then sometimes combines several photos into one painting.

The Art Teacher Is the Artist in the Classroom

The art teacher is the best model of an artist for the students. He is strategically located and knows his students and their needs for learning in art. Therefore, it is imperative for him to work at his art in order to serve as the most direct and effective example of what an artist can be. The art teacher *is* the model of the artist for classroom, school district, and community.

As an art teacher for many years in both public schools and college, as well as an artist, this author would like to share some ideas on how to begin and create art.

I hope these suggestions will be helpful to you as you initiate or continue to grow in your artistic vision. There are both two- and three-dimensional types as artists. The two-dimensional people become drawers and painters, while the three-dimensional people work in sculpture, ceramics, and so forth. I have always kept in mind a basic definition of what an artist is. *An artist is someone who combines eye, hand, and mind into a skillful and artistic product.* With this in mind, look at yourself as an artist, no matter how inexperienced. It is important to think about being creative, original, unique. These are the marks of art. Getting into the right image frame is essential to making artistic ideas emerge. Carry a sketchbook where ever you go. With a pen or 2B pencil sketch everything in your vision. Don't worry about perfection. Improvement will come in time. Be persistent and patient, and not overly critical in order to give yourself a chance to grow. As you practice the methods of art, start your classes along the same lines.

I chose drawing and painting as the media that I enjoy best. You may find that clay, wood, fibers, jewelry, or photography will be more to your choosing.

Here is how I create my art. I am constantly searching for interesting figural relationships. That is, I study faces and forms to discover the unusual characteristics of people. As I like to draw the figure, I observe how people bend, sit, stand, slouch, sleep, pause, run, walk, and whatever else the body can do. At the same time, I keep in mind a myriad of imaginative situations that my figures could be in. Some people paint portraits. I like to portray experience and human emotion. I'm interested in adventure, mystery, love, death, excitement, romance!

Here is a statement that I wrote which provides insights into what I like to draw and paint.

For me, the imaginative world of my art is a slam-bang, dynamite adventure that derives from selective and aesthetic experiences. Just as Matisse did not wish to become a "prisoner of reality" in his art, I too have taken the raw stuff of life and invented a panorama of electric personalities that exist in media. I choose to create a new reality in my work, rather than to replicate a given subject or form.

I am very much a traditionalist in the sense of pictorial composition. That is, the space must work for me. In this reference, I seek to thrust forms back and forth in order to achieve an infinity of depth on a flat surface. At times, the forms can ride on top of the plane, or they can drop back. Each part must relate to the whole. The classical ideas of balance, rhythm, harmony, are all present, yet interpreted in a contemporary context.

Color is used to heighten and express form in both an emotional and intellectual sense. For me, it has to be gutsy and speak for itself. I constantly try to find new modes for the manner in which a color, a line, a shadow, etc., can imply or suggest the form or the idea; the manner in which two colors meet, or edges merge, or the slash of a line, or the implication of events beyond what is not apparent — all have pertinence for the way in which I search for expressive form. And it is this search that captures me completely — the artistic ideational merging of what the skilled hand and the skilled mind can create.

There is another factor of my art that has special appeal for me. It deals with a fantasy of the sinister-the suspense of impending danger (that can grip each of us at times). I know it is all in good fun, and therefore all of the stops are out, and the high speed chase of the imagination is what counts, expressed in the best possible artistic result.

Countless figurative types dominate the works. Among them are Commander Evil, Dr. Thrill, the Snake Lady, and the Factory Director, all of whom I have encountered somewhere in the stream of my life. Doubtless, the viewer may see many more archetypes of his or her own choosing.

My art springs from thousands of hours across childhood up to now of watching gangster films, reading suspense stories, devouring hundreds of — "gold age" comic books, as well as examining the works of other artists, and the crystalizing of it all through years of drawing, painting, and art teaching.

For me, the art falls together as a visual novel or illustrated fiction with no words necessary. There is no time setting for the art, yet one might think of the thirties and forties for they are the years of my experiences. Yet the works are timeless, for I am very much interested in universal themes—the big ideas that deal with life-death-love-hate-mystery-suspense-adventure. But I also enjoy the lighter, humorous aspects of such heavy subjects. Who has not laughed when they might have cried.

Many of the accoutrements that appear in my works, such as cigarettes, snakes, boats, hats, and light bulbs are what provide the accents to the streaky characters who pervade my work.

My drawings become the "studies" for my paintings. I work out the pictorial organization in the drawing. This means the artistic handling of the art elements of color, line, shape, space, and so on. I won't always get a great drawing, but many of them will be just right and serve as the basis for paintings to come. The reason I use my drawings as forerunners to the paintings is that the difficult compositional challenge has been solved ahead of time. This leaves only the equally difficult task of manipulating the paint on the surface into a pleasing result, according to my own critical standards of artistic excellence. When everything goes well, I have both a drawing and a painting of the idea.

I always tell my students to get a good idea, work out the composition in the drawing, and then bring it to an exciting climax in a painting! However, it should be understood that drawing in itself could be all that is necessary for an artist to do. But not for me. The oil painting, for me, is the ultimate achievement in a media. It is my definition of high art, for it is the most difficult of media to work with. I think that every artist chooses his own challenge in art. He then combines idea and skill into an artistic result.

If a student wanted to major in art as a career, I would advise him to practice constantly. One should practice improving his ideas as well as his skill. It would also be very important to increase his sense of vision through looking and discovering what established artists have done before him. Art growth takes a great degree of conditioning, and it requires much patience and indulgence. But to me, there is no other experience like it. It is totally creative and fulfilling, and will remain with you your entire lifetime. In the photographs which follow are several examples of my drawings and paintings.

"Backstage at the Blu Wolf"
by Earl Linderman
Oil on Canvas
58" x 70"

It is important to solve the compositional problems in the drawing, for this information can then be adapted to the painting. The challenge of the pigment will be a great adventure to solve in itself.

Study for "Backstage at the Blu Wolf"
by Earl Linderman
Oil and Pastel
11" x 14"

Study for "After the Performance"
by Earl Linderman
Oil Pastel
11" x 14"

"After the Performance"
by Earl Linderman
Oil on Canvas
58" x 70"

I always do a study before starting the painting.
The oil pastel drawing above enabled me to
solve the compositional problems in creating
the art work. Notice the similarity between
the two products.

"Midnight at the Blu Wolf"
by Earl Linderman
Oil on Canvas
56" x 66"

"The Snake Lady"
by Earl Linderman
Pastel and Ink
11" x 14"

Building a Secondary School Art Library

Basic Design

ADAMS, EDWARD, DAVID VAN DOMMELEN and GEORGE PAPPAS, *Design at Work: Its Forms and Functions*, Pennsylvania State University Press, University Park, 1960.

ANDERSON, DONALD M., *Elements of Design*, Holt, Rinehart & Winston, New York, 1961.

BALLINGER, LOUISE B., *Design*, Reinhold Publishing Corp., New York, 1965.

BATES, KENNETH F., *Basic Design*, World Publishing Co., Cleveland, Ohio, 1960.

CHEVREUL, M. E., *The Principles of Harmony and Contrast of Colors*, Reinhold Book Corporation, New York, 1967.

COLLIER, GRAHAM, *Form, Space, and Vision: Discovering Through Drawing*, Prentice-Hall, Inc., Englewood Cliffs, N.J., 1963.

DESAUSMAREZ, MAURICE, *Basic Design*, Reinhold Publishing Corp., New York, 1964.

DOWNER, MARION, *The Story of Design*, Lothrop, Lee, and Shephard Co., New York, 1963.

GARRETT, LILLIAN, *Visual Design*, Reinhold Publishing Corp., New York, 1966.

ITTEN, JOHANNES, *Design and Form*, Reinhold Publishing Corp., New York, 1963.

LINDERMAN, EARL W. and HERBERHOLZ, DONALD W., *Developing Artistic and Perceptual Awareness*, Wm. C. Brown Company Publishers, Dubuque, Iowa, 1964.

LINDERMAN, EARL W., *Invitation To Vision: Ideas and Imaginations for Art*, Wm. C. Brown Company Publishers, Dubuque, Iowa, 1967.

NEUMANN, ECKHARD, *Functional Graphic Design In The 20's*, Reinhold Publishing Corp., New York, 1967.

SNEUM, GUNNER, *Teaching Design and Form*, Reinhold Publishing Corp., New York, 1965.

Drawing

ALBERT, CALVIN, and SECKLER, DOROTHY, *Figure Drawing Comes To Life*, Reinhold Publishing Corp., New York, 1962.

BRANDT, REX, *The Artist's Sketchbook And Its Uses*, Reinhold Publishing Corp., New York, 1966.

BRODATZ, PHIL, and WATSON, DORI, *The Human Form In Action and Repose*, Reinhold Publishing Corp., New York, 1966.

BUCHANAN, NORMAN, *Learn To Draw*, Warne, Frederick & Co., Inc., New York, 1964.

BURNETT, CALVIN, *Objective Drawing Techniques*, Reinhold Publishing Corp., New York, 1966.

CSOKA, STEPHEN, *Pastel Painting*, Reinhold Publishing Corp., New York, 1962.

JACQUES, FAITH, *Drawing In Pen and Ink*, Watson-Guptill Publishing Co., New York, 1964.

ROTTGER, ERNST, *Creative Drawing*, Reinhold Publishing Corp., New York, 1964.

THOMPSON, BEATRICE, *Drawings By High School Students*, Reinhold Publishing Corp., New York, 1966.

WIGG, PHILIP, *Figure Drawing*, Wm. C. Brown Company Publishers, Dubuque, Iowa.

Painting

BRANDT, REX, *Watercolor Technique*, Reinhold Publishing Corp., New York, 1963.

BROOKS, LEONARD, *Painting and Understanding Abstract Art*, Reinhold Publishing Corp., New York, 1964.

BROOKS, LEONARD, *Watercolor A Challenge*, Reinhold Publishing Corp., New York, 1967.

CHAVATEL, GEORGE, *Exploring With Polymer*, Reinhold Publishing Corp., New York, 1966.

DANIELS, LES, *Learning How To Paint In Oils*, Doubleday & Co., Inc., New York, 1964.

GORE, FREDERICK, *Painting*, Reinhold Publishing Corp., New York, 1965.

GUTIERREZ, JOSE, and ROUKES, NICHOLAS, *Painting With Acrylics*, Watson-Guptill Publishing Co., New York, 1966.

MARKS, MICKEY K., *Painting Free*, Dial Press, New York, 1965.

ROGERS, W. C., *A Picture Is A Picture*, Harcourt Publishing Co., New York, 1964.

RICHARDSON, E. P., *Painting In America*, Crowell Publishing Co., New York, 1965.

Drawing and Painting Techniques and Artists

1. NELSON, ROY PAUL, *Cartooning*, Chicago: Henry Regnery Company, 1975.
2. LAIDMAN, HUGH, *The Complete Book of Drawing and Painting*, New York: Viking, 1974.
3. NICOLAIDES, KIMON, *The Natural Way to Draw*, Boston: Houghton Mifflin Company, 1941.
4. MAYER, RALPH, *The Artist's Handbook of Materials and Techniques*, rev. ed., New York: Viking Press, Inc., 1957.
5. WATROUS, JAMES, *The Craft of Old Master Drawings*, Madison, Wisconsin: University of Wisconsin Press, 1957.
6. MAYER, RALPH, *The Painter's Craft*, Princeton, New Jersey: D. Van Nostrand Company, Inc. 1948.
7. MENDELOWITZ, DANIEL C., *Drawing*, New York: Holt, Rinehart & Winston, Inc., 1967.
8. ALBERT, C. and SECKLER, D., *Figure Drawing Comes to Life*, New York: Reinhold Publishing Corp., 1957.

9. SACHS, PAUL J., *Modern Prints and Drawings*, New York: Alfred A. Knopf, 1954.

10. GOLDSCHEIDER, LUDWIG, *Michelangelo Drawings*, London: Phaidon Press, 1951.

11. CHOMICKY, YAR G., *Watercolor Painting*, Englewood Cliffs, N.J.: Prentice-Hall, Inc., 1968.

12. DIBBLE, GEORGE, *Watercolor: Materials and Techniques*, New York: Holt, Rinehart, & Winston, Inc. 1966.

Crafts

ALLER, DORIS and DIANE, *Mosaics*, Lane Book Company, Menlo Park, Colorado, 1960.

ANDREWS, MICHAEL F., *Creative Printmaking*, Prentice-Hall, Inc., Englewood Cliffs, N.J., 1963.

ARGIRO, LARRY, *Mosaic Art Today*, International Textbook Company, Scranton, Pa., 1961.

BROW, FRANCIS, *Collage*, Pitman Publishing Corporation, New York, 1963.

BRUNSDON, JOHN, *The Techniques of Etching and Engraving*, Reinhold Publishing Corp., New York, 1966.

CHIEFFO, CLIFFORD, *Silk Screen As A Fine Art*, Reinhold Publishing Corp., New York, 1967.

CLARKE, GEOFFREY; FEHER, FRANCIS and IDA, *The Techniques of Enamelling*, Reinhold Publishing Corp., New York, 1967.

ERIKSON, JANET DOBBS, *Block Printing on Textiles*, Watson-Guptill Publications, Inc., New York, 1961.

ERICKSON, JANE and SPROUL, ADELAIDE, *Printmaking Without a Press*, Reinhold Publishing Corp., New York, 1966.

JOHNSTON, MEDA PARKER and KAUFMAN, GLEN, *Design on Fabrics*, Reinhold Publishing Corp., New York, 1967.

KREVITSKY, NIK, *Batik*, Reinhold Publishing Corp., New York, 1964.

KREVITSKY, NIK, *Stitchery*, Reinhold Publishing Corp., New York, 1966.

PETERSEN, GRETE, *Creative Leathercraft*, Sterling Publishing Co., New York, 1960.

PROUD, NOVA, *Textile Printing and Dyeing*, Reinhold Publishing Corp., New York, 1965.

STERNBERG, HARRY, *Woodcut*, Pitman Publishing Corporation, New York, 1962.

WANKLEMAN, WILLARD F.; WIGG, PHILIP; and WIGG, MARIETTA; *A Handbook of Arts and Crafts for Elementary and Junior High School Teachers*, 4th ed., Dubuque, Ia.: William C. Brown Company Publishers, 1978.

WILLIAMS, ELSA S., *Heritage Embroidery*, Reinhold Publishing Corp., New York, 1967.

WILSON, JEAN, *Weaving Is For Anyone*, Reinhold Publishing Corp., New York, 1967.

WINTER, ED, *Enamelling for Beginners*, Creative Hands Bookshop, Worcester, Mass., 1962.

WING, FRANCIS S., *The Complete Book of Decoupage*, Coward-McCann, Inc., New York, 1965.

ZARDENBERG, ARTHUR, *Prints and How To Make Them*, Harper & Row, Publishers, New York, 1964.

Advertising Design

BALLINGER, RAYMOND A., *Lettering Art In Modern Use*, Reinhold Publishing Corp., New York, 1965.

BIEGELEISEN, J. I., *Careers and Opportunities In Commercial Art*, E. P. Dutton and Co., Inc., New York, 1963.

GARLAND, KEN, *Graphics Handbook*, Reinhold Publishing Corp., New York, 1966.

GILL, BOB, *Illustration*, Reinhold Publishing Corp., New York, 1964.

KLEPPNER, OTTO, *Advertising Procedure*, Prentice-Hall, Inc., Englewood Cliffs, N.J., 1966.

LEACH, MORTIMER, *Letter Design In The Graphic Arts*, Reinhold Publishing Corp., New York, 1960.

LEACH, MORTIMER, *Lettering For Advertising*, Reinhold Publishing Corp., New York, 1965.

LESIAK, MICHAELINE, *The Art of Fine Lettering*, University of Notre Dame, Press, New York, 1965.

LEVITAN, ELI, *Animation Art In The Commercial Film Production*, Reinhold Publishing Corp., New York, 1962.

MAURELLO, RALPH, *How To Do Paste-Ups and Mechanicals*, Tudor Publishing Co., New York, 1960.

SCHARF, AARON, *Creative Photography*, Reinhold Publishing Corp., New York, 1965.

SCHLEMMER, RICHARD M., *Handbook of Advertising Art Production*, Prentice-Hall, Inc., Englewood Cliffs, N.J., 1966.

STONE, BERNARD, *Preparing For Printing*, Reinhold Publishing Corp., New York, 1965.

WILDBUR, PETER, *Trademarks*, Reinhold Publishing Corp., New York, 1966.

WIRSIG, WOODROW, *Principles of Advertising*, Pitman Publishing Corporation, New York, 1963.

Art Appreciation

CHASE, ALICE E., *Looking at Art*, Crowell Publishing Co., New York, 1966.

CHENEY, SHELDON, *A Primer of Modern Art*, Liveright Publishing Corporation, New York, 1966.

FLEMING, WILLIAM, *Arts and Ideas*, Holt, Rinehart, & Winston, New York, 1961.

GETTINGS, FRED, *The Meaning and Wonder of Art*, Golden Press, Inc., New York, 1963.

GOMBRICK, E. H., *The Story of Art*, New York Graphic Society, New York, 1966.

HAMLIN, TALBOT, *Architecture Through The Ages*, Putnam's G. P., Sons, New York, 1963.

JANSON, H. W., *History of Art*, Prentice-Hall, Inc., Englewood Cliffs, N.J., 1966.

KAINZ, LUISE, *Understanding Art*, Abrams Publishing Co., New York, 1966.

READ, HERBERT, *The Meaning of Art*, Pelican Publishing Co., Baltimore, Maryland, 1966.

WELLER, ALLEN S., *Contemporary American Painting and Sculpture*, University Press, New York, 1967.

WILSON, FORREST, *Architecture*, Reinhold Book Corporation, New York, 1968.

Ceramics

BALL, F. CARLTON, *Making Pottery without a Wheel*, New York: Reinhold Book Corporation, 1965.

BARFORD, GEORGE, *Clay in the Classroom*, Worcester: Davis Publications, 1963.

BINNS, CHARLES F., *Ceramic Technology*, London: Scott Greenwood and Company.

BINNS, CHARLES F., *The Potter's Craft*, New York: Van Nostrand.

CALIFORNIA (STATE) UNIVERSITY: Irvine Art Gallery, *Abstract Expressionist Ceramics*, 1966.

COX, WARREN E., *The Book of Pottery and Porcelain*, New York: Crown Publishers, 1953.

DUNCAN, JULIA HAMLIN and D'AMICO, VICTOR, *How to Make Pottery and Ceramic Sculpture*, New York: Simon and Schuster, 1947.

FORD, BETTY DAVENPORT, *Ceramic Sculpture*, New York: Reinhold Publishing Corp., 1964.

HAYETT, WILLIAM, *Display and Exhibit Handbook*, New York: Reinhold Publishing Corp., 1967.

HOFSTED, JOLYON, *Step-by-Step Ceramics*, New York: Golden Press, 1967.

ISENSTEIN, HAROLD, *Creative Clay Work*, New York: Sterling, 1960.

KENNY, JOHN B., *Ceramic Sculpture*, New York: Greenberg, 1953.

KENNY, JOHN B., *The Complete Book of Pottery Making*, New York: Greenberg, 1949.

KRUM, JOSEPHINE R., *Hand-Built Pottery*, Scranton: International Textbook Co., 1960.

LAKOFSKY, CHARLES, *Pottery*, New York: Brown Publishing Company, 1948.

LUNDKVIST, LIS and HANS, *Making Ceramics*, New York: Reinhold Publishing Corp., 1967.

MOSELY, JOHNSON and KOENING, *Crafts Design*, Belmont: Wadsworth Publishing Company, Inc. 1963.

NELSON, GLENN C., *Ceramics*, New York: Holt, Rinehart & Winston, 1966.

NORTON, F. N., *Ceramics for the Artist-Potter*, Reading: Addison Wesley Publishing Company, 1959.

RADA, PRAVASLAV, *Book of Ceramics*, London: Spring Books.

RAPHAEL, MAX, *Prehistoric Pottery and Civilization in Egypt*, Washington: Pantheon Books, 1947.

RHODES, DANIEL, *Clay and Glazes for the Potter*, New York: Clinton Book Company, 1957.

RHODES, DANIEL, *Kilns Design Construction and Operation*, New York: Clinton Book Company, 1968.

ROTTGER, ERNST, *Creative Clay Design*, New York: Reinhold Publishing Corp., 1963.

ROY, VINCENT A., *Ceramics*, New York: Chilton Company, 1960.

SANDERS, HERBERT H., *Pottery and Ceramic Sculpture*, Menlo Park: Lane Books, 1964.

SANDERS, HERBERT H., *The World of Japanese Ceramics*, Tokyo: Kodasha International, 1967.

STILES, HELEN E., *Pottery of the Ancients*, New York: E. P. Dutton Company, 1938.

STILES, HELEN E., *Pottery of the Europeans*, New York: E. P. Dutton Company, 1940.

STILES, HELEN E., *Pottery X of the American Indians*, New York: E. P. Dutton Company, 1939.

TREVOR, HENRY, *Pottery Step-by-Step*, Reseda: Watson Publishing Company, 1966.

WATKINS, LURA WOODSIDE, *Early New England Potters and Their Wares*, Cambridge: Harvard University Press, 1950.

WEISS, HARVEY, *Ceramics—from Clay to Kiln*, New York: Young Scott Books.

WILDENHAIN, MARGUERITE, *Pottery: Form and Expression*, New York: Reinhold Publishing Corp., 1962.

Jewelry

BAERWALD, MARCUS and TOM MAHONEY, *Gems and Jewelry Today*, New York: Marcel Rodd Company, Inc., 1949.

BOULAY, R. *Make Your Own Elegant Jewelry*, New York: Sterling Publishing Co., 1973.

BOVIN, MURRAY, *Jewelry Making*, Forest Hills, N.Y.: Murray Bovin, 1953.

BRYNNER, IRENA, *Modern Jewelry*, New York: Reinhold Publishing Corp., 1968.

CHOATE, SHARR, *Creative Casting*, New York: Crown Publishers, Inc., 1966.

CONWAY, VALERY, *Introducing Enameling*. New York: Watson-Guptill Publications, 1973.

DAVIDSON, PETER WYLIE, *Educational Metalcraft*, New York: Longmans, Green, and Co., 1913.

FRANKE, LOIS E., *Handwrought Jewelry*, Bloomington, Ill.: McKnight and McKnight Publishing Co., 1962.

FRANKOVICH, GEORGE R., *The Jewelry Industry*, Cambridge: Bellman Publishing Co., 1955.

HALD, ARTHUR and SVEN ERIK SKAWONIS, *Contemporary Swedish Design*, Stockholm: Nordisk Rotogravyr., 1951.

HARDY, R. ALLEN and JOHN J. BOWMAN, *The Jewelry Repair Manual*, New York: D. Van Nostrand Co., Inc., 1956.

KERR MANUFACTURING CO., *Lost Wax the New Modern Craft*, Detroit: Kerr Manufacturing Co., 1948.

MARTIN, CHARLES J., *How to Make Modern Jewelry,* New York: The Museum of Modern Art, 1949.

MEYEROWITZ, PATRICIA, *Jewelry and Sculpture through Unit Construction,* New York: Reinhold Publishing Corp., 1967.

MILLS, JOHN M., *The Technique of Casting,* New York: Reinhold Publishing Corp., 1967.

MUSEUM OF MODERN ART, *Jewelry by Contemporary Painters and Sculptors,* New York: The Museum of Modern Art, 1967.

NEWBLE, BRAIN, *Practical Enameling and Jewelry Work,* New York: The Viking Press, Inc., 1967.

OSTIER, MARIANNE, *Jewels and the Woman,* New York: Horizon Press, 1958.

PACK, GRETA, *Jewelry Making,* Princeton: D. Van Nostrand Co., 1957.

RATHBONE, R. LL.B., *Simple Jewelry,* London: Constable and Co., Ltd., 1910.

SELWYN, A., *The Retail Jewellers' Handbook,* New York: Chemical Publishing Co., Inc., 1950.

STORY, MICKEY, *Centrifugal Casting as a Jewelry Process,* Scranton: International Textbook Co., 1963.

VON NEUMAN, ROBERT, *The Design and Creation of Jewelry,* Philadelphia, 1961.

WEINER, LOUIS, *Hand Made Jewelry,* New York: D. Van Nostrand Company, Inc., 1948.

WILCOX, S. M., *The Jewelers' Journal Book of Recipes,* Entered according to act of Congress in the year 1889, in the office of the Librarian of Congress, at Washington.

WILSON, H., *Silverwork and Jewellery,* London: John Hogg, 1903.

WINEBRENNER, D. KENNETH., *Jewelry Making as an Art Expression,* Scranton: International Textbook Co., 1955.

WORSHIPFUL COMPANY OF GOLDSMITHS, *International Exhibition of Modern Jewellery, 1890–1961,* London, 1961.

ZECHLIN, KATHARINA, *Creative Enamelling and Jewelry Making,* New York: Reinhold Publishing Corp., 1966.

Photography

ATJET, EUGENE and MARCEL PROUST, *A Vision of Paris,* New York: The Macmillan Company, 1963.

BONI, ALBERT, ed., *Photographic Literature—A Bibliographic Guide,* New York: Morgan and Morgan, 1963.

CARTIER-BRESSON, *Photographs by Cartier-Bresson,* New York: Grossman Publishers, 1963.

COBURN, ALVIN LANGDON, *Portfolio of 16 Photographs,* Rochester: Eastman House, 1962.

COLGAN, JAMES W., "The Pinhole Camera: Easy to Make, Easy to Use," *Arts and Activities,* 71 (June 1972).

The Encyclopedia of Photography, New York: Willard Morgan Greystone Press, 1963–1964.

KOMROFF, MANUEL and NATHAN RESNICK and KONRAD CRAMER, *The Third Eye,* New York: Walker and Company, 1962.

NEWHALL, NANCY, *Ansel Adams: The Eloquent Light,* San Francisco: Sierra Club, 1963.

PORTER, ELIOT, *In Wilderness is the Preservation of the World,* San Francisco: Sierra Club, 1962.

PORTER, ELIOT, *The Place No One Knew—Glen Canyon on the Colorado,* San Francisco: Sierra Club, 1962.

STRAND, PAUL, *Tir A'Mhurain: Outer Hebrides,* London: Macgibbon and Kee, 1962.

Sculpture

AUERBACH, ARNOLD, *Modelled Sculpture and Plaster Casting,* New York: Thomas Yoseloff, 1961.

BALDWIN, JOHN, *Contemporary Sculpture Techniques,* New York: Reinhold Publishing Corp., 1967.

CASSON, STANLEY, *Some Modern Sculptors,* New York: Books for Libraries Press, 1928.

CHENEY, SHELDON, *Sculpture of the World,* New York: Viking Press, 1968.

CLARKE, GEOFFREY and CORNOCK, STROUD, *A Sculptor's Manual,* New York: Reinhold Book Corporation, 1968.

CRAVEN, WAYNE, *Sculpture in America,* New York: Thomas Y. Crowell Company, 1968.

COLEMAN, RON, Wm. C. Brown Company Publishers, Dubuque, Iowa.

DAINGERFIELD, MARJORIE, *Fun and Fundamentals of Sculpture,* New York: Charles Scribner's Sons, 1963.

ELISCU, FRANK, *Sculpture Techniques in Clay, Wax, Slate,* Great Neck: Arts and Crafts Book Club, 1961.

FITZ, JOHN and MAURICE MILLS, *The Pergamon Dictionary of Art,* New York: Pergamon Press, 1965.

GRANSTROM, K. E., *Creating with Metal,* New York: Reinhold Publishing Corp., 1968.

GROSS, CHAIM, *The Technique of Wood Sculpture,* New York: Arco Publishing Co., 1965.

HALE, NATHAN CABOT, *Welded Sculpture,* New York: Watson-Guptill Publications, 1968.

JOHNSTON, MARY GRACE, *Paper Sculpture,* Worcester: Davis Publications, 1964.

KOEPF, HANS, *Masterpieces of Sculpture,* New York: G. P. Putnam's Sons, 1966.

LANTEN, EDOUARD, *Modelling and Sculpture,* New York: Dover Publications, 1965.

LYNCH, JOHN, *Metal Sculpture,* New York: Studio Crowell, 1957.

MARKS, MICKEY KLAR, *Sand Sculpturing,* New York: Dial Junior Books, 1962.

MILLS, JOHN W., *The Techniques of Sculpture,* New York: Reinhold Publishing Corp., 1965.

MURRAY, PETER, *Dictionary of Art and Artists,* New York: Frederick A. Praeger, 1965.

PRESS, FRED, *Sculpture at Your Fingertips*, New York: Reinhold Publishing Corp., 1962.

RASMUSSEN, HENRY and GRANT, *Sculpture from Junk*, New York: Reinhold Publishing Corp., 1967.

READ, HERBERT, *A Concise History of Modern Sculpture*, New York: Frederick A. Praeger Publishers, 1965.

SELZ, GEORGE, *Modern Sculpture*, New York: George Braziller, 1963.

SLOBODKIN, LOUIS, *Sculpture Principles and Practice*, Cleveland: World Publishing Company, 1949.

TROWELL, MARGARET, *Classical African Sculpture*, New York: Frederick A. Praeger Publishers, 1964.

TUCHMAN, MAURICE, ed., *American Sculpture of the Sixties*, Los Angeles: Los Angeles County Museum of Art, 1967.

Lettering

DOUGLASS, RALPH, *Calligraphic Lettering*, New York: Watson-Guptill Publications, 1967.

GEORGE, ROSS F., *Speedball Textbook for Pen and Brush Lettering*, Philadelphia: Hunt Manufacturing Co., 1965.

HUNT, W. BEN, *101 Alphabets*, Milwaukee: The Bruce Publishing Co., 1954.

LEACH, MORTIMER, *Lettering for Advertising*, New York: Reinhold Publishing Corp., 1963.

LINDEGREN, ERIC, *ABC of Lettering and Printing Types*, Vols. 1, 2, 3, Sweden: Eric Lindegren Grafisk Studio, 1964.

MUSEUM OF MODERN ART, *Lettering by Modern Artists*, New York: Museum of Modern Art, 1966.

RONDTHALER, EDWARD, ed., *Alphabet Thesaurus*, Vols. 1, 2, New York: Reinhold Publishing Corporation, 1965.

SHAHN, BEN, *Love and Joy about Letters*, New York: Grossman Publishers, 1963.

WRIGHT, HARRY B., *Lettering*, New York: Pittman Publishing Company, 1962.